RUSTED DREAMS

HARD TIMES IN A STEEL COMMUNITY

**David Bensman
and
Roberta Lynch**

UNIVERSITY OF CALIFORNIA PRESS
BERKELEY AND LOS ANGELES

This book is dedicated
to Marilyn Bensman,
to Joseph Bensman,
to Antoinette Rita Lynch, and
to the memory of James Francis Lynch

University of California Press
Berkeley and Los Angeles
This edition by arrangement with McGraw-Hill Book Company.

First Paperback Printing 1988.

1 2 3 4 5 6 7 8 9

Library of Congress Cataloging-in-Publication Data

Bensman, David, 1949–
     Rusted dreams : hard times in a steel community / David Bensman
and Roberta Lynch.
         p. cm.
     Reprint. Originally published: New York : McGraw-Hill, c1987.
     Bibliography: p.
     Includes index.
     ISBN 0-520-06302-3 (pbk.)
     1. Chicago (Ill.)—Economic conditions.   2. South Chicago (Ill.)—
Economic conditions.   3. Unemployment—Illinois—Chicago.   4. Plant
shutdowns—Illinois—Chicago.   I. Lynch, Roberta.   II. Title.
[HC108.C4B45   1989]
330.9773'11—dc19   87-32619
                                                              CIP

ACKNOWLEDGMENTS

From the moment we began defining our conception of this book, and all throughout its writing, we have had the generous assistance of friends and colleagues. In addition, many people whom we had never met before this undertaking provided enormous help. We would like to express our gratitude to all those who made this book possible; we can thank by name only a few.

Jack Metzgar was our closest collaborator in this work. It is impossible to overstate his intellectual influence or to imagine a more supportive friend. Jack's rigorous analyses of the economics of the steel industry and the dynamics of the labor movement constantly challenged us to refine our own thinking. And his perceptive analysis of mill community life permeates the book's pages.

Kevin Fitzgibbons also aided us from this project's earliest days. He provided skillful guidance through the complexities of local politics, generously shared source materials, and gave us insightful readings of several chapters. Moreover, Kevin's unflagging support was critical to sustaining our belief in the importance of chronicling Southeast Chicago's story.

William Kornblum was both intellectual mentor and practical advisor. Kornblum's classic study of South Chicago, *Blue Collar Community*, taught us much about the mill neighborhood. And his suggestions regarding potential signs of the community's transformation proved of great value to our research.

Edward Sadlowski's seemingly boundless knowledge of local history and of labor-management relations in the steel industry was vital to our efforts. Ed was also generous with his time and advice: He introduced us to local leaders, answered numerous questions, and corrected early manuscript drafts.

Throughout much of the time we worked on this book, the late Alice Peurala was fighting what proved to be a fatal disease. Nevertheless, she spent many hours talking with us, just as she continued to spend countless hours fighting for her vision of a more humane workplace. We deeply value both the information and the inspiration that she gave us.

Ann Markusen's brilliant analysis of the steel industry helped to define two of these chapters, and Ann's encouragement and advice have been a constant source of sustenance throughout the vagaries of the writing/revising/publishing process.

Tom Geoghegan provided a thoughtful reading of several chapters, as well as important insights into the decline of Wisconsin Steel. He also graciously shared relevant material and recommended key issues for further research.

We have benefited greatly from the work of Tom Dubois, Greg Leroy, Dan Swinney, and others at the Midwest Center for Labor Research in analyzing the contemporary steel industry. Rob Persons helped our understanding of how local unions respond to concessions. And Julie Putterman's incisive research on the impact of job loss provided data that confirmed the impressions gleaned in our interviews.

Miriam Rabban provided initial contacts and thoughtful reflections on her own research on Southeast Chicago. From Father Dennis Geaney we learned much about the role of the church in the steel communities. Phyllis Janik and her father, Phillip Janik, shared with us their unique and creative approach to keeping the history of mill work alive. And the staff and resources of the Southeast Chicago Historical Project helped to give faces and voices to the community's past.

We owe a special debt of gratitude to the staff of *The Daily Calumet*, both present and past, particularly Robert Bong, John Wasik, and John Kass. The newspaper's files and ongoing reportage were of invaluable assistance.

We value the cooperation we received from former officials of Wisconsin Steel, as well as from the personnel of International Harvester (now Navistar), and of Envirodyne, Inc. Former staff members and consultants of the federal Economic Development Administration were especially helpful, repeatedly responding to our phone calls and answering our questions. Unfortunately, U.S. Steel, now U.S.X., had imposed a news blackout for virtually the entire time we conducted our research and company officials were not available for interviews.

National, district, and local officers of the United Steelworkers of America (USWA) gave us considerable amounts of time—when they had very little to spare—and much useful information. Frank Lumpkin and other leaders of the Save Our Jobs Committee frequently extended themselves to arrange interviews and provide periodic updates. Former officers of the Progressive Steelworkers Union also lent their cooperation to this project.

No contribution to this book was more valuable than that made by the dozens of Southeast Side residents who took the time to speak with us. Many willingly shared painful experiences and emotions in the hope of helping others. We should note that while some of these individuals are named in the pages of this book, others who spoke of very personal problems are identified only by pseudonyms in order to safeguard their privacy. But whether or not their names appear in these pages, all of those Southeast Chicagoans whom we interviewed helped to shape this work in ways varied and incalculable. They have our deepest gratitude.

The wealth of material that we amassed contributed to an unwieldy original manuscript that benefited greatly from the perceptive editing of Elisabeth Jakab, our editor at McGraw-Hill.

Finally, we would like to acknowledge those whose help was less direct, but no less important.

Two passionate analysts of the American experience, Robert Lekachman and the late Herbert Gutman, shaped our understanding of economic change and its social consequences. We owe them a very considerable debt.

Our agent, Jane Jordan Browne, gave unstintingly of her time, her wise counsel, and her skillful advocacy. She also contributed expert editorial assistance. Without Jane's extraordinary efforts, this book would never have seen the light of day.

Carol Becker was hard at work on her own book during the writing of this one. Yet she was unfailingly available to empathize, encourage, and advise. Her generosity of spirit and strength of conviction helped to sustain us through the inevitable periods of doubt, discouragement, and difficulty.

The friendship and support of the late Edmund Fuller helped to make this book possible. And as she has done so often, Deborah Willen Meier provided generous assistance.

Contents

Prologue

Steve Szumilyas, Ron Turner, and Joe Smetlack worked together in a rolling mill at Wisconsin Steel on Chicago's Southeast Side. At 4 P.M. on Friday, March 28, 1980, Steve was working at the reheater furnace when his foreman came by with news that would shatter his world: the gates were being locked at the end of the shift; the mill was going down; 3400 steelworkers were out of a job.

Steve immediately phoned his buddies Joe and Ron (who were on vacation) to tell them what had happened. Then he went back to work, "like they asked me to," and finished out the shift.

In the meantime, his friends rushed over to the trailer on 106th Street where the Progressive Steelworkers Union had its headquarters. While they sat in their car in the pouring rain, members of the union's board of delegates began climbing out of the entrance. Joe swears there were tears in their eyes.

Wisconsin Steel's sudden shutdown was not a complete surprise: workers had known their mill was in trouble ever since the late 1960s, when its owner, the International Harvester Corporation, began to cut back on maintenance. But when Harvester sold the mill to Envirodyne Industries in

1

1977, and then the government guaranteed a $90 million loan to Envirodyne in the fall of 1979, Wisconsin's steelworkers assumed they would be able to keep their jobs and maintain the lives they had built around them.

Steve Szumilyas certainly was counting on staying at Wisconsin. His father had worked there for forty years; he expected to do the same. He liked his job, checking the billets before they went into the reheating furnace to make sure they corresponded to the customers' orders. "It was a high-pressure job, one mistake and the whole mill could be down," but Steve loved "working that job. Boy, I tell you, it could have been a nice life."

Just three months before, Steve had bought a house in the suburbs for his wife and son. Now that house is a millstone around his neck. The mortgage payments ate up his meager savings. When his son had to be hospitalized, the family faced a major crisis, for Wisconsin Steel workers had lost their health insurance when the mill closed, and Steve had no money for private coverage.

Steve's been out of work for more than half the time since the shutdown. Although he had been against his wife's taking a full-time job before the mill closed, he admits that her salary was "about the only thing that saved us." He's back at work now, driving a laundry truck at half his former wages, but Steve doesn't think he'll ever be the same again. "I'll never give another company what I gave them. I try my darnedest, don't get me wrong, but then again, if I can get away with anything, I do it. I don't care about a company no more. They made me feel that way."

The closing of Wisconsin Steel was followed by massive layoffs at other mills and the shutdown of dozens of steel-related businesses on Chicago's Southeast Side in the next three years. By the end of 1983, U.S. Steel's great South Works was almost closed, with 9000 of its original 10,000 employees gone for good.

The decline of Chicago's steel industry was but part of a larger crisis. The closing of Singer's sewing machine factory in Elizabeth, New Jersey, of Goodyear's tire factory in Akron, Ohio, of Chrysler's assembly plant in Hamtramck, Michigan, all signaled a profound transformation of America's economy.

As corporations pursue business opportunities around the world, our nation's basic industries are withering. Steel, rubber, electrical appliances, machine tools, automobiles, and auto parts are all shrinking drastically. The recessions of 1979–1982 accelerated a long-term decline, producing record numbers of bankruptcies, the highest unemployment rates since the Great Depression, and hundreds of plant closings. In 1982 alone, there were 2696 incidents of mass layoffs or plant shutdowns, causing over 1,287,000 job losses. Although the recovery of 1983–1984 restored corporate profits in some quarters, it did little to reverse the rapid decline of America's industrial core. Thus, the booming auto industry's unemployment rate remained as high as 17.2 percent in the winter of 1984; employment stood 210,000 below its 1978 peak.

But no industry has been as ravaged as steel, long the backbone of our industrial economy. The U.S. Commerce Department reported in 1985 that more jobs have been lost in steelmaking than in any other industry: employment in production and maintenance has fallen from more than 570,000 in 1953 to just 200,000 today. Much of that decline occurred between 1979 and 1982, when more than 150,000 jobs were lost.

With all this, we are told not to worry. Prophets of high technology and defenders of the free market consider the demise of our smokestack industries the inevitable by-product of economic progress. They counsel that the "creative destruction" of old forms of production is essential if new forms are to arise. And indeed, while manufacturing staples like steel have found themselves mired in red ink, new industries are emerging amid great fanfare. Computers, information

processing, financial services, fast foods, and health care—
these, we are assured, are the wave of the future. Workers
displaced by plant shutdowns can find better jobs in this new
information/service sector.

This is the conventional wisdom that provides the un-
derpinning for our current political and economic policies.
Unfortunately, it is seriously mistaken on several counts.

Steve's friend Ron has been without a steady job for more
than three years. "All I do is side jobs, like painting houses.
I keep filing applications and they throw them right in the
garbage can." He'd gotten divorced just before the mill closed
and now "my wife won't let me see the kids 'cause I can't send
her no money."

Ron moved in with his parents two years ago, after declaring bankruptcy and selling the trailer that had been his
home. He lost his car, too. "They came and got it. Repos-
sessed, they call it. That was the first year the mill shut down."
But he keeps on trying and his old friends Steve and Joe help
keep his spirits up. They come by frequently to pick Ron up
for a night of card playing or hanging out.

"I'll find something soon. I will. I ain't giving up. That's
what happens to a lot of people. They've given up. They don't
keep looking. If you don't keep looking, a job ain't going to
come to you. Sure, sometimes you get depressed. You don't
want to go out and look any more. But my dad helps me. He
tells me, 'Don't get disappointed.'"

What's wrong with the optimistic scenario of the high-
tech advocates? First, there is no evidence that displaced workers in old industrial centers will be the beneficiaries of expanded employment opportunities in newer ventures. Barry
Bluestone and Bennett Harrison's study, *The Deindustrialization of America*, reported that only 3 percent of those displaced
from New England's textile mills found jobs in that region's
high-technology sector. "Losing one's job as a result of dein-

dustrialization tends to propel one downward in the industry hierarchy toward lower productivity jobs—not upward," they concluded.

In reality, the bulk of the new jobs that have been created over the last decade are low-level service jobs—some paying no more than minimum wage. As Emma Rothschild pointed out in 1981, "the increase in employment in eating and drinking places since 1973 is greater than total employment in the automobile and steel industries combined." The late Otto Eckstein of Data Resources, Inc., projected that more than 90 percent of the new jobs in the 1980s and beyond would be in services and sales. The crisis in our basic industries means that we are replacing higher-paying unionized jobs with low-wage nonunion work, replacing hard-won economic security with marginal employment. The result is not an upgrading of former industrial workers but a downgrading of the entire blue-collar middle class. Over the last decade, the proportion of American families with incomes between $15,000 and $35,000 dropped from 53.4 to 43.9 percent.

Secondly, there is nothing "creative" about the "creative destruction" wreaked by plant closings in communities across our nation. All too often, the dimension of human suffering is conveniently omitted from a political agenda filled with eager talk of "sunrise industries." The proponents of a new economic order simply close their eyes to the immense dislocations that such massive job loss leaves in its wake.

Manufacturing firms have been the economic backbone of cities all across America. More often than not, such firms have sunk deep roots into a community. Generations of the same families have worked for them. Labor unions have been shaped and sustained. And individuals have found not only their daily sustenance but a measure of personal meaning.

As industries die, these industrial communities unravel. The victims of unemployment are stripped of the work routines, the personal bonds, and the goals that shaped their identities. They no longer can count on a steady income, on adequate health coverage, on a secure retirement. Families are rocked by new tensions. Small businesses, dependent on the industrial giants, give up the ghost. If there is a high-tech nirvana, these workers have not learned the mantra that could take them there.

Contrary to the pronouncements of high-tech gurus, this painful course of industrial decline is not inevitable. Rather it is merely the product of a complex chain of choices made by corporate managers and government officials. For several decades, American industries have neglected to modernize domestic facilities in favor of investment in more immediately lucrative ventures at home and abroad. At the same time, the industries of other nations—most notably Japan—have enjoyed considerable government support. As international competition intensified, amid a worldwide economic slump, America's free-trade ideology and free-market policies placed it at a distinct disadvantage. Different policies could bring us very different results.

Ron and Steve's friend Joe Smetlack has been "pushing" a cab for the last two years. He's very angry. Joe's thoughts are never far from the money he believes he was cheated out of. When Wisconsin Steel closed, Joe was entitled to severance pay, supplementary unemployment benefits, and vacation pay totaling $23,000 by his count. But he's gotten nothing—for complex reasons that will be explained in Chapters 3 and 6. Instead, Joe ended up on the public aid rolls and in bankruptcy. The experience has made him bitter. "I resent very much what they did to us. Right now, I'm looking for revenge." Three and a half years of desperation and futile anger have killed Joe's former idealism. "I stood behind the government in the 1960s. I would have went to 'Nam. The form of government we have here, you can't beat it. But it's being corrupted. . . . The American Dream? That's dog eat dog. Rip off as good as you can. Integrity don't mean a damn thing anymore."

*   *   *

The Southeast Side of Chicago is a microcosm of America's industrial decline. Combined with the adjacent area in northwest Indiana, it was, until just recently, the largest steel-making region in the world.

For about thirty years, from the onset of America's post-World War II prosperity until the sudden collapse of the steel industry, the residents of Southeast Chicago were able to create a stable and orderly world for themselves. It was a world where people could realize their personal aspirations for decent and productive lives, and fulfill as well their sense of obligations to their families, their communities, and their God.

It was an insular world, protected from the tides and trends that swept over much of American society. As long as the mills kept belching out their smoke and producing steel for America's skyscrapers, automobiles, tractors, and trucks, the men and women of the Southeast Side were able to preserve their own community.

Today, over half the local work force has been laid off; many will never work again. The community's institutions, values, and traditions have been shaken to the core.

The closing of the mills has brought Southeast Chicago a visibility it never wanted. The mills' death agonies, the desperate, vain efforts to start up abandoned facilities, the trauma of displaced steelworkers—this saga became a continuing prime-time story in the local media.

If the closing of the mills made the people of Southeast Chicago visible to a wider public, the closing of the mills also made visible to the people of Southeast Chicago a fact they had long ignored: their fate was, and had always been, inextricably entwined in the fate of America's steel industry and her larger industrial economy.

As distressed citizens called for help, politicians too were forced to face unfamiliar problems. Some sought to capitalize on the crisis to bolster their prestige; others applied traditional remedies, only to see them flop—at great expense; a very few experimented with new approaches that might stem their region's decline.

The story of Southeast Chicago's wrenching encounter with economic decline was similar to the experiences of scores of cities throughout the United States. It was enacted in a dozen mill communities, like Johnstown, Pennsylvania, Youngstown, Ohio, Lackawanna, New York, and Birmingham, Alabama. It was played out in Akron, Ohio, which lost its rubber industry, and in Flint, Michigan, where auto employment dropped steeply. It occurred in cramped industrial cities in northern New Jersey, where America's leading electrical machine manufacturers pulled up stakes.

This book examines what happened in Southeast Chicago as a way of illuminating the grim realities of deindustrialization across our country. By looking at the international economic forces that brought down local mills, at the corporate and governmental decisions that accelerated the region's decline, and at the futile efforts of political leaders to apply traditional solutions to new and different problems, we will be exploring one particular, and rather typical, instance of a historical process that is unfolding throughout industrial America.

Yet there is also a unique dimension to Southeast Chicago's story. This steel community brought its own, singular, historical identity to bear on the worldwide process of economic change. This was not Pittsburgh, where the Steelworkers International Union and the steel companies' corporate headquarters could bring their centralized bureaucracies to bear on a new situation. This was not Johnstown, Pennsylvania, an isolated mill community, where steel was a culture all townspeople shared. Southeast Chicago was a mill community within a large metropolis, separated by geographical, ethnic, and industrial barriers, but also connected by the political system and the media. This unusual configuration shaped the way Southeast Chicagoans defined their public roles in the glory years, and it shaped the way they responded to the closing of the mills.

Thus, understanding the particular way Southeast Siders coped with deindustrialization requires more than an analysis of economic and political trends; it requires a look back in history. In the pages of this book, the past is not prologue to the present, but rather a living force, shaping the memory of citizens, coloring their perception of new problems and opportunities, channeling their energies in some directions rather than others.

Yet in the final analysis this book is as much about the future as about the past. Though the industrial depression of 1979–1982 has passed into history, the future of American manufacturing industry remains in question, the fate of displaced workers like Ron, and Steve, and Joe has not been resolved, and the future prospects for Southeast Chicago are cloudy.

In the pages that follow, we will look at the larger forces impacting on Southeast Chicago. We will situate the area's industry in the wider arena of corporate and governmental decision-making. We will examine how these policies shaped the respective fates of Wisconsin Steel and U.S. Steel, once two of the region's largest employers. And we will describe possible alternate programs to help restore the steel industry to health.

The problem of industrial decline is as much political as it is economic. In recent years, the dire consequences of plant closings and mass layoffs have nudged new ideas onto the political stage. At the local level, there has been a growing interest in employee buy-outs of endangered firms and in legislation to require advance warning of shutdowns. At the national level, various proposals for "industrial policy" have sparked heated debate.

The chaos and pain left in the wake of America's rapid economic decline in the years 1979–1982 pose a difficult challenge for a society like ours, in which the pursuit of profit is considered the surest path to public progress, and government intervention, however well-intentioned, is usually seen to just make matters worse. Can America plan for a future where displaced workers are reemployed and old communities preserved? Can we shape a smooth transition to a global economy where American workers must compete with billions of people eager for the fruits of economic growth?

Through their unions, churches, and community organizations, the people of Southeast Chicago are trying to play a role in shaping their future. Whether or not our country finds a way to take their needs and values, their dreams and aspirations into account, as it makes the decisions that will define America's role in the new world economy, will give form to the future of our nation's democracy.

By looking at how Southeast Chicago is responding to threatening and painful change, this book explores the new nation that America is becoming.

1

The World As It Was

On the block that I lived, next door was Hungarian people
and on the other side was Slavic people and across the street
was Swedish people. Then we had German people. It was just
a League of Nations. . . . When you got mad, it was "Oh you
dirty Polack," "Oh you dirty German." But then let
something happen in the neighborhood. Mrs. Vistecki got
very sick. Right away, chicken soup is being made, noodles
are being made, and everyone comes to the house. . . . So,
you see, there was much unity. There was love.

Frances Bughaski
Southeast Chicago

FOR MOST OF ITS LENGTH, the Chicago Skyway is an ordinary
freeway rising to modest heights over South Side streets. Its
name derives from a three-mile stretch where it soars high
above the city, swooping down again only at the Indiana border. Glimpsed from afar, its immense steel girders suggest a
bridge that spans some vast waterway. In reality, the Skyway
bridges rail yards, scrap heaps, and factories, allowing Chicago's citizens and visitors to pass speedily over the densely
industrial landscape of the city's Southeast Side.

11

Viewed from this privileged altitude, the area below seems a maze of smokestacks and train tracks, dull maroon buildings, and occasional splotches of green parkland. Vast steel mills dwarf the soldierly rows of houses encrusted with decades of industrial grime.

At one time, the quickest route to Indiana was through the neighborhoods of Southeast Chicago. In those days, the passing traveler couldn't miss the local residents—mowing tiny patches of lawn, shoveling snow-filled sidewalks, or setting off to work in thick-soled boots. But when the Skyway was built in 1956, all that changed. Now travelers are lofted high above the nitty-gritty of life on these streets. Through car windows shut tight against the acrid air, they see Chicago's steel mills merging with those of Whiting and Gary to form an immense, continuous industrial chain.

In effect, with the coming of the Skyway, the steel mills lost their human context. The actual men and women who passed daily through the carefully guarded millgates—the roll hands and chippers, the scarfers and spark testers, the laborers and electricians—were no longer visible. Invisible as well were the communities they had created.

Southeast Chicago is an odd necklace of neighborhoods strung along the Calumet River from Lake Michigan to Lake Calumet, just 15 miles south of downtown Chicago. Only three of the region's 21.7 square miles are zoned for residential use; undeveloped marshes, waste disposal sites, and a potpourri of mammoth factories and tiny job shops fill out the terrain.

More than 100 years ago, Southeast Chicago attracted entrepreneurs hoping to build an industrial empire amidst its empty swamps and scraggly forests. They were drawn by its access to Lake Michigan and the whole Great Lakes chain, and by its proximity to central Chicago, with a market potential and labor force growing by leaps and bounds.

From the time that Joseph Brown, one of the most enterprising of these early settlers, built the area's first steel mill on the banks of the Calumet River in 1875, native and immigrant workers have come to live and work in Southeast Chicago. For a century, they have struggled against the soggy soil, piercing winds, foul smells, and never-ceasing waste effusion. Over the generations, they shaped a blue-collar world—a series of balkanized neighborhoods anchored by the three largest mills.

At the northern tip of the Southeast Side, U.S. Steel's South Works stretches for more than a mile along Lake Michigan's shore. The poorest, most recent immigrants have long settled in the unpretentious rows of houses pressed against the mill's perimeter. Just a few blocks away are aging brick two-flats that have withstood the rigors of Midwest winters and factory emissions with stoic fortitude. These tree-lined streets are home to older Polish-Americans, comfortably retired on steelworker pensions, and young Mexican-American and black families, growing into middle-class stability on steelworker salaries. This is South Chicago, a vibrant, polyglot neighborhood that is the heart of the steel region.

Its main street, Commercial Avenue, is the central business district for all of the Southeast Side. Although suburban shopping malls have slowed the pace of trade here in recent years, law and medical offices, banks and travel agents, clothing stores and restaurants still occupy the handsome low-rise buildings that recall the avenue's better days.

Commercial Avenue is also the main artery linking the disjointed mill neighborhoods. Running south, it wends its way through Slag Valley, a residential islet marked off by an enormous expanse of slag heaps, piles of scrap metal, and crisscrossing rail lines. From there, it charts a chaotic course into South Deering, home of Wisconsin Steel.

Tucked away in the far southwest corner of the mill region, South Deering looks like the relic of an earlier era. Its streets are poorly paved; its frame houses sag with the weight of almost a century; its air reeks of sulfur dioxide. Wisconsin

Steel occupies more of its acreage than all the homes, schools, churches, and stores combined. The neighborhood seems almost an afterthought, an ungainly adjunct to the looming presence of the mill.

Across the Calumet River, to the east of Wisconsin Steel, lies the East Side, Southeast Chicago's largest and most influential neighborhood. The homes here are neat, square bungalows with well-tended lawns and backyards dotted with giant plastic pools. A wide array of ethnic groups—the descendants of Swedes, Irish, Italians, Serbs, Poles, and Croatians—mingle on its streets. Many of them work in the Republic steel mill which sprawls along the neighborhood's southern border.

More than a mile south of Republic is the last residential outpost of the Southeast Side—Hegewisch. Surrounded by the region's only remnants of wetlands and a sprawling auto assembly plant, Hegewisch is a sleepy community that treasures its clean streets and well-maintained homes.

The neighborhoods of the Southeast Side are divided by ethnic differences, topographical barriers, and economic gradations. But they are united by a powerful bond—the steel industry.

The Daily Calumet, America's oldest daily community newspaper, symbolizes the area's unique identity. Like a small-town paper, it is the primary source of news for local residents, far more important to them than the metropolitan dailies. Few small-town papers, however, could lay claim to the singular combination of local gossip and high drama that is *The Cal's* stock in trade.

On the one hand, Southeast Chicago is a community as close-knit as a mountain village. Ethnic and church ties cement associations that were first formed in schoolyards and on Little League teams. The stories of people's lives matter here. Marriages, deaths, births, crimes of greed and passion—these are events of note. And *The Daily Calumet* features them all.

On the other hand, Southeast Chicago is a hub of international commerce. Here the steel rails and plates that undergird America's highways and railroads were forged. Here the steel companies tested new technologies and tested the endurance of mill workers as well. And here some of the fiercest battles to organize the United Steelworkers union were waged. This story, full of conflict and striving, has been unfolding for over a century now, in the pages of *The Daily Calumet.*

The region beneath the Skyway is fundamentally a steel town. But it is more. The mills provided the foundations of life in Southeast Chicago, but on that base, the people built a community.

MAKING STEEL

The South Works of the North Chicago Rolling Mill was erected in 1880, when Southeast Chicago was still a land of swamps, notorious for its mosquitoes and bullfrogs. Twenty years later, the mill became part of a new corporate giant, the United States Steel Corporation. Soon, four of U.S. Steel's competitors built new mills in Southeast Chicago and another three mills went up across the Indiana border. By the early decades of the twentieth century, the Calumet basin had become the world's premier steel center.

The mills were a mighty magnet, drawing immigrants by the thousands from every corner of Europe. At first, steel manufacturers counted on their employees' returning to their homelands after a few hard years of labor. But after the First World War cut off the heavy two-way traffic between the Old World and the New, employers increasingly attempted to "Americanize" the immigrants in order to improve their work habits. In improvised factory classrooms, mill hands learned English, their duties as citizens, and the blessings of the free enterprise system. Company-supported churches preached to them the virtues of sobriety and obedience. And company-backed newspapers lectured them on the Red Menace to the steel industry and the nation.

But if newspaper editorials and Sunday sermons were intended to edify the human spirit, they stood little chance against the punishing regimen of the mill. The mills ran twenty-four hours a day; to keep the furnaces hot and the rolls turning, men put in a standard twelve-hour shift, seven days per week. It was grueling work. In summer, the heat could be unbearable, sometimes exceeding 110 degrees. In winter, the cold waged merciless war on hands and feet.

Furthermore, it was dangerous work. Often, the air was thick with dust and vapors; it was decades before any connection was made between these pollutants and the short life spans of mill workers. Nevertheless, the mills gained notoriety for the toll they took in human lives. In 1906, forty-six men were killed at South Works alone.

Progressive-era muckrakers zealously exposed the carnage wreaked by the mills. In 1911, *American Magazine* summarized work conditions as "a daily and weekly schedule of hours, both shockingly long; a system of speed-up that adds overstrain to overtime; and, crowning all, a system of repression that stifles initiative and destroys healthy citizenship."

Revelations such as these sparked public outrage and helped to pressure the steel companies to make modest reforms. However, it was only when steelworkers began to unionize that the potential for far-reaching reform developed. It would take more than three decades to organize the United Steelworkers of America (USWA), but as a result of that long and rough fight, by the 1940s working conditions in the American steel industry would be transformed.

It is fashionable now to deride labor unions, but the fashion has never really caught on in the Calumet region. There are still too many who remember what work was like before the unions achieved recognition.

Stanley Bughaski sums up the gut-level conviction that

prompted workers to risk harassment and even firing in the hard-fought battles to win union representation: "I'm strictly for unions. They're really something that people—well, if they're working people—they should unite and have a union. Because when you're dealing with the big boys, you're not going to get anything unless you have a little something to show."

When the USWA was formally established in 1942, the workers in the mills of Southeast Chicago finally had something to show, and in the ensuing years, they could see the fruits of their collective strength. "The unions were a great thing," opines Father Schopp, pastor of St. Kevin's Church in South Deering. "They limited the hours the company could demand out of a person, set a standard for safety, gave people a living wage, provided needed benefits, and gave the workers a bargaining voice." By any standards, an enviable record of accomplishments.

But the union was more than an institution that provided services to mill workers; it was a proud tradition with which activists allied in order to battle daily on behalf of their own. They won their terrain by nickel and dime, by job categories defined, by firings prevented. And although being a union steward brought no financial rewards, it offered an outlet for the serious intellects and prodigious energies that accidents of birth or school tracking systems had consigned to a lifetime of shearing steel.

Union elections were often hard-fought, gritty contests that required workers to develop a range of political and technical skills. Candidates had to negotiate alliances with men and women from different departments, ethnic backgrounds, and racial groups. They had to write their own campaign literature, learn how to get out voters, and familiarize themselves with a range of work issues. The stakes were high. Victory in the quest for one of the handful of full-time, paid union positions could mean escape from the mill and the acquisition of power and status in the larger community. In a world offering few ladders for upward mobility, this was a prize worth fighting for.

Within the local unions, a lively, chaotic democratic life flourished. Leadership rarely became entrenched. Meetings were often filled with complaints and suggestions. Bargaining committees gave a variety of members a taste of the complicated process by which contract settlements were reached. And the local union was one of the very few arenas in which steelworkers could feel free to express their views, to assert their ambitions, and to exercise a measure of control over their lives.

As the USWA grew to become one of the nation's largest and most powerful unions, some members began to grumble that it was slipping away from them. By the 1960s, they believed, the international union had become more concerned with administering complex collective bargaining agreements than with battling employers, and the officers at the Pittsburgh headquarters had grown far removed from the daily routines of work in a blast furnace.

"People tend to see the union in much the same way as they see an insurance policy," says USWA activist Rob Persons. "It's there, you pay into it every month, and in case you ever really need it, it's a good thing to have. But you don't have any real identification with your insurance company."

Moreover, the union had become isolated from its former allies and supporters. As labor-management relations stabilized in the postwar era, the USWA became progressively less involved in the public life of the Calumet region. By the 1970s, influential local church and business leaders had come to doubt the USWA's continuing value. Despite his respect for the union's record of achievements, Father Schopp believes that it no longer plays a positive role. "They didn't know when enough was enough," he declares. "They became too powerful."

Schopp's view is shared by a wide array of public figures

and media commentators. Images of power and greed—these are the twin demons that have turned many fair-minded people against the labor movement. But power is relative. While the USWA may have more of it than other groups in the halls of Congress, it has far less than the adversary against whom it is unfailingly matched—the steel corporations.

And what of greed? Again, it's all relative. The average wage for a steelworker is $28,000 a year, substantially above the average for industrial workers in America. But in order to earn that kind of money, a steelworker likely had twenty or more years in the mill—or worked an awful lot of overtime.

Overtime is a fact of life in the steel industry—mandatory overtime. There are union rules about trying to find a replacement for someone who's put in eight hours, but once the company has tried and failed, the person is back on the job. It's not uncommon for a steelworker to work sixteen hours straight, and there are those who tell of being kept on even longer.

Moreover, to earn their above-average wages, steelworkers had to surrender a significant measure of control over their lives. Jack Metzgar, a steel industry specialist at Roosevelt University, explains:

> High wages were granted to steelworkers partly in exchange for allowing management a nearly unfettered right to organize production . . . A typical steelworker might work 7 A.M. to 3 P.M. one week, 3 to 11 P.M. the next and 11 P.M. to 7 A.M. the following week. . . . Some mills follow a strict rotation. But at many mills . . . a steelworker often doesn't know what day and what shift he'll be working until a week beforehand. This makes it hard to buy tickets for football games or to plan family outings. . . . It also makes it hard to sleep.

And while most steelworkers live comfortably, they are far from affluent. Many had put in most of their years before mill wages took their big jump. (As late as 1969, the average hourly rate in steel was just $3.77.) And all of them have had to live through the boom-and-bust cycle of the steel industry, digging deep into savings in times of layoff.

"After twenty-two years, I make twelve dollars an hour," says Don Jordan, a product tester at South Works. "It's ridiculous to say we're greedy. There's only one reason to work in those mills—to make as much money as you can."

Jordan's belief that only good money draws workers into the mills reflects the fact that for all the union's accomplishments, steelmaking remains a demanding and often harrowing occupation.

Steve Szumilyas, who worked at Wisconsin Steel through the 1970s, insists that the company "expected you to put yourself at risk. You've gotta work in a rolling mill to appreciate" the dangers. "What you don't want is for a bar to land on you because they go right through you like a knife through butter."

Phillip Janik was a foreman at Wisconsin for more than thirty years and he saw many technological changes during his tenure there, but the philosophy that directed the work process never varied. "They'd say that production and safety were clasped like this," he recalls, lacing the gnarled fingers of his two hands together, "but it wasn't that way. Production always came first."

In response to the companies' unceasing push for production, steelworkers have developed a sense of pride, perhaps even of bravado, in their ability to get the job done. This pride is reinforced by the special demands of the steelmaking process itself. The manufacture of steel is hardly an assembly-line operation: it requires skill, teamwork, and courage to transform iron ore into steel products.

To begin with, iron ore must be purified by heating it in a blast furnace to which limestone and coke have been added. Next, the purified molten iron goes to a basic oxygen furnace, where burning oxygen combines with the carbon remaining in the iron ore, producing molten steel and a waste called slag. The hot metal may then be poured into molds to produce semifinished shapes for rolling, or it may be poured into the top of a relatively new machine, the continuous strand caster, which slowly cools and shapes the steel so that it can then be rolled.

The casting department provides a good example of the difficulties and dangers encountered throughout the steel-making process. Here the temperature is usually over 100 degrees. Overhead cranes swing ladles filled with 200 tons of molten steel across the vast room, jets of cold water shoot into contact with boiling steel, and the hydrogen gas that feeds the reheating ovens is always in danger of exploding.

If the machinery jams, hundreds of tons of steel may be ruined. Then the workers must swing into action. One crew member has to shove a lance over and over again into the boiling metal, while standing on two half-inch-thick sheets of steel a hundred feet from the ground. While shoving the lance, he pushes forward closer and closer to the mouth of the ladle until he's on the verge of falling in, and only the men and women standing by his side can protect him. A mistake can not only shut down an entire casting department, it can cost a fellow worker an arm, an eye, a life.

The work's constant danger bred camaraderie, a sense of mutual responsibility. "I used to watch the other fellas and if it looked like they were going to get hurt, I'd do something about it," observes Phillip Janik. "It became second nature." Another Wisconsin employee, Wayne Schwartz, remembers the close-knit feeling: "One man would help another no matter if he were black, white, purple, green."

The solidarity that the steelworkers created in their mills extended to their life outside as well. Members of work crews drank together at local taverns, came to know each other's families, shared occasions of celebration and sorrow. Furthermore, the intense personal bonds of trust forged in the workplace provided the basis for a host of local institutions

—ethnic clubs, church groups, and political associations. This dense web of interconnections has made Southeast Chicago the kind of community that people cling to, despite its antiquated streets and sewers, despite the pollution and the grime.

HOME GROUND

The food at the East Side Restaurant is hearty and plentiful. The waitresses know most people by name and their banter flows freely. Retired or unemployed men will sit at the counter for an hour or more over a bottomless cup of coffee. At the tables, women, small children in tow, visit with friends and neighbors.

Like dozens of restaurants, taverns, and stores on the Southeast Side, this eatery is home ground, familiar, comfortable, accessible. You may be a stranger downtown, but here you belong.

"Everybody knew each other's business," says Phillip Janik of the block where he grew up half a century ago. "And people would help their neighbor any way they could. If my mother had a couple dollars to spare and Mrs. Goetzinger needed a couple dollars, then she'd give it to her."

Petra Rodriquez has found this same casual generosity in South Deering for over fifty years. "You can find beautiful homes in the suburbs," she avers. "But you will never find the warmth and kindness—the amount of it—that exists in a place like this."

Statistics bear out these sentiments. In a survey of eight Chicago neighborhoods, Dr. Richard Taub of the University of Chicago found that the mill region's East Side placed highest in satisfaction and a sense of security. Over 87 percent of local respondents felt that they could call on their neighbors for help if they were sick, 97 percent said they could call on their neighbors to watch their homes when they went away,

and 88 percent felt they could borrow money from their
neighbors in an emergency.

The sense of belonging fosters stability. When Frances
and Stanley Bughaski got married, they bought a house on
the same Hegewisch block on which Stanley had grown up.
Frances moved there from her parents' home two blocks away.
More than forty years later, they still live in that same house.
"I only moved once," Frances says fervently, "and I hope to
God I never have to move again."

People on the Southeast Side share a feeling that they
control their own turf, and outsiders of every kind are suspect. Corporate officials in pinstripe suits, academics with
sophisticated jargon, social workers with professional
sympathy—they're all out of place in these neighborhoods.

The social wall that residents have erected around their
community is an outgrowth of the immigrant experiences of
the early settlers. The immigrants who poured into the mill
region in its early years did not find the gold-paved streets
that labor recruiters had promised them. In many cases, the
streets they found were not paved at all. Nor were there
adequate sewage or sanitary facilities: after a heavy rain, pud-
dles of garbage would sit for days.

In the mills, the most recent immigrants were assigned
the dirtiest and most difficult jobs. They were scorned by
native workers, like the one who wrote: "Here I am with these
Hunkies. They don't seem like men to me hardly. They can't
talk United States."

It didn't take the new arrivals long to realize that their
voyage to America did not end when they stepped off the
boat. It was, rather, a journey that took place over generations, a gradual adaptation to a new culture that was constantly frustrated both by a longing for the world left behind
and by the incessant labor required simply to survive.

In the early days, religion was often the only sustenance
to which immigrants could turn. Churches of many denominations sprang up in Southeast Chicago almost as quickly as

the community was settled. There were Lutheran, Methodist, Baptist, and even Jewish congregations. But it was the Roman Catholic church that claimed the allegiance of the great majority of the new arrivals, and each nationality soon established its own parish.

In the square mile that is the heart of the Southeast Side, there are eight Catholic churches. By the 1930s, the Poles, the Irish, the Croatians, the Slovenes, and the Mexicans had all built their own parishes, complete with religious objects from the Old Country, and priests who spoke the mother tongue.

The parish provided material aid and spiritual succor, and it played the key role of educator. Dominic Pacyga, historian of the Poles of South Chicago, stresses that the immigrants saw the establishment of parochial schools as critical to preserving their cultural heritage. This defensive posture was not the product of naivete: public education in America did aim at eradicating ethnic identities. A University of Chicago doctoral student, writing at the turn of the century, noted approvingly:

> It is the testimony of principals who have been in South Chicago for from 15 to 20 years that children of all nations. . . . go out from the 8th grade or the high school. . . . essentially Americanized, even looking with contempt on their parentage and mother-tongue.

Small wonder that each ethnic group struggled mightily to establish its own parish school. Frances Bughaski remembers her years at St. Florian's in Hegewisch as an idyllic time: she was taught by Polish nuns, sang in a Polish choir, and celebrated Polish holiday rituals. The pride she gained in her cultural traditions has stayed with her throughout her life.

But at the same time as the Catholic church reinforced ethnic identity, it also helped overcome ethnic insularity. The fact of shared belief served to unify the diverse ethnic groups. Richard Balcerzak, a lifelong resident of Southeast Chicago, recalls that "it was a united community. We had a common bond. Most of us were of the faith."

Forces outside the mill community eventually caused the church to modify its ethnic policies, however. The distrust felt by America's Protestant majority, exemplified by accusations that church members owed their ultimate allegiance to a "foreign power," the Pope in Rome, convinced American Catholicism to throw off the mantle of immigrant church.

The new church made patriotism its proud banner. And after World War II, when the United States became locked in cold war with the Soviet Union, this patriotic impulse merged seamlessly into a passionate opposition to atheistic communism.

Aside from such concerns, modern Catholicism maintained a discreet silence on public issues while emphasizing private morality. The zeal to demonstrate its Americanism produced a church uneasy with any protest against the dominant culture. Thus, an East Side resident described a local politician: "Everyone feels that he goes to church every Sunday and he's very good to his family. They don't care about all these rumors of payoffs and backroom deals—that's just part of politics."

As the role of the church shifted, ethnicity took on a larger secular dimension. Ethnic clubs, dance groups, musical societies, and other cultural activities became widespread, often independent of any particular church. In addition, ethnicity became a critical part of the political nexus of the community. Where group loyalties had once provided a shield against the wider world, they came to provide a stepping-stone into that world, a power base that enabled group leaders to negotiate advancement in the local Democratic party, the trade unions, and the business world.

At the same time, the church was able to integrate some of the cultural traits most central to the immigrant traditions into the American ethos it had come to articulate: respect for hard work, personal charity to those in need, and, perhaps most importantly, fulfillment of family responsibilities.

BLOOD TIES

The extended family is the central institution of the mill communities. From cradle to grave, Southeast Siders live within a thick web of blood ties to grandparents, uncles and aunts, parents, siblings, cousins, nephews and nieces, and children. The great waves of change in American family patterns in the last two decades—the rebellion of the young against parental values and the entry of women into the work force—were experienced here as minor ripples in a placid sea.

For generations there have been dual worlds on the Southeast Side. Men have tended to dwell in the realm of mill work and neighborhood taverns, while the home was women's domain.

Taverns are everywhere on the Southeast Side—across from the mill, along the shopping strip, next to the corner grocery. When mill work was a deadening seven-day-a-week routine, alcohol provided the only respite. Drinking became part of the mill worker's way of life, with alcoholism its unacknowledged by-product. Tony Vicik ran a tavern near South Works in the 1940s. "We had terrible drinkers in the mill," he recalls. "They'd come into my place at 7 A.M. and drink till 10 or 11. Them guys worked hard in that mill and they earned it. But many died young because of the drink."

Most tavern-goers drink more moderately. They come as much for the companionship as for the solace of whiskey. In these dark rooms, the anger and resentment that build up during the working day can be argued and joked away. Mill bonds can be reinforced.

While men work to the point of exhaustion and then drink

away their weariness, their wives often work equally hard, shouldering the responsibility for running and maintaining the home. "Women perceive themselves as very traditional," Theresa Marzullo says of her neighbors in Southeast Chicago. "But here they are taking on the husband's jobs. They're mowing the lawn, taking out the trash, fixing the pipes. These are women with five, six, seven, eight kids."

Bridging the separate worlds of men and women is a common concern for their children's education. Among Catholics, parochial school is a high priority, despite the strain it places on the family budget. Public school parents also are involved in their children's education, through PTAs and school activities. But despite the sacrifices made to ensure a good education, the image of working-class parents desperate to educate their kids into middle-class America does not fit Southeast Chicago. Upward mobility is a more ambiguous issue than it might appear at first glance.

First, there is the economics of advancement. Few steelworker families can afford the cost of college for their many children. A student will need scholarship help and a part-time job as well. Only the brightest and most motivated can apply.

Equally important are the social barriers. The public high schools in the mill neighborhoods track students into blue-collar jobs. Ed Sadlowski recalls:

When you're a kid in school, about 12 and 13, the questionnaire would say: What's your name? You'd say: Sadlowski. What does your dad do? You'd put down: steelworker. The counsellor would put you into industrial arts. A fancy name for you know what. That's where me and my pals wound up: making little holes in glass to make chimes. . . . All the kids I knew wound up in the steel mills. The son of a gun from U.S. Steel would come at graduation time and recruit guys.

Finally, there are psychological factors at work. Steelworkers may complain about the dirt and hours, but they take
pride in their work. Sometimes directly, sometimes merely by
example, their attitude is passed on. Ken Wychocki expresses
the contradictory emotions of a steelworker family, as he wryly
notes that "I can always remember my grandfather didn't
want my father to work in the mill. And my father didn't
want me to work in the mill. And I *know* I don't want my son
to work in the mill. But, it was just taken for granted: if your
father was in the mill, you were in the mill. It was never
thought of that you'd go anywhere else. Your father didn't
want you to, but when you were of age and ready to go to
work, he was the guy that got you the job, for crying out loud."

For their part, children often identify with their parents
and want to follow in their footsteps. Many young people
grow up, marry someone from the community, and buy a
home nearby. Sons will ride to work with their fathers; daughters call or visit their mothers almost daily.

Southeast Side parents know that only a minority of the
area's young people will complete college and leave the mill's
shadow. The rest will work and raise their own families within
this familiar territory. Sociologist William Kornblum has noted
that in these neighborhoods, the most important legacy parents leave their children is the family's standing in their community.

This strong adherence to shared values and traditions has
provided a sense of continuity in Southeast Chicago, but it
has also produced a certain narrowness. John Cronin grew
up on the Southeast Side and recently returned there after
living in the suburbs for many years. He says that he loves
the warmth of his East Side neighborhood but adds, "I hate
to sound elitist, but there's a provincialism here. They're not
too much in touch with the outside world and they don't care
to be." Carol Treno, who grew up on the East Side, shares
this assessment. While prizing the community's closeness, she

acknowledges that "there's a strong hostility to outsiders. That's the one bad thing about it. It can make them act very crummy."

DIVIDING LINES

Although black Americans have been part of the mill community since its earliest days, they have always been treated as outsiders by the white majority.

The first flare-up of racial hatred came during the 1919 steel strike when U.S. Steel brought blacks into the mills as strikebreakers. The sight of black workers crossing picket lines reinforced old prejudices and created new resentments among the whites. When the strike was broken, company officials crowed that "niggers did it."

Management showed little appreciation for this assistance, however. Steel executives deemed the turnover rate among black workers too high and soon turned to Mexico as their primary source of new labor. In some mills, blacks were entirely eliminated from the work force. Where they remained, black workers were relegated to the hardest and the dirtiest jobs.

Nonetheless, by the time of the massive industrial union drives in the 1930s, blacks were thoroughly entrenched in the mills and sufficiently disenchanted with their lot to throw in with the CIO. The advent of the USWA brought improvements in wages and working conditions, but it did not challenge the discriminatory practices that kept blacks at the bottom of the employment hierarchy. Former South Works employee Steve Alexander describes how discrimination was perpetuated for more than two decades:

It started at the personnel office. If you were black, you were sent to the blast furnace or coke oven. If you were white, you were sent to the machine shop or electrical

service department. Both started at the same level, but
blacks advanced through a seniority unit that locked them
into lower-paying jobs. Whites were in seniority units that
gave them the opportunity to bid into the journeyman
crafts.

It wasn't until the civil rights movement stimulated blacks
to organize in the 1960s that they finally gained access to the
highest-paying production jobs. And it took a federal lawsuit
in 1974 to crack the last bastion of white privilege and open
up craft positions to black apprentices.

Black advancement in the union paralleled gains in the
industry. In 1974, Local 65 at South Works elected its first
black president, and from that time forward, it became all
but impossible to win the leadership of a local union in Southeast Chicago unless a black worker had a prominent slot on
the slate. This increase in black representation produced material gains as well: more blacks were hired in staff positions
with the union; grievances were filed against job
discrimination—and won; and ongoing civil rights committees were established in many locals.

By 1980, more than sixty years after blacks had entered
the mills, they had gained formal equality and mechanisms
for combatting the discrimination that remained. In the process, they had forced the trade union movement to confront
its own prejudices and to live up to its own ideals of justice.
Furthermore, access to better jobs was combined with an overall jump in steel wages to increase the standard of living of
black steelworkers significantly. They could now afford the
kind of homes, cars, and clothes that symbolize middle-class
respectability.

The long and often bitter struggle to integrate blacks into
the mill's work force seems almost effortless when compared
to the difficulties encountered in cracking the color barrier
in Southeast Chicago neighborhoods.

South Deering's Trumbull Park was designed by the Olmstead brothers, masters of urban greenery, in 1911. Its swimming pool and stately field house have made the park the community's most prized attraction. It is also the symbol of the one ineradicable conflict that has marked this community for more than three decades.

Adjacent to Trumbull Park is one of the first low-income public housing developments built in Chicago, the Trumbull Park Homes. The project was never welcomed by the community because Chicago Housing Authority (CHA) policies largely excluded local residents. A 1941 study found:

> The people in the community that applied for a flat were mostly unsuccessful in attaining one. When the steel mills were running at full capacity, their wages were above the level set down by the housing authorities and when the mills were running slower, they were far below.

By the 1950s, the CHA was coming under fire for maintaining segregation in its projects. In July of 1953, the first black family was assigned to the Trumbull Park Homes; within a year, the black population of the project exceeded half a dozen families. The surrounding community reacted with dismay and anger, convinced that these first few families were only a vanguard for an entire army of blacks who would soon settle in its midst. When their protests to the CHA proved futile, the white residents of South Deering turned their fury on the black residents of the Trumbull Park Homes. Black people could not walk through the streets without being vilified. Their lawns were strewn with garbage. Their homes were defaced. Their sleep was shattered by the explosions of aerial bombs overhead.

Through it all, the blacks stood firm. By the end of the decade, a solid minority of black families lived in the Trumbull Park Homes and a tenuous calm had descended over the wider community.

Peace did not reign for long. In 1966, Dr. Martin Luther King, Jr., was greeted by rock- and bottle-throwing crowds when he led a march for open housing through the East Side. And in the years that followed, racial antagonisms flared anew as resistance to court-ordered busing plans grew.

Today, the handsome middle-class neighborhoods that ring the mill area—Pill Hill, The Manors, and South Shore —are predominantly black. South Chicago is an integrated neighborhood, where whites, blacks, and Hispanics live side by side. South Deering has a growing black population, but it is confined to a few discreet areas. The East Side, Hegewisch, and Slag Valley remain overwhelmingly white. In all these neighborhoods, fear—even hatred—of blacks lingers on.

There is a line down the middle of Trumbull Park. It is an invisible line, but those who regularly use the park have no doubt as to its location. One side of the park is reserved for Mexicans and whites; the other, for blacks.

On July 12, 1983, Rudolf Rice, a 22-year-old black man on the wrong side of the line, was shot and killed in Trumbull Park. Police arrested a 26-year-old Mexican in connection with the slaying but refused to release his name for fear of reprisals. Reprisals, however, are hard to avoid. A few weeks later, a Mexican man was stabbed and seriously wounded in the vicinity of the park; a black teenager was arrested for that attack.

Despite the racial tension that still holds South Deering in its grip, a solitary bicyclist circles Trumbull Park every evening. Like many others, Petra Rodriquez has never honored her community's dividing lines. In the aftermath of the Trumbull Park riots, Petra joined neighbors of all national- ities to organize activities for South Deering's children. To- day, she insists that the Park should be for all the people. "We have a divided park now," she says sadly. "The dark side and the light side. It's so foolish. Here we have two groups of people [Mexicans and blacks] who weren't ever wanted and still aren't wanted in some places. Why are we separated? We should be together. When I go bike riding, I feel I have to go to that dark side. Otherwise, what is it all about?"

POWER PLAYS

The contrary impulses of the mill communities—solidarity and prejudice, greed and generosity—all have their expression in a complicated and intense political life.

Politics on the Southeast Side has always been a brusque business, with scant room for good government gentility or the high-minded clash of ideas. One of the earliest political battles was fought in 1867 over the odiferous practices of a fertilizer company in South Chicago. By the turn of the century, politics had strayed little from such earthy matters. The 1901 aldermanic election was fought chiefly over the city's refusal to allow any sewers south of 95th Street.

But the real meat and potatoes of Southeast Chicago politics has never been the issues that are debated on election platforms. Rather, it has been jobs and services for local residents. The early immigrants' desperate need for "patrons" —people who could intercede for them with the authorities, help them find work and housing, translate their letters— helped to create a political system that came to be known as the Machine. Although machines flourished in immigrant communities across America, few proved to be as potent or as enduring as the Regular Democratic Organization of the City of Chicago.

The patronage system has ruled on the streets of Southeast Chicago for decades. Its methods have become more sophisticated, but its underlying approach hasn't changed: jobs or favors are provided in return for political support. After the steel mills, city government is the region's largest employer. And estimates of the number of jobs that are controlled by the Regulars range as high as 3000—many of them in the private sector.

With so many jobs at stake, politics is taken very seriously. Nothing of import, not union elections, nor chamber of commerce meetings, nor ethnic festivals, escapes entanglement in the web of local political alliances. Furthermore, the Organization is almost the only force that can make things happen—help teenagers find summer jobs, get parking tickets "taken care of," cut through the red tape for a liquor license.

Southeast Chicago falls largely within the boundaries of the city's seventh and tenth wards. Until the advent of the tenth ward's current alderman, the region was something of a political stepchild, rarely receiving the attention or resources that went to other parts of the city. Worse, it did receive something that almost no other ward got: the city's garbage. Because of its proximity to water, and its industrial concentration, the area became a prime location for waste disposal facilities.

There are many problems inherent in Machine politics in a mill community. While the Machine undoubtedly does much to help individuals with problems ranging from the minor—getting a trash can—to the fundamental—finding a job—there is usually a steep price for this assistance: the passive acceptance of a political culture that tends to abandon any responsibility for the overall condition of the community.

The Regular Democratic Organization's strength has at times been reinforced by the muscle of the United Steelworkers union. In the 1940s, the USWA set out to make its own political mark. Joe Germano, the powerful and autocratic Calumet district director, threw the union's weight behind Adlai Stevenson in the 1948 gubernatorial race. His victory boosted the Steelworkers into the top ranks of influence in state government.

Germano had a nose for winners. His next big gamble

was even more on target. In 1954, he helped unseat Chicago Mayor Martin Kennelly, lending his support to the plodding, paunchy Cook County clerk, Richard M. Daley. Once in office, a grateful Daley repaid the favor by appointing USWA staffers to city posts.

Soon the union was making endorsements in congressional and state legislative races and backing them up with money and manpower. In the state capital, the union brought its weight to bear on behalf of dozens of measures that improved working conditions and social supports for Illinois workers.

While the USWA has, in the main, supported the candidates of the Regulars, dissidence within its own ranks has often spilled over to spark political rebellions in the community. It was true that the union's pragmatism led it to seek alliances with those powerful enough to help secure its prestige and efficacy in political circles. But it was also true that a labor tradition of justice, equality, and democratic participation created a countervailing force, leading key unionists to play a role in shaping an independent political movement in Southeast Chicago. The social ideals and the material resources of the USWA provided the sustenance for independent challenges to the Machine's hegemony that were rare in the wards of Chicago.

While the Machine has been powerless to prevent union insurgency from achieving electoral expression, it has been successful in impeding the development of most other alternative institutions. Neither social service agencies nor activist community groups have flourished in the neighborhoods of Southeast Chicago. Some observers see this lack as a natural result of the community's self-reliance; others, as a deliberate policy on the part of political leaders who want to centralize power.

Among Southeast Siders themselves, the attitude toward social agencies is mixed. On the one hand, people will note

with considerable bitterness how services always bypass their
borders. "We pay our taxes and get nothing in return" is the
feeling. On the other hand, there is a scorn for institution-
alized charity. When people do need help they tend to turn
to family, to friends, or to their precinct captain down the
block.

Community activism, especially when associated with
"outsiders," is also suspect. When a citywide organization mobilized a core of local activists against the area's rampant pollution in the early 1970s, the operation was put to sleep almost
overnight. Local John Birchers attacked it, the politicians
threatened it, and the community recoiled from it in dismay.

This reluctance to engage in community protest grows
out of the fierce union battles of the past. During the CIO's
organizing drives of the 1930s, charges of communism and
anarchy stung Southeast Siders deeply, and they're still trying
to live down the stigma. What's developed is "a kind of schizo-
phrenia between work life and community life," says East Side
native Kevin Fitzgibbons. "It's okay to strike, but not to stir
things up in the community."

A pattern has emerged over time. Local residents depend
on their politicians to serve as their ambassadors to the
larger—and often alien—world. The Machine has given them
a measure of clout, if not respect. They have little faith in
their own ability to reshape the conditions of life in their
community; nor, until recently, did they feel any deep necessity to try.

At the same time, the citizens of Southeast Chicago do
not see themselves as atomistic individuals struggling to get
ahead. Instead, they have a strong sense of their interdependence. As a result, they readily and frequently band together to provide help to the needy and improve their
neighborhoods. Groups such as the East Side Golden Agers,
the Sunshine Club, Mothers of World War II, and the Mexican Patriotic Club all make a contribution to the common
good. While the politicians struggle for power, the people set

themselves the practical tasks of renewing the bonds forged over a centruy.

THE WORLD THEY HAVE MADE

The immigrants who came to Southeast Chicago from Eastern and Southern Europe, from Mexico, and from the Black Belt in the South found a world dominated by giant mills and larger corporations. For decades they worked hard in the mills, and just as hard outside them, striving to learn the ways of a strange and new culture while holding on to old traditions.

Across the generations, the lessons they learned about leadership, coalition building, compromise, and struggle enabled the men and women of the Southeast Side to gain a measure of control over their own terrain. While the tides of suburbanization and secularism swept over America in the post-World War II years, the citizens of this steel community carried on undisturbed, in the shadow of the mill smokestacks and the Skyway's sweeping arc. Little noticed by outsiders, they preserved their blue-collar world, with its commitment to family, to hard work, to God, to one's own people, and to labor solidarity. Their local schools taught children to value the ways of their parents. Their ward organizations provided jobs and services. And their labor unions helped workers share in the prosperity of the American steel industry in all its glory.

Over time, the mills came to be seen not as appendages of giant corporations but as part of the local landscape. If the people of these neighborhoods still knew that they depended on the mills for their livelihoods, they had also come to believe that the mills depended on them to make one of the world's most important commodities—steel.

There was a sense of pride and power in this view of the universe. There was also security. Life was predictable, and despite all the discomforts of the job, there was comfort in the certainty that it offered: steady work at decent wages and a secure retirement.

But this sense of security was rudely shattered on a chilly spring day in 1980 when the locks went up on the gates of Wisconsin Steel. Before long the illusion of interdependence between the companies and the community would be shattered as well.

Just as the people of Southeast Chicago were invisible to the travelers who passed high above them on the Skyway, so too the workings of the U.S. steel industry—with its diversified conglomerates, its overseas investments, its outdated technology—were invisible to the people who lived beneath the Skyway's trestles. While they worked countless hours of overtime, watched their paychecks grow, saw new blast furnaces installed, bought new houses or cars, choices were being made in Pittsburgh, in Washington, D.C., in Tokyo, and in Brazil that would radically alter the nature of the steel industry. The people of Southeast Chicago would not be consulted about those choices, yet they would alter the face of Southeast Chicago—perhaps irrevocably.

2

Shutdown at Wisconsin Steel

THE SMOKESTACKS of International Harvester's Wisconsin Steel mill had loomed over the houses of South Deering for seventy-five years. Harvester was a family firm, tied to the values of America's farmers—to hard work, patriotism, and benevolent charity. And South Deering was part of the Harvester family.

When International Harvester first came to South Deering in 1902, it was hailed as a savior. On the site of a deserted steel mill, the giant farm implement manufacturer erected a large new facility to produce plate and bars for the company's bright red tractors.

And Harvester brought more than a steel mill. The company laid gas lines, strung electric wires, and even paved some streets.

Chuck Grande's father came to South Deering to build the mill. He worked there forty years, and his son fifty. Together they span the Harvester era.

For seventy-five years, Harvester, Wisconsin Steel, and South Deering were a large and, Chuck thinks, happy family. Fully three-quarters of the men who lived in South Deering worked in the mill. The company provided coal and electricity for local churches for half a century. When South Deering residents campaigned for a park near the mill, management added its muscle to their lobbying efforts. And during the Depression, Harvester made land available so its idled employees could grow their own food.

Harvester's paternalism was most clearly marked in its labor relations. Company efforts extended from the organization of "tug-of-war" teams that demonstrated the mill workers' "pull-together" spirit to the establishment of an employee organization called the Works Council in 1919.

The Works Council's most popular activity was the promotion and support of community gardens, but at times, more momentous matters also came within its purview. That was the case in September 1919 when the National Committee for Organizing Steel Workers (AFL) called for a general strike at steel mills throughout the United States. While picketing steelworkers clashed with policemen in Pittsburgh, Youngstown, Gary, and South Chicago, South Deering stayed calm. At the company's request, the fledgling Works Council asked its members to stay home at first; when Harvester called its men back to work three weeks later, they responded with enthusiasm.

The McCormick family rewarded their loyalty with relatively generous sickness and accident protection, vacation plans, and time-and-a-half pay for Sunday and holiday work. But most of all, company managers made Wisconsin Steel what Chuck Grande calls "a good place to work."

This is best symbolized by the fact that for seventy-three years, Wisconsin Steel employees did not have to punch a time clock. Foremen loosely controlled their crews' comings and goings, allowing the men leeway if work was slow or if something special came up.

The mill was renowned for the family feeling among the men. Work buddies became lifelong friends. Employees operated a credit union to help finance homes and cars, a Goodfellows Club to help the needy, and a baseball league. Harvester management assisted all three activities, providing office space, donations, and even uniforms.

Wisconsin Steel's special blend of corporate paternalism and worker cooperation found its fullest expression when its independent trade union, the Progressive Steelworkers Union, was organized in 1937. PSWU leaders didn't take orders from any international union headquarters in Pittsburgh or Detroit, nor were they bound by industrywide labor agreements. The PSWU negotiated its own contracts with Harvester management, represented workers in grievance proceedings, and brought cases to arbitration.

The union spread its roots deep in the soil of South Deering and neighboring communities. Mike Drakulich won election as president in 1955 and held on to the reins of power for twenty years by allying himself with the heads of South Deering's leading families. His caucus was a well-oiled machine, piling up votes for the tenth ward Democratic organization in political elections as well as for the Drakulich slate in the mill.

But Harvester paternalism put limits on the PSWU's independence. While the bigger steel companies endured long and bitter strikes by the United Steelworkers of America in 1937, 1941, and 1959, Harvester management assured continuous steel supplies for its plants by giving the PSWU whatever wages and benefits the USWA achieved in its strike settlements. In addition, company officials allowed the PSWU leadership a certain amount of influence over decisions on hiring, job assignments, and promotions.

Not that the PSWU's cozy relationship with management was necessarily a "sellout" deal. Although the union refrained from striking for forty years, it did orchestrate "wildcat" walkouts from time to time. Eli Stranich, a long-time PSWU officer, recalls: "I could settle a problem without going through a lot of steps. If the spark testers had a gripe, I would tell them, 'Call in sick, you all got the flu.' The company would threaten to fire each one who didn't show up for work. So I

said, 'Go ahead, go ahead.' And nobody was ever fired." The
union won its point often enough to repel repeated CIO
attempts to bring Wisconsin Steel into the mainstream of organized labor. It was to remain independent until its dying
day.

Over time, the Harvester family began to lose its cohe-
siveness. Economy-minded executives discontinued company
Christmas parties after the Second World War. Not long afterwards, management cut back on its aid to athletics and the
baseball and basketball leagues had to be disbanded. Worst
of all, Harvester began neglecting the mill. By the end of the
1960s, Chuck Grande, who worked in the office as a payroll
clerk, could "see the machinery deteriorate. Management made
a little money, and instead of plowing it back into the equipment they didn't do it. Maybe they had other ideas."

But Chuck still retained his trust in Harvester. When the
company sold the mill to Envirodyne in 1977, he figured that
management "knew who it was putting in there. We had faith
Harvester knew what it was doing."

Three years later, Chuck was retired, though he kept up
with news from the mill. On March 27, 1980, he attended a
union meeting at which Wisconsin Steel's new owners assured
a jam-packed audience, "Don't worry. For a long time to come,
everything looks real good."

The next day, workers on the three o'clock shift were told
to go home because the mill was closed and headed for bankruptcy. Chuck couldn't believe the news. "It took a week or
so for the truth to sink in. At first, I felt sorry for all the
people who had homes here and big families. And then I
started to worry about us pensioneers."

It took about a year before Chuck could find out that he
would continue to receive his pension. But when the government took over paying pensions that Harvester had not fully
funded, Chuck's monthly check was cut 10 percent.

Chuck Grande tries hard not to get angry. He acknowledges, however, that "there are some things that do irritate

the people around here. We don't get straight answers." He'll even confess that "when something like this happens, you carry a little chip on your shoulder. It's something you can't control."

But Chuck is not sure that his anger is justified. His uncertainty is rooted in his respect for the corporation. He believes that Harvester, Envirodyne, and even the government must have had good reasons for what they did.

Perhaps what Chuck Grande feels more than anger is sadness. Some mill workers are leaving South Deering to seek better job opportunities elsewhere. However, the majority of the people who worked at Wisconsin still remain. Chuck thinks of them as "die-hards." "We set our sights on long range dreams, and we hung on. Now those dreams are shattered."

THE DECLINE OF WISCONSIN STEEL

From the day Chuck Grande's father came to South Deering to build the mill to the day, seventy-eight years later, when Chuck learned it had been shut down, Wisconsin Steel's fortunes were tied to the International Harvester Corporation. The mill owed its birth to the fact that Harvester executives were unwilling to be at the mercy of the steel oligopoly J. P. Morgan organized in 1901. Fearing that U.S. Steel would use its market power to raise prices artificially, as the railroads had done, Harvester organized its own steel division, with iron ore and coal mines, a fleet of ore boats, and the steel mill in South Deering.

For half a century, U.S. Steel's success at keeping steel prices high and technological change slow ensured Wisconsin Steel's survival, for it required no great investment on Harvester's part to maintain its mill's competitiveness. Wisconsin also benefited from the fact that it fit a special niche in America's steel markets: its rolling mills produced small batches of high-quality steel shaped for farm equipment and auto parts manufacturers; most large steelmakers disdained such orders.

That was the pattern until 1960, when South Deering got a break. Harry Bercher, who'd once managed the Wisconsin Steel division, rose to the presidency of International Harvester determined to make the Torrence Avenue mill an industry leader. Within two years, Bercher invested $30 million in new technology, including two of America's first basic oxygen furnaces and an innovative continuous caster. Suddenly Wisconsin Steel had become a jewel. Observers from all over the country toured the new facilities and praised them in the business press.

Then, just as suddenly, things went sour. Harry Bercher left Harvester in 1969, and Wisconsin Steel stopped receiving funds for modernization. The cutoff resulted from more than a change in personalities. The businesses that had long formed the core of the Harvester empire—tractors and pickup trucks—had fallen into trouble.

Harvester had emerged from World War II dominant in the farm market, but its success bred excessive ambitions. When the corporation entered the construction equipment and over-the-road truck markets, it got in over its head. The company simply lacked the capital to finance its varied businesses, especially since 74 percent of corporate earnings went for dividends. Soon, Caterpillar trounced Harvester in bulldozers, and Deere took the lead in tractors. These defeats shook up corporate management. Brooks McCormick, Harry Bercher's successor, announced a new emphasis on profitability. To boost the bottom line, the company would concentrate on its money-making operations. No more capital would be poured into Wisconsin Steel. Why modernize a marginal business when more important facilities were starving?

Had Harvester sold the mill in 1969, tragedy might have been averted, according to Chuck MacDonald, then president of the Wisconsin Steel division. "We were riding the crest then," he says. But Harvester is not a fast-moving company. Four years passed before top management decided to unload the aging mill. In the meantime, MacDonald remembers, "I'd spend four to five million a year, and my competition would spend twenty million. Three or four years of that, and you fall behind seriously."

Passage of environmental protection legislation in 1970 clinched Harvester's decision to let go of the mill. For decades, Wisconsin had polluted South Deering's skies with carbon monoxide, and its waters with cyanide, iron, and lead. After Congress passed the Clean Air and Waters Act, Wisconsin Steel managers had to clean up their act or face heavy fines.

In 1973, Harvester hired a consultant to assess the mill's viability, and learned that it would take more than $150 million to bring Wisconsin into compliance with antipollution requirements, to restore its efficiency, and to operate it for five years. To the Harvester brass, that amount was unthinkable.

But Harvester could not afford to close the mill either. One reason was that the company had $62 million in unfunded pension liabilities that it would have to pay if the plant closed. In addition, Harvester's labor agreements called for the payment of millions more dollars in pension supplements and severance pay in the event of a shutdown. Finally, if the company had to write off the mill's $200 million book value, red ink would be smeared all over the corporate ledger.

Brooks McCormick decided to try to sell Wisconsin Steel rather than close it down. He assigned Chuck MacDonald and James Doyle, Harvester's vice president for corporate affairs, to conduct a top secret search for a company interested in buying a steel mill.

To Doyle, selling Wisconsin Steel was a job. But for Chuck MacDonald, who'd worked at the mill for twenty-three of his twenty-six years at Harvester, it was a trial. As he searched for a buyer, old friends would ask why he was not replacing dilapidated equipment, and countless rumors spread through the mill about an impending sale, but MacDonald had to express "absolute confidence that it was not going to be sold." Then on August 17, 1975, a *Business Week* interview with Brooks McCormick let the cat out of the bag. The magazine's cover story was headlined "Wisconsin Steel on the Block," thereby confirming the worst fears of the people of South Deering.

Doyle and MacDonald spent four years (1973–1977) looking for a buyer. At one time or another probably every steelmaker in the country looked at Wisconsin's prospectus, but the mill's deteriorated condition scared them off.

All but McLouth Steel of Detroit. McLouth needed Wisconsin Steel's coke ovens badly; it negotiated with Harvester right up to the point of sale. But at the last moment, McLouth management pulled back; the deal was off.

Years of neglect had begun to take their toll on the mill. In 1969, mysterious explosions in an old battery of coke ovens terrified South Deering residents. A year later, seven men suffered burns on their hands and faces when a pocket of gas exploded underneath the coke oven they were cleaning. In 1973, fire broke out in the number 4 coke battery, causing extensive damage. Then in 1976, the number 3 coke battery had to be shut permanently to bring the mill into compliance with Clean Air laws. Finally, in 1977, four men working on an old blast furnace were overcome by gas and killed.

As the mill deteriorated, it began to lose money. By now Harvester was absolutely desperate to sell Wisconsin Steel.

A MINNOW SWALLOWS A WHALE

Envirodyne Industries was the answer to Harvester's prayers. Formed in California in the early days of the high-tech revolution, Envirodyne was the brainchild of a young engineer with entrepreneurial ambitions. Dr. Ronald Linde was director of physical sciences at the Stanford Research Institute. Growing restless with the life of an academic administrator, he decided to enter the marketplace in 1969.

Linde's plan was to concentrate on acquiring promising young firms and developing their projects commercially. After eighteen acquisitions, nearly all accomplished with stock swaps, Envirodyne's revenues exceeded $24.4 million in 1976. Its businesses ranged from the development of pollution treatment equipment to the design of bridges to the harnessing of ultrasonic waves as an energy source. Yet for all its early successes, Envirodyne seemed stuck in place. Profits for 1976 totaled just $242,000 and the stock had declined from $16.00 a share to $3.25. Linde decided it was time for a change. His new strategy was to find a small manufacturing operation that some large corporation wanted to get rid of, to buy that operation with borrowed money, and to restore it to profitability.

Linde hired George Sealey, an engineering salesman and vice president of the giant Bechtel Corporation, to find this next acquisition. Sealey immediately began calling friends and acquaintances around the country in search of a suitable firm. One day in February 1977, while Sealey was having lunch with his old friend James Doyle, his search hit pay dirt. "How would you like to get into the steel business?" Jim Doyle asked.

Sealey laughed at first: after all, neither he nor Ron Linde knew the first thing about the industry; and besides, Envirodyne was looking to acquire a company its own size, not one ten times as big. But Doyle was serious. On the back of a paper place mat, he showed Sealey how the deal could be arranged. Envirodyne would buy Harvester's entire Wisconsin Steel division without putting up any money and without taking any risk. This magic trick could be simply accomplished: Abracadabra—Envirodyne would set up a limited liability subsidiary which would mortgage Wisconsin's assets to buy the mill. Presto—for no money down, Envirodyne was in the steel business.

To Ron Linde and George Sealey, Doyle's proposal was an exciting opportunity to create a profitable business out of a conservative old money-loser. They saw Wisconsin Steel as the victim of old-fashioned management and of its captive-supplier relationship with the Harvester Corporation. Modern marketing methods would improve sales, high technology would boost production, and smart management would cut costs. Besides, what did they have to lose?

They would need, of course, more money to modernize the mill. But here too, Envirodyne's executives had a plan: if they could just show positive operating results for the first years, private lenders would provide the funds. Those assets. not mortgaged in the sale could serve as collateral.

Envirodyne's enthusiasm was not matched in Harvester's executive suites. The deal was enormously tempting, for it would rid the company of its pension obligations and its operating losses, while assuring a continued supply of steel bars, but there were serious questions. Could Envirodyne, with its ignorance of the steel business, really make a go of it? Could the firm raise sufficient capital for modernization? What would happen if the mill went belly-up? Most important of all, would the Pension Benefit Guaranty Corporation (PBGC), the federal agency charged with protecting workers' pensions, challenge the sale?

As soon as Harvester actually contemplated the deal with Envirodyne, alarm bells began ringing at the PBGC. If Harvester was allowed to transfer its unfunded liabilities to an assetless firm, and if the mill then were to fail, the agency would be obligated to pay out Wisconsin Steel pensions to the tune of more than $50 million.

Alarm bells were also keeping Chuck MacDonald awake at night. An experienced steelman, he wasn't convinced that Envirodyne could turn the mill around. How could people who didn't know what shift work meant, who didn't know the difference between a blast furnace and a basic oxygen furnace, run a steel mill?

When MacDonald raised these objections at corporate headquarters, he met a hostile reception. And this posed a dilemma:

> I was not a decision-maker for Harvester. I was an officer of the company. I could not singlehandedly stand up to management and say, "You can't sell the mill to Envirodyne." Wisconsin Steel management had come off three or four years of being hailed as inefficient, do-no-goods. But I could see the pitfalls. No one wanted to listen to those. I was branded a negative thinker. So I quit talking.

Brooks McCormick shared MacDonald's concerns, however. Wisconsin had been part of the Harvester "family" for seventy-five years; the company had a responsibility to treat its employees fairly. And so McCormick decided to call on the investment banking firm of Lehman Brothers Kuhn Loeb to analyze the viability of the deal Jim Doyle had proposed.

Peter Peterson, former secretary of commerce in the Nixon administration, was Lehman Brothers' president. The verdict he delivered to Harvester's board of directors was negative. Peterson's reservations were twofold: Envirodyne lacked the expertise in the steel business necessary to turn Wisconsin Steel around, and it lacked money to operate and modernize the mill.

The fact that the consultants Brooks McCormick had hired to examine the prospects of Wisconsin Steel in Envirodyne's hands brought in a negative verdict did not kill the deal. After the Harvester board of directors heard another consultant, Phillip Brothers, deliver a more positive evaluation, it agreed to allow the sale to proceed.

It's not hard to see how PhiBro could have concluded that Wisconsin Steel had a chance to survive under new ownership: commonly accepted projections for the steel industry in

1978–1983 showed a strong expansion of the market for the mill's products. On the other hand, PhiBro was not entirely disinterested; the firm was a party to the sale agreement, having agreed to take a "put" on the mill's output, which meant that if the mill shut down, PhiBro would pay the lenders an agreed-upon sum for inventory and then sell it for whatever price it could get.

At any rate, Harvester now had what it wanted—an expert opinion that the mill could survive under Envirodyne. Whatever private reservations Brooks McCormick might have felt, he gave his approval.

The agreement consummated between Harvester and Envirodyne on July 31, 1977, was complex. The key was Harvester's promise to buy a specified proportion of its steel bars from Envirodyne for the following ten years. Furthermore, the company agreed to back an unrelated Envirodyne project—Envirosonics. That this was no small matter is attested to by the fact that the sale agreement explicitly stipulated that Envirodyne could use some of the mill's earnings to finance that venture.

With these agreements in place, Envirodyne's subsidiary, EDC Holding Company (assets $1.5 million), was to pay Harvester $65 million for the entire Wisconsin Steel division, including ore boat, coal and ore mines, steel mill, and land. Envirodyne borrowed $50 million of that total from Harvester by giving the company 8.5 percent notes payable beginning in ten years. As collateral for these notes, Harvester took a first lien on the iron and coal mines. EDC Holding Company paid the remaining $15 million in cash, money it received by borrowing an additional $35 million from the Chase Manhattan Bank. Chase's collateral for that loan was Wisconsin Steel's inventory and accounts receivable. Finally, EDC Holding Company assumed all of the debts of Harvester's Wisconsin Steel division, including the $62 million in unfunded pension liabilities.

The business press reported: "Minnow Swallows Whale."

Each of the parties to the sale protected itself very carefully. Envirodyne shielded its assets by establishing a limited-liability subsidiary. Harvester took care to have EDC Holding Company sign over the deeds to the ore and coal mines, so that Harvester could claim possession of them at any time. And Chase established a network of auditors and security guards on site at Wisconsin Steel to make sure that there always existed sufficient collateral to cover its loan exposure.

Even the government protected itself. Although the PBGC decided not to declare Harvester's pension systems terminated at the time of the sale, a move which would have obligated the firm to meet all its unfunded pension liabilities, the agency reserved the right to take action at a later date. Five years later, in fact, the PBGC did file suit against Harvester on the ground that the sale was a spurious transaction, an allegation Harvester denies. But in 1977, only one organization challenged the sale. It was the Progressive Steelworkers Union.

By the time of Wisconsin Steel's sale to Envirodyne, Leonard "Tony" Roque had replaced Mike Drakulich as president of the Progressive Steelworkers Union. While growing up amidst South Chicago's Mexican community, Roque had gained the friendship of the future alderman of the tenth ward, Edward Vrdolyak.

From the beginning of his own political career Vrdolyak had coveted the PSWU as a power base. When Drakulich's health declined in the early 1970s, "Vrdolyak" made his move. The two men assembled a coalition of Mexicans hungry for power, blacks frustrated by years of exclusion from the better jobs in the mill, and whites opposed to Drakulich's rule. After a narrow election victory, in 1973, Roque and Vrdolyak consolidated their base by securing preferred job assignments for those who pledged loyalty.

Tony Roque learned of Wisconsin Steel's impending sale

only days before its completion. This was no accident. Harvester officials had urged Ronald Linde and George Sealey not to meet with the PSWU until arrangements were concluded. Roque believes that Doyle feared the union would try to discourage Envirodyne from buying the mill.

In any case, when Roque learned of the sale, he frantically sought information about the new owner. Upon learning that Envirodyne had little capital, Roque became a man obsessed. He immediately fired off telegrams to executives of the two companies, demanding information about the terms of their agreement.

Transcripts of Roque's subsequent meetings with Harvester officials record a rather confused dialogue. That confusion stemmed from the fact that three different sets of benefits were at stake. The first were those pension benefits spelled out in earlier collective bargaining agreements and which were covered by the government's Pension Benefit Guaranty Corporation. Second, there were other contractual pension benefits which PBGC policy did not cover, and which would be lost to union members unless Harvester agreed to pay them in the event of an Envirodyne bankruptcy. Third, there were benefits, in areas other than pensions, that Harvester was contractually obligated to pay if it shut Wisconsin Steel down.

Transcripts of Harvester's negotiations with the PSWU appear to indicate that Tony Roque did not understand that the bulk of Harvester's pension liabilities were guaranteed by the PBGC under the ERISA Act of 1974. Roque concentrated so heavily on attempting to win Harvester's promise to pay these already largely guaranteed benefits that he did not effectively bargain for the other two sorts of benefits which were provided for by Harvester's contract with the PSWU and which were not guaranteed by the PBGC.

To illustrate this confusion, consider an exchange which occurred between Harvester's Robert Crowel and the PSWU's

Tony Roque, at the second meeting between company and union representatives on August 11.

CROWEL: In all our negotiations, IH made a very careful analysis of our legal obligations under the law and under ERISA [the pension act of 1974]. We also gave very careful consideration to our moral obligation and we think both legal and moral obligations are covered in the sales agreement. We went over ERISA last time we met. We pointed out that the protection of the people doesn't come from IH or Envirodyne, it comes from the PBGC. An employee has as much protection as he can get by virtue of that. . . . If you are seeking to have IH go further than the legal requirements in guaranteeing unfunded liability, we are not going to do that. No other company has that obligation today.

ROQUE: That is your opinion. We feel there is a sweetheart deal here. We do not think IH would have given Wisconsin Steel to Envirodyne if they had to fund the pension benefits. We have no choice but to go after Harvester for the money we believe is owed our people. We do not think you have a moral right to let someone assume something that they do not have (money) to pay. We want you to be a third party guarantor in the event that the plant shuts down.

In the end, Harvester management gave up trying to make Roque understand the PBGC's role in guaranteeing pensions in the event of a bankruptcy. The agreement signed by Harvester and the PSWU bound Harvester to pay steelworkers whatever pension benefits Envirodyne's Holding Company and the PBGC did not pay, if the mill closed within five years. In exchange, the union agreed to relinquish all other claims against Harvester, including the nonpension contractual benefits, which were not covered by PBGC's guarantee.

Upon signing the agreement, Roque told cheering PSWU members that their pensions were now safe. They breathed a collective sigh of relief.

Years later, steelworkers were to form a different judgment of the agreement Roque had signed. What Harvester had actually given them was a promise to pay the difference between the pensions due them under their contract and what the PBGC would pay. By the time the mill actually closed, this amounted to perhaps $5 million. But the union had waived its rights to a good deal more than that.

Roque had signed away four major benefits: severance pay, accrued vacation pay, extended vacation pay, and supplementary unemployment benefits. If the mill had shut down under Harvester on July 31, 1977, steelworkers would have received more than $12.5 million from these four sources. In addition, Roque had waived pension supplements for those workers forced to retire before age 62. These supplements were worth another $12 million.

How did Tony Roque come to sign an agreement which he would later testify that he didn't understand, waiving millions of dollars in benefits to steelworkers who would so sorely need them? It was here that the PSWU and its members paid dearly for their independent status. Henry Szesny, the lawyer assigned by Vrdolyak Ltd. to handle the negotiations with Harvester, has testified that he told Roque that he (Szesny) didn't know ERISA fully and advised him to seek the services of another lawyer. But Roque did not do so.

In September 1977, having concluded his ill-fated negotiations with Harvester, Tony Roque turned his attention to Envirodyne. It was a strange encounter. Envirodyne management came to South Deering convinced they could reduce labor costs. Roque had other ideas. He believed that Envirodyne would run the mill into bankruptcy, but in the meantime, the company's weakness made it easy pickings.

Both sides got some satisfaction. While Envirodyne did not get the wage and benefit cuts it hoped for, it did secure

Roque's cooperation in boosting productivity by discouraging worker complaints about speedup or job assignments.

In return, Roque obtained a new employee benefit, which boosted his standing with the members: free vision care. This was to be provided by NCI Industries, a new company which established a clinic in the building housing Alderman Vrdolyak's law firm. And there was more. After the union signed its contract with Envirodyne, Alderman Vrdolyak received a campaign contribution from Wisconsin Steel; the union's lawyer was taking campaign contributions from the company with which the union negotiated.

Once the labor agreement was concluded, Envirodyne launched its campaign to make the mill profitable. Two new executives came to Chicago to lead the effort. They couldn't have been more different.

James Morrill was a lifetime steelman whose forte was operations. He came to Chicago after heading Penn-Dixie's steel division in Kokomo, Indiana. When stories about corruption in Penn-Dixie's management began to fill the business press in 1978 and 1979, there were rumors in Chicago and Washington that Morrill was implicated in the scandal. Despite the fact that he was never indicted for any alleged wrongdoing, the fact that Morrill had been named in rumors took some of the luster off Envirodyne's effort to rescue Wisconsin Steel.

Michael Lyon was a veteran of an agrarian reform program in Chile, a businessman-lawyer at the Hyatt Corporation, and a professor at Stanford Law School. When his friend Ron Linde asked him to come to Chicago to help raise private-sector funds to modernize the mill, Lyon agreed.

His plans changed radically on December 1, 1977, however, when President Carter announced a new federal program to aid the steel industry. Dramatic plant shutdowns and the layoff of thousands of steelworkers in Democratic districts had prompted the president to establish a task force on the steel industry early in his administration. The task force had determined that foreign competition was eroding domestic markets, causing U.S. steelmakers to lose their incentive to invest. The remedies suggested were twofold: a trigger-price mechanism that set minimum prices for steel exports to the United States on the basis of foreign production costs, and a $500 million loan guarantee program to enable small steel companies to modernize. Why target small companies? The task force reasoned that the larger companies would not need guarantees; once the trigger-price mechanism went into effect, large firms like U.S. Steel would use their vast resources to modernize their mills.

Once Carter's task force announced its plans to save America's steel industry, Michael Lyon's—and Envirodyne's —hopes for desperately needed capital were centered squarely on public support.

The Government Lends a Hand

Congress approved the steel loan guarantee in February of 1978. The Economic Development Administration (EDA) was assigned to administer the new program. This was not a simple task. EDA had been established in 1965 to aid small businesses; it was accustomed to evaluating $5 to $10 million loans, most of them for projects in rural areas. Agency personnel seldom dealt with larger transactions, and none of them were familiar with the steel industry.

Moreover, the legislation creating EDA left the agency ill-suited for carrying out its new mandate. For example, one section of the original legislation prohibited the agency from making loans to businesses making products for which there was already excess capacity. Under the steel loan guarantee program, EDA found itself constantly having to determine whether or not there was excess capacity in specialized steel markets. On two occasions, the competitors of companies receiving federal loan guarantees actually sued EDA on the grounds that its subsidies were spurring the construction of steelmaking capacity which would glut the market and depress prices, thereby damaging the plaintiffs' profitability.

But despite these flaws, to George Sealey and Michael Lyon the Carter program looked like manna from heaven. The day after the president announced his steel policy, Sealey flew to Washington to meet with EDA officials. He came away convinced that the loan was in the bag; agency staffers had told him that Wisconsin Steel was exactly the kind of mill their program had been established to help.

At Envirodyne's new offices in Chicago's Wrigley building, the future looked bright. The mill was doing a great business, and $50 million in federal loan guarantees would soon be forthcoming. The run-down, loss-plagued mill would be transformed.

But before long, procedural delays began to play havoc with Envirodyne's plans: the EDA demanded a complete financial history of Harvester's steel division. Only one Harvester employee knew where the records were kept and it took him months to amass the required data. Only after this hurdle was passed did EDA hire a consultant to study the loan application, and five months were to pass before his report was filed.

Procedural delays were only part of Envirodyne's problem. The EDA also made it clear that Wisconsin Steel could not get a loan guarantee until it complied with environmental regulations. Harvester had resisted federal orders to clean up the mill right up to the day of the sale; by then, violations were rampant. Ronald Linde had hoped to finance pollution-control equipment from the projected EDA loan, but environmental regulators were not satisfied with the company's timetable.

As the loan application process snarled, Wisconsin Steel's performance began to falter. During the summer of 1978, two of the old blast furnaces broke down. Each passing month saw operating costs escalate and production decline. Every new ounce of red ink necessitated revision of the loan application; in the end, EDC Holding Company filed twelve different sets of figures with EDA, and the loan request ballooned from $50 million to $90 million. EDA wasn't thrilled.

As Wisconsin Steel's finances declined, politics became increasingly important to Envirodyne's game plan. Illinois' second district congressman, Morgan Murphy, became point man in its efforts to overcome federal resistance to making the loan guarantee.

Morgan Murphy was the ideal candidate to play that role. As Ed Vrdolyak's ally, he had a vital interest in protecting his political power base. Furthermore, Murphy was chairman of the congressional steel caucus, a bloc whose membership included more than half the members of the House of Representatives. When it came to federal policy for the steel industry, Murphy packed a lot of clout. Nor did it hurt matters that he was second ranking Democrat on the House Rules Committee, at a time when the committee's chair, Edward Bolling of Missouri, was seriously ill. The congressman from Illinois was very important to the Carter White House. Finally, Murphy's own personality was helpful. A handsome Irishman with the gift of gab and great personal charm, Murphy loved the drama of politics. He cast himself as the people's champion, defending the jobs of worthy mill workers against heartless bureaucrats. It was a role for which his enthusiasm knew no bounds.

Now in private law practice, Murphy remains committed to the cause: "Call it pork-barrel, call it what it was. I was just concerned about 4000 jobs. The effect on the community, on small specialty shops, the cobbler, the presser, the restaurant owner, the church. I used my influence as best I could. I plead guilty to that."

Some other men might have been deterred by the warnings Murphy heard as he toiled on behalf of his constituents. Friends within the administration leaked damaging information about Envirodyne to the congressman, to save him from the embarrassment of going out on a limb for an unworthy ally. They informed him of the clouds over Morrill's past; they passed on confidential allegations that Envirodyne was draining the mill of capital. To no avail. Even when Murphy learned that the EDC official with whom he'd formed the closest bonds was misleading him about the mill's actual condition, he carried on.

Murphy's efforts were not in vain. With all the skills of an old Chicago pol, he arranged a meeting involving Envirodyne executives, state and federal environmental regulators, and the chairmen of appropriate congressional committees, and told the participants to stay until they had reached agreement. The resultant decree brought Wisconsin Steel into compliance with EDA requirements to install $34 million worth of pollution equipment.

With the pollution knot untied, Murphy turned to the EDA. One day, Murphy recalls, Vice President Mondale, on the tennis court of his Washington residence, told the congressman that the EDA was ready to approve the loan guarantee. And oh, yes, it would be nice if Murphy would help out the administration's bill to create a new education department. For the congressman, the price was steep; he'd received a personal letter from Chicago's Cardinal Cody urging him to oppose the legislation. But Murphy paid that price. And when EDA approved the loan guarantee on August 1, 1979, there was Morgan Murphy announcing South Deering's good fortune, flanked by Jack Watson of the Carter White House, Chicago's mayor Jane Byrne, and tenth ward alderman Edward Vrdolyak.

Bob Hall, the man then responsible for approving EDA's loan guarantees, disputes Murphy's account: "One of the interesting things about the Carter White House—perhaps it was our weakness—was that we very rarely had political pressure to do things. In hindsight, if I had been told to do it, my conscience might be clearer. But that would be untrue and unfair. The congressman tried to exert pressure, but in terms of a $90 million deal, that wouldn't have been sufficient." In the end, Hall argues, there was only one question: Did Wisconsin Steel have a reasonable chance?

Peter Bohn, the consultant to the EDA on Wisconsin Steel, played a large part in answering that question. In a Marriot hotel suite high above Chicago's lakefront, Bohn began his study of Wisconsin Steel in February 1979.

He wasn't happy with what he found. He was appalled by the mill's condition, and by Envirodyne's ignorance of the steel industry. For Bohn, Wisconsin's travails were America's problems in a nutshell—businessmen wanting to make money without getting their hands dirty.

The first of several serious problems was the management structure of Envirodyne Holding Company. The board of directors consisted of Michael Lyon, Ronald Linde, and George Sealey, none of whom was a steelman. This arrangement, Bohn declared, was "totally inadequate." Then Bohn also discovered that EDC Holding Company management lacked a financial director, thus seriously handicapping its ability to plan and monitor its costs. Even worse, there was no standard system to tell Jim Morrill what it cost to manufacture various products.

Finances were the biggest problem. When Bohn began analyzing Wisconsin Steel's plans, they projected a slight profit for the year. A bad winter changed that to a small loss. But then in May, hot iron breached the brick lining of the number 3 blast furnace, forcing it to shut down for three weeks of repairs. As a result, the company had to cancel millions of dollars of orders. Projections for 1979 had to be revised once again—downward.

The blast furnace's problems had drained Wisconsin Steel of money for working capital and to pay its bills. Without an immediate infusion of cash, bankruptcy was imminent.

Even worse, if EDA made the loan and then the mill were to close down in 1980, the government would be out millions of dollars. The total sum the EDA could hope to raise by selling the mill property, Bohn estimated, was much less than what the agency would be obligated to pay to the financial institutions that had lent the $90 million.

As Bohn shared his findings with EDA and Envirodyne officials, frantic negotiations ensued, aimed at correcting the problems. Adviser Eric Richards of Chase Manhattan Bank recalls that "it was an intense period. I probably saw more of Ron Linde at this time than I saw my wife." Together with Mike Lyon, Richards spent day after day talking to executives at Chase, Harvester, PhiBro, and the U.S. Department of Housing and Urban Development—mostly requesting additional loans. At the same time, Envirodyne executives searched for solutions to the managerial shortcomings Bohn had exposed.

Most intense of all were the negotiations between Harvester and the EDA over the issue of collateral. After Bohn pointed out the government's exposure, EDA officials told Harvester that there would be no guarantee unless the company surrendered some of its collateral. Specifically, EDA wanted Harvester's first lien on the coal and iron mines. But here, Harvester drew the line; it had gone to great lengths to secure its liens on the mine properties in the 1977 sale. It was not about to surrender that protection just two years later.

EDA negotiators were equally adamant. They pointed out that Harvester stood to gain materially from the loan guarantees; therefore, the company should share the government's risk. Finally, Peter Bohn worked out a compromise with Jim Doyle of Harvester. The company would hold onto its lien on the mines, but if the mill should fail, and the government find itself more than $30 million in the red, Harvester would pay the government up to $30 million, in payments stretched over 20 years.

The crisis had passed. By June 14, 1979, when Peter Bohn submitted his final report, all the necessary pieces were back in place. EDC Holding Company had a vice president for finance, $30 million in working capital had been raised, and the government had sufficient collateral. Bohn recommended that EDA grant the loan guarantee.

Yet the nightmare was far from over. Just as Congressman Murphy made his triumphal announcement that Wisconsin would get its $90 million loan guarantee, new problems arose to jeopardize the mill's very existence.

Phillip Brothers triggered the first crisis when it reneged on its commitment to guarantee the 10 percent of the $90 million loan that the EDA was not allowed by law to cover. Somebody had to guarantee that 10 percent, and neither the insurance companies who had signed onto the deal the year before nor Chase Manhattan was willing to take on the risk. Congress had required the 10 percent private sector guarantee as a way to safeguard the government: if no commercial lender would deem the loan reasonably safe, why should the government expose itself?

As the harried negotiators saw their package unraveling, their eyes turned to Harvester. Since that company stood to gain from Wisconsin Steel's modernization, why shouldn't it take on the burden?

Congressman Berkeley Bedell (D.-Iowa) would later complain that Harvester's participation wasn't really what Congress had in mind when it wrote the law requiring private guarantees. Precisely because Harvester stood to gain from the loan, its participation as a guarantor did not serve the safeguarding function. In short, the deal flouted congressional intent.

Nevertheless, the deal was legal. The question was, would Harvester bite?

As Envirodyne officials anxiously awaited Harvester's response, days passed into weeks. Until the problem was resolved, repairs on the blast furnace had to be postponed, more orders had to be canceled, and Wisconsin Steel's lifeblood was draining away.

By the time Harvester finally agreed to guarantee 10 percent of the loan, the mill's output had diminished even further, knocking Wisconsin Steel's business plan into the dustbin of history. Before EDA could "close" on the loan, a new plan would have to be developed.

Once again, the mill's woes were in iron production. Now all three of Wisconsin Steel's blast furnaces were malfunctioning. Their repeated breakdowns wreaked havoc with Morrill's plans. He had accepted a $5 million order for hot iron during the summer, but with the blast furnaces crippled, Wisconsin had to buy the metal elsewhere to fulfill its contract, taking a loss on the whole transaction.

At the same time, a major part of Wisconsin Steel's fund of working capital evaporated. Ten million dollars due from the HUD in the form of an action grant would not be available for use as working capital. Instead, the department insisted, it could only be used to reimburse Wisconsin Steel for the purchase of pollution control equipment.

Should the $90 million loan guarantee be canceled? As Peter Bohn prepared yet a second report for the EDA, things looked grim. By the end of the year, Bohn projected, the mill's losses would total $41 million. Furthermore, the number 3 blast furnace would have to be rebuilt, not simply relined; the additional cost was $15 million that EDC Holding Company didn't have.

Bohn, Lyon, Richards, Doyle, and the EDA officials returned to the drawing board. Their new plan called for Chase to increase its line of credit to $50 million with the help of PhiBro and Citibank. It was a complicated arrangement, but for the moment at least, it gave Wisconsin Steel the needed working capital.

On October 29, just two days before EDA was scheduled to close on the loan to EDC Holding Company, Peter Bohn sent in his amended report. Once again, he recommended that the loan guarantee be granted, but he did so guardedly. "The financing plan for Wisconsin Steel is complex and this is a high risk undertaking with a 60–40 chance of success in terms of repayment of obligations." Failure of HUD to come through with the UDAG grant could scuttle the project. So could the PSW, if it failed to cooperate in reducing labor costs. And high interest rates or a steel recession would throw the plan out of kilter.

Even if nothing went wrong, the loan's success would depend on management's performance. Jim Morrill would have to cut costs aggressively and maintain strict controls in every area. There was no room for "technical errors" or the sort of expensive research programs Envirodyne was fond of. A financial officer would have to be recruited to augment EDC Holding Company's management.

And there was more. In what was perhaps the most astonishing feature of the loan guarantee package, Bohn's report concluded that "constant monitoring by the EDA, of a type not normally supplied, is strongly recommended to detect and cause to be corrected minor deviations from plans which could grow into catastrophes." In concrete terms, this resulted in Richard Rodgers, Bohn's associate at Worden and Risberg, being sent to South Deering to work on EDC Holding Company's payroll, to ensure that mill management adhered to the plan.

After Bohn issued his sobering report, EDA's Robert Hall was on the spot. The mill was losing millions of dollars, the blast furnaces were breaking down, the government's own consultant didn't trust the mill management, and the financing package was still very shaky. There was a substantial chance that the project would fail and the loans would be partially defaulted.

Hall recalls: "It was a tough decision to make. It was chancy. We knew it was going to be a close call in terms of whether it was going to work." He laid out the problem to White House officials "and was told to make the best professional judgment on it." Within EDA there was no consensus. Many officials involved with the project had opposed the guarantee. But to Hall, the paramount issue was jobs. If he canceled the loan guarantee, 3500 people would be out of work. He approved the loan, and on November 1, 1979, funds began flowing to Wisconsin Steel.

Four years later, one question remains. Why did EDA approve a loan package containing, as an essential element, a $10 million HUD grant for *working capital*? Bob Hall's explanation is that HUD originally committed the money and then withdrew it. "I think it was at the time we decided to go ahead that the UDAG thing came into question, and then we were on a committed course." But Margaret Sowell, who administered the UDAG program in 1979, denies that her agency ever agreed to supply a grant to Wisconsin Steel for working capital. And George Karras, who was EDA's liaison to HUD, supports Sowell's denial.

November 1, 1979, should have been a banner day for Wisconsin Steel. More than two years after Envirodyne had bought the mill, money was finally available to modernize operations. Within a matter of months, the mill would have a new blast furnace, a working continuous caster, and equipment to purify water and gas emissions. However, on November 1, International Harvester, Wisconsin Steel's largest customer, shut down for a six-month strike.

The End of Wisconsin Steel

Harvester had a new chairman, Archie McArdle. He had come to Chicago with a glamorous reputation: the financial magic he'd worked at Xerox was supposed to turn the old Harvester empire into a modern enterprise.

McArdle was resolved to be tough. Old ways of doing business would have to be changed: unprofitable areas would be abandoned, incompetents given the boot, outdated facilities shut down, inefficient work practices eliminated.

Labor costs were McArdle's first target. Congressman

Murphy, today still bitter about the strike's deadly impact on Wisconsin Steel, believes that McArdle "had no more conception of dealing with labor relations than I have of, flying a space ship." But to McArdle the issue seemed simple: union work rules at Harvester plants were stricter than those prevailing at Deere or Caterpillar, which meant that Harvester's labor costs were higher. They'd have to be reduced.

McArdle knew that the United Automobile Workers union (UAW) would not acquiesce to the changes he wanted, so he prepared for a strike. During the very months that Jim Doyle was negotiating with the EDA over terms of the federal loan guarantee for Wisconsin Steel, McArdle ordered Harvester plants to run overtime to build up inventory in anticipation of a strike.

When bargaining began on August 9, 1979, Harvester's new labor negotiator, Grant Chandler, presented to union officials a list of seven work-rule concessions he considered essential to any contract. Those demands "will be here when the strike begins and when it ends," he said.

UAW representatives knew there was no way their local unions would accept compulsory overtime or a limit on members' seniority rights. Unionists had paid dearly for those protections years before. Furthermore, why was McArdle insisting on these changes in 1979, when the company was announcing record profits? To the union leaders, just one explanation made sense—McArdle was out to break the union.

For three months, company and union bargainers went through the motions of collective bargaining, knowing a strike was all but inevitable. Nevertheless, when UAW members set up picket lines on November 1, EDA officials were surprised and chagrined. Their $90 million loan guarantee was being jeopardized by the actions of one of the loan's participants: How could Harvester have concealed its plans for the strike? Why had no one at EDA known what was coming?

Ed Levin, EDA's chief counsel, is still troubled by these questions. "After the strike began, there were some meetings here to discuss whether anybody knew," Levin recalls. "And it isn't clear in my mind that nobody knew. The people who made the actual decisions did not know. There was no information to that effect in any of the papers that went through the agency. But I'm told that our program people who worked on the loan thought there was going to be a strike. And they later claimed they told people about it. But the people they claimed they told later said they had no recollection of it."

The loss of Harvester orders hit Wisconsin Steel hard. Suddenly 40 percent of the mill's income was gone. There was no cash to repay loans, no cash to pay suppliers, no cash for equipment. As a result, the mill was fast approaching both bankruptcy and a total breakdown.

Frank Lumpkin, who worked at Wisconsin Steel for thirty years, remembers the winter of 1979–1980 as a scary time on the scarfing docks, where workers burned imperfections off steel bars using torches with worn-out hoses. People were constantly getting burned when leaking gas exploded. Whenever Frank needed to replace equipment, he had to wander through the mill in search of a piece he could "borrow." In the rolling department, there were no spare parts. Whenever one of the guides that steer the steel bars through the rolling mill broke, management had to close down the mill until the craftsmen could improvise a new piece. And the brick linings of the blast furnace were worn so thin that the outside walls had to be sprayed with cold water to keep them from burning up, and even this makeshift procedure didn't keep the furnaces from breaking down over and over again. As iron production plunged, Wisconsin Steel fell ever further behind its production schedule, until by March, the mill's backlog of orders had reached the enormous sum of $39.7 million.

As the Harvester strike dragged on, Envirodyne's executives made a last-ditch effort to salvage Wisconsin Steel. At one memorable meeting in February, Michael Lyon, Ed Levin, and Jim Doyle assembled in William Butcher's offices at the Chase Manhattan Bank in New York to discuss whether money could be raised to keep the mill afloat until repairs to the blast furnace were complete and the Harvester strike settled. The talks were hard. Everyone wanted somebody else to ante up. When Jim Doyle hinted that perhaps Butcher really preferred the mill to close, Butcher exploded and threw everyone out. One wonders what he would have done had he known that Harvester was already lining up alternate sources of steel.

The end came in March of 1980 after Envirodyne filed its annual report with the Securities and Exchange Commission. Wisconsin Steel had lost $44 million over the previous twelve months and needed a cash infusion to survive. In addition, management admitted, the company needed relief from vendors and waivers of default from creditors simply to continue operations. To sum it up, Wisconsin Steel might fail, though Envirodyne management still held out the hope that a short-term rescue package could be worked out.

Harvester's management did not take kindly to Envirodyne's pleas for help, for their company had troubles of its own. The strike had entered its fifth month, and losses were mounting. Envirodyne's inability to meet the monthly payments on its share of the Michigan iron ore mines meant that Harvester had to pay up lest its title to the mines be forfeited. These payments drained badly needed cash.

At the end of the business day on March 27, while steelworkers toiled over the coke ovens, blast furnaces, and rolling mills on Torrence Avenue, Harvester reclaimed title to the mines it had sold to Envirodyne thirty-two months earlier. Within twenty-four hours, it was all over. When news of Harvester's action reached Wall Street the next morning, Chase Manhattan froze EDC Holding Company's bank accounts. Gun-toting agents of Chase's Collateral Control ordered a halt to steel shipments out of the mill.

The abrupt closing meant that a mill worth hundreds of millions of dollars would have to lie idle during bankruptcy proceedings, that repair work on the blast furnace would remain incomplete, that thousands of tons of steel would have to be sold unfinished. The mill's sudden shutdown reduced its value to an estimated $20 million below what it would have brought in an orderly closing. Why the hurry?

Simply put, Harvester and Chase moved as they did to protect themselves from what they judged to be Wisconsin Steel's imminent collapse. Had they waited for EDC Holding Company to exhaust all possibilities before declaring bankruptcy, both creditors would have had to file motions in bankruptcy court to recover their collateral. Neither Harvester nor Chase would have received anything until all of Wisconsin Steel's assets and debts had been enumerated. There would have been months—perhaps years—of delay. Chase and Harvester avoided all of that by reclaiming their collateral before the mill went bankrupt.

Harvester settled its strike and resumed operations on April 14, 1980. But that was too late for Wisconsin Steel. By then, Envirodyne's affairs were a mass of confusion, as creditors lined up in a courtroom in Chicago's Loop to press their competing claims. Ten miles to the south, steelworkers waited in lines at the unemployment center, weighing the wild rumors that arose in profusion and then died without a trace.

For years afterwards, steelworker families would search for signs that Wisconsin Steel would reopen. Despite the evidence of a decade that Harvester no longer needed the mill, few believed it would remain shut permanently.

Even fewer Southeast Siders realized that Wisconsin Steel's shutdown was the beginning of the end of an era that had spanned their lifetimes. The world into which they had been born and come of age was a world of steel. They could not imagine another one.

Had Wisconsin Steel's closing been an isolated event, solely the product of bad breaks and mismanagement, the steelworkers' stubborn refusal to accept the reality of the shutdown might have been justified. As it was, Wisconsin's bankruptcy was but an early casualty of an epidemic of industrial failures that raged throughout the Calumet region, and indeed throughout what soon came to be known as the nation's Rust Belt. The steel industry was afflicted by a new disease, one which would soon bring other mighty industrial giants down into the dust.

3

South Works and the Decline of the American Steel Industry

As THE GATES of Wisconsin Steel clanged shut, America's steel industry was plunging into the worst slump it had known in fifty years. The back-to-back recessions of 1979–1980 and 1981–1983 sharply reduced demand for steel, from a peak of 100 million tons in 1979 to just 65 million tons in 1982. Compounding the problem was a wave of imports that depressed steel prices to unprofitable levels. By mid-1983, more than half the nation's steelworkers were jobless, and *Business Week* was warning, "Time Runs Out for Steel."

The collapse of American steel rang alarm bells throughout industrial America. Mass layoffs were not confined to "Rust Bowl" centers like Pittsburgh and Buffalo; the mill towns of the Sunbelt suffered equally. As mill shutdowns spread from coast to coast, the collapse of America's steel industry made prime time television. On Capitol Hill, worried congressmen called for federal action.

The decline of U.S. Steel's South Chicago Works exemplifies that of America's steel industry. Unlike Wisconsin Steel, which was a small mill dependent for orders on one customer,

South Works was a large and modern facility whose products were major factors in several steel markets. Nevertheless, in just one decade, 1973–1983, South Works' booming prosperity disappeared.

Back in 1973, South Works' steel orders outpaced supply, and its parent, U.S. Steel, made record profits. The big blast furnaces poured out three million tons of pig iron annually to be made into steel in the basic oxygen furnaces. The finishing mills made plate for Caterpillar tractors, bars for General Motors cars, and beams for Chicago's office buildings.

Its nine thousand steelworkers had all the overtime they wanted. For the men and women of the Bush, the East Side, South Deering, and Hegewisch, high wages, steady work, decent pensions, and comprehensive medical coverage added up to a secure present and the promise of a better future. Newcomers shared in the prosperity: young blacks from the South Side, immigrants from the Mexican countryside, women eager for a crack at decent pay.

A decade later, the vast mill complex was as silent as a tomb. Weeds had taken over the parking lot south of 85th Street. The number 8 furnace, built as recently as 1968, had been closed since 1981; the bar, plate, and rod mills were shut forever. The entire southern end of the mill, all the way to the ore dock at 95th Street, was up for sale. Only South Works' electric furnace and beam mill were still running; fewer than 1000 steelworkers were hanging on to jobs that could end any day.

Whenever TV newscasters report some new development in the story of South Works' decline, they usually note that the mill is 100 years old and looks every day of it. But the mystery of the South Works story is deepened by the fact that South Works is not an antiquated mill; it has modern steelmaking and finishing facilities, some of which have never been used. Take number 8 blast furnace, for example. In 1981–1982, U.S. Steel had spent $91 million to reline it; if that job had ever been completed, number 8 would have become one of the company's largest, most efficient facilities. Nor is South Works afflicted with obsolete open-hearth furnaces; instead, there are two basic oxygen furnaces and three electric furnaces as well as a continuous billet caster. On South Works' finishing end there is a rod mill which was hailed for its "ultramodern" design when it was built in 1975.

U.S. Steel's decision to shut down so many modern facilities at South Works is not exceptional. Much of the $10 billion that American steelmakers spent on modernization in the 1960s and 1970s went for facilities that were quickly dismantled. Bethlehem modernized and abandoned its huge mill in Lackawanna, New York, much as U.S. Steel did South Works.

Why did South Works and so many other mills decline so rapidly in the past decade? Interviews with steelworkers, corporate executives, and steel industry analysts suggest three explanations. First, slow growth in the world industrial economy in the 1970s and 1980s deprived American mills of their markets. Second, poor management kept South Works and other mills from becoming world class. And third, and most important, the decline of America's steel industry stems directly from the fact that domestic steelmakers now must compete in world markets where they cannot earn the profits they need to survive in our capitalist economy.

INADEQUATE DEMAND FOR STEEL

South Works' rapid decline began in 1979. In that year, the Iranian revolution battered the world economy by taking millions of barrels of oil out of production. OPEC's subsequent decision to boost oil prices triggered steep inflation in the West and stripped third world nations of the ability to import manufactured goods. By the end of 1979, the U.S. economy had plunged into its third recession of the decade.

The combination of rapid inflation and stagnant output led Federal Reserve chairman Volcker to abandon Keynesian

economic management. He feared that if he tried to follow
the Keynesian formula of stimulating the economy in the
midst of recession, inflation would zoom out of sight. Volcker
decided to experiment with monetarism—the theory that the
size of the money supply determines price levels. So he launched
a brutal campaign to reduce the money supply, and soon, to
the bewilderment of millions around the world, American
interest rates shot up to record heights. Automobiles and
housing were quickly priced out of the reach of most Americans. With these prime markets in decline, the steel industry
went into a tailspin.

After a brief recovery in 1981 helped steelmakers recover
from the traumas of the previous year, Reaganomics precipitated a second, deeper slump. The President's policies of
cutting taxes, clamping down the money supply, raising military expenditures and slashing social spending produced another spectacular rise in interest rates and another steep drop
in industrial output. This recession was the "direct cause,"
according to economist Hans Mueller, of the "severe problems" facing "most of the steel industries in the Free World."
The impact on U.S. Steel's South Works was dramatic: with
its chief customers in the capital goods sector flat on their
backs, sales of steel plate and bars all but disappeared.

The high interest rates produced by Volcker's monetarism had a second perverse impact on America's steel
industry—they sent the value of the dollar soaring on world
currency markets. Suddenly the dollars Americans paid for
steel were worth 20 to 35 percent more to foreign producers;
the discrepancy made the U.S. market irresistible to foreign
steelmakers, who themselves were suffering the effects of
worldwide recession. Imports flooded into the United States,
not only from European steelmakers who had long coveted
our market, but from third world countries like Brazil and
Korea as well. By July of 1984, imports accounted for more
than 30 percent of domestic steel use, twice the previous level.

Unfortunately, steel's problems went beyond the short-term disruption caused by economic recession and misaligned currency markets: demand for steel has been declining steadily for twenty years. When U.S. Steel began its modernization program at South Works in the mid-1960s, it based its decision on forecasts of sustained and rapid long-term industrial growth. Had those forecasts been accurate, the demand for steel would have grown 3 percent every year and America would soon have found itself short of capacity to meet the growing need. The projections proved false, however. From 1970–1979, American steel consumption grew 1.5 percent per year, just half what steel companies projected. After 1979, consumption actually declined; by 1983, it had fallen 10 percent below what it had been thirteen years earlier.

As a result, steel companies had more manufacturing capacity than they needed. Mills like South Works ran well below capacity, which meant that unit production costs were high. And weak demand meant prices were low. The resulting profit squeeze eliminated the incentive for steel companies to modernize.

Critics of American steel complain that failure to build new, fully modern "greenfield" mills rendered our industry unable to compete with overseas producers. But the critics fail to take into account the impact of high interest rates on investment. When U.S. Steel considered building an entirely new (greenfield) mill in Conneaut, Ohio, in the late 1970s, it envisioned substantial cost savings: the new mill would produce steel for $60 per ton less than a modernized old (brownfield) mill like South Works could. But, as Robert Crandall points out in his book, *The U.S. Steel Industry in Recurrent Crisis*, that wasn't enough: high interest rates meant that the cost of building a greenfield plant would have been $160 more per ton than brownfield modernization. There was no way to justify the investment. Foreign steelmakers who did build greenfield plants gained an ever-widening cost advantage over U.S. producers.

Thus, the decline of America's steel industry was caused

in large part by a combination of short-term and long-term economic trends—worldwide recession, an overvalued dollar, and slow economic growth—which decreased demand for steel well below the level domestic companies needed for satisfactory profits. But it would be a mistake to blame all of the steelmakers' problems on forces over which they had no control. Steel's decline must be blamed in part on the incompetence of industry executives, who had grown complacent in the days when they dominated world markets, allowing their mills to become woefully inefficient—inviting targets for foreign competitors. When they had to face an unexpected loss of dominance, American steelmen were slow to adapt. The signs of their failure are easy to read at U.S. Steel's South Works.

EXPENSIVE MISTAKES

Tales of inefficiency at South Works abound. Discussions with workers at the mill reveal a picture of management ineptitude that would be hard to credit were it not drawn in such minute and graphic detail. Corruption was widespread in management ranks. One case involved one of the general superintendents, who was fired when higher-ups discovered he was the mastermind of a kickback scheme. The superintendent was ordering and paying for large quantities of supplies that were never delivered; in return, contractors provided vacation trips and call girls for him as well as other managers.

In another incident, a plate mill foreman was stopped by a plant guard who noticed that the rear end of his car was dragging. Inside his trunk was a fortune in new brass bearings. It turned out that a nearby scrap yard had been buying this booty for months.

Pilferage was rampant. Foremen ordered fancy light fixtures for plant washrooms and air conditioners for offices and took them home. Blast furnace foremen stole enough sheet, lumber, and steel from their department to build a house. One craftsman confided that he actually built an entire 40- by 40-foot building for his boss, who took it out of the plant in sections in the rear of his station wagon.

In South Works' garage, while one mechanic worked on plant business, several others fixed their bosses' cars. One foreman ordered an exhaust system at company expense. Another had a whole new engine installed.

Bob Samano, who worked for twenty years in the plant maintenance division, believes that stealing declined after South Works got a new superintendent in 1978. But, Samano says, nepotism, and the incompetence it fosters, remained in full force. He grows irate as he tells of one boss—who got his job through his high-ranking brother-in-law—who ordered a craneman to pick up a particularly heavy load. The craneman pleaded that it couldn't be done, but his foreman insisted. When the craneman tried to pick up the load, the $100,000 crane toppled over to the ground.

Mistakes like these are expensive. Alice Peurala, who was Local 65's president from 1979 to 1982, recalls that company engineers tried to save money on a repair job on the number 8 furnace by starting in the middle of the furnace, instead of at the bottom, as it's usually done. It didn't work. After the furnace had burnt out five times, the company had to rip out all the brick and start over from the beginning. The loss totaled millions.

Peurala believes that the problems of South Works management go beyond errors in judgment: they are built into the structure of decision making at the mill. The plant superintendent approved a separate budget for each of the mill's departments; department managers cared only about meeting their budget projections, regardless of the mill's overall needs. This system produced selfish, uncoordinated decision making, as the testimony of Local 65's grievance committee chairman, Mike Ally, reveals. "I worked in an area where there was a lot of overtime," Mike recalls. "We worked six days a week, twelve hours a day. There was no work for us to do. But you had to stay. The way they worked it, a particular department was allowed so many hours to do a job. (The chief foreman) never wanted to turn the job in ahead of time. If they were allowed 18,000, they wanted to make sure you worked 18,000 hours, so the next time the budget came out, they'd be allowed 18,000 hours. So we were forced to stay there and do nothing. They paid us time and a half premium to do nothing."

The most costly instance of wasteful management occurred in the fall of 1981, when U.S. Steel announced an emergency program to completely reline the big number 8 blast furnace. The work had to be done in ninety days, so the mill could fulfill big orders for steel in the winter. Outside contractors would be needed to get the job done in time. Contractors began working at $17 per hour in November; eighteen months later, the project still wasn't done, and its cost had grown to $91 million.

Distressing as these stories may be, plant level mismanagement is not a primary cause of South Works' decline. It is, rather, a symptom of a deeper problem—mismanagement at the top of the corporate hierarchy. U.S. Steel executives at company headquarters in Pittsburgh allowed nepotism, poor coordination, and corruption to flourish under their supervision because, in the days when the American steel oligopoly dominated world markets, U.S. Steel could afford to be lax.

Donald Barnett, former chief economist for the steel industry's research arm, the American Iron and Steel Institute, believes, along with other analysts, that U.S. Steel, like most of the steel companies in America, has followed an ineffective investment policy. The problem was never one of lack of investment. Just as South Works got a continuous billet caster, basic oxygen furnaces, and a rod mill, Gary Works, Homestead, Edgar Thompson, Fairfield, and Fairless also had some of their facilities renovated. Unfortunately, Barnett says, the corporation simply did not get its bang for the buck. For the $10 billion it has spent on modernization in the past twenty years, U.S. Steel should have been able to create several highly efficient mills capable of competing against all comers. Instead the company got a dozen mediocre mills, or else ones that couldn't compete. For instance, says Barnett, U.S. Steel's decision to build a rod mill at South Works in 1975 was a disaster. The new facility, designed to be the largest, most modern rod mill in the country, proved unable to compete with the minimills. Within a few years, it was closed down and dismantled.

U.S. Steel only partially modernized all of its mills because it wanted to preserve as much of its assets as possible. Further, executives reasoned that huge productive capacity would come in handy whenever steel markets boomed: as supply conditions tightened, U.S. Steel would be able to fill orders beyond the reach of other companies, and some new orders would become permanent customers.

This strategy was not unique; Donald Barnett and Louis Schorsch, authors of *Steel: Upheaval in a Basic Industry*, argue that it was typical of the investment policy of oligopolistic industries (where a small number of firms dominate a market and restrict competition). Here we have a key to understanding U.S. Steel's poor performance in the 1960s and 1970s. During those years, investments consistently generated smaller than expected returns not because company managers were personally incompetent but because they failed to realize that the world around them was changing. Competition had intruded on the American steel industry for the first time in sixty years. When executives continued to employ the oligopolistic strategies that had worked in the past, they produced disastrous balance sheets and became the butt of derision in the business press.

Steel company managers can be faulted up to a point for pursuing outmoded strategies, but beyond their personal failure loomed the third and most important cause of the decline of America's steel industry—the growth of worldwide competition.

THE SPECTER OF COMPETITION

Americans assume that competition is the normal state of affairs, that our corporations compete not only with each other but with producers around the world. If businesses fail in that contest, it is either because foreigners are competing unfairly or because American firms have become inefficient.

The U.S. steel industry does not correspond to this economic model. Steelmakers abandoned competition as a way of life eighty years ago. A brief look at the history of steelmaking in America will explain this argument.

The last third of the nineteenth century was the heroic age of American steelmaking. In one generation, a small, backward iron trade was transformed into the world's largest, most advanced steel industry. Production increased tenfold, while prices dropped drastically. By 1900, U.S. mills were far ahead of their British and German counterparts in size, modernity, and efficiency.

During this era, the steel industry worked as free-market theory said it should. Dozens of entrepreneurs competed to cut production costs by increasing efficiency, for each competitor hoped to gain new orders by underbidding rivals. As they did, the price of steel plunged rapidly, while demand exploded.

An inexorable trend developed. Steel companies grew ever larger in size and complexity, as they sought economies of scale, bought up sources of raw materials, built transportation facilities, and developed new product lines. Small manufacturers fell by the wayside. Successful enterprises, like

Carnegie Steel in Pittsburgh, and Illinois Steel in Chicago, absorbed enormous amounts of capital.

By the late 1890s, the competitive game had lost its savor. Steel companies feared the cutthroat price cutting brought on by the depressions that afflicted the economy five years out of every ten. Overhead costs at giant mills like Illinois Steel's South Works threatened all but the most solvent operations.

The end of competition in the steel industry was precipitated by Andrew Carnegie when he announced plans to build a huge tube mill in Conneaut, Ohio, in an attempt to break the monopoly on tube production recently attained by the National Tube Company. Industry leaders decided it was time to call a halt to the murderous business struggle, for if Carnegie built a tube mill, what would prevent Illinois Steel from entering the steel sheet business, or American Spring and Wire from entering the raw steel market? In short, as *Fortune* magazine would later write: "the steel industry was poised on the brink of a ruinous competitive conflict."

In order to save their industry, American steelmen decided to kill off competition. Led by J. P. Morgan, Wall Street's foremost investment banker, in 1901 they organized the United States Steel Corporation, which immediately became the world's largest business enterprise. The Corporation, as it came to be known, was a vast holding company, with 200 subsidiaries in every branch of the steelmaking trade. It included the two largest raw steel-producing companies, Carnegie Steel and Illinois Steel, as well as recently formed trusts that dominated markets for wire, rods, plate, tube, sheet, and structural beams. Altogether, 65 percent of the nation's steel capacity was concentrated in the hands of one vast enterprise.

Under The Corporation's dominance, the steel industry took on a new character. Gone were ruinous competition, relentless innovation, and massive investment in new production facilities. Under the leadership of Judge Elbert Gary, the essence of U.S. Steel's policy was, in *Fortune*'s words, "to

avoid the appearance of monopoly, while keeping, as much
as possible, the reality." This meant: set prices high, keep
them high, and preserve the value of your existing assets. To
that end, Judge Gary invited his fellow steelmen to an annual
dinner where they agreed to "stabilize" prices while listening
to speeches about business ethics. It worked: for a full decade,
the price of steel rails held firm despite a depression in 1904
and a boom in 1909. The Corporation's profits averaged 12
percent, high for the time.

After government antimonopolists challenged Gary's price-
fixing scheme, the industry adopted another variant, called
Pittsburgh-plus, which set steel prices at the level charged by
mills in the Pittsburgh area, plus freight charges based on the
cost of shipping orders from Pittsburgh, regardless of where
the customer actually purchased his shipment. The system
proved as effective as the Gary dinners had been and had the
additional benefit of preserving U.S. Steel's many high-cost
eastern mills, which might otherwise have been threatened
by more modern mills located on the Great Lakes.

American steelmakers operated comfortably, if not effi-
ciently, for sixty years under the oligopolistic arrangements
of 1901. As long as competition could be averted, the steel
companies could keep prices high enough to assure adequate
profits. Of course, steel users paid higher prices than they
otherwise would have paid, but steelmakers believed that wasn't
important; they didn't think consumption of their product
was closely related to price. So much for the laws of supply
and demand.

THE NEW COMPETITION

Unfortunately for the steel companies, complex changes
in the world economy undermined their hold on the American market just when conditions seemed most favorable. By
the end of the 1950s, the industry again faced what it dreaded

most—competition. But this time it was foreign producers who threatened to cut prices.

U.S. steel's complacency might have lasted forever had the Mesabi iron ore range in northern Minnesota been inexhaustible. For sixty years, the range had provided domestic mills with cheap, high-grade ore at minimal transportation costs. Nowhere in the Western world could comparable ore be mined so cheaply. But after World War II, yields from the range declined; the best ore was gone, and the taconite that remained was much more expensive to make into pig iron.

By the late 1950s, Venezuela's iron ore deposits, which once had seemed so expensive, were the world's cheapest source. Huge oceangoing freighters made the ore accessible to steel producers thousands of miles away. America's primary cost advantage had suddenly evaporated.

To Japanese industrialists, the availability of Venezuelan iron ore signaled a new opportunity; they saw steel as a possible export industry which could fuel the rebirth of their shattered economy. The Japanese began building huge new steel mills in deep-water ports. Into these new mills they put the newly developed basic oxygen furnaces, which reduced labor costs significantly. American steelmakers were slow to adopt this new technology. U.S. Steel, for example, had built huge open-hearth furnaces at the Fairless Works near Philadelphia in 1952; it wanted to continue to use those furnaces, not build new ones.

Once the Japanese had modern mills, access to cheap iron ore, and oceangoing freighters, it was only a matter of time before they invaded U.S. markets. Their opening came in 1959, when the U.S. steel industry experienced a 116-day strike over management efforts to eliminate local work rules. While the companies and steelworkers dug in for a test of power, steel users searching for an alternate source of supply discovered that foreign steelmakers could deliver large quantities of steel at competitive prices.

For the next decade, imports surged and ebbed in three-year cycles; the approach of labor negotiations sent steel users searching for foreign suppliers. Each time the cycle repeated itself, imports jumped to a higher level than in previous years; by 1968, they had garnered 18 percent of the U.S. market. That figure held steady for the next fourteen years, until overvaluation of the dollar made the U.S. market attractive to third world producers; imports jumped to 22 percent in 1982.

Japanese steelmakers triumphed in international markets because their industry did not play by the competitive rules that free-market theorists hold out as ideal for world economic growth. In the early 1950s, the Japanese government promoted the industry by loaning the fledgling steel companies 40 percent of the funds they needed for modernization. Equally important, they enacted stringent protective legislation to keep out imports. These formal restrictions were later dropped in favor of informal restraints, but the effect has remained; *as late as 1978, less than 1 percent of Japan's steel consumption came from imports.*

Once the steel industry was on its feet, government support continued in new forms. The Ministry on International Trade and Industry (MITI) coordinated low-interest bank loans to finance modernization, and during recessions, anti-trust laws were relaxed to permit steel companies to form cartels to limit output and keep prices high. Government protection made it possible for Japanese companies to build up huge capacity, far in excess of domestic needs, without having to worry about possible losses. When steel markets contracted, domestic consumers paid higher prices, and low-priced exports boomed. These policies freed Japanese steelmakers and lenders of risk.

We can see how Japan's steel industry worked by looking at its response to the worldwide depression in steel markets following the OPEC price increases in 1974. By October 1975, with Japanese steel in the worst slump in its history, MITI set "guideposts" requiring steel producers to reduce their output. With production down, steelmakers were able to increase domestic steel prices.

This wasn't sufficient to maintain the financial health of Japan's steel companies, however, because their huge production overcapacity meant they were saddled with heavy debt loads. The only way they could make their interest payments was to boost exports, and this they did; by October 1975, Japan was exporting steel to the United States at prices 14 percent below the average for the period April–September. According to the *Japan Metal Bulletin*, these prices were "not enough to cover the cost and proper profit," but they certainly were low enough to penetrate the U.S. market, which was already reeling from the effects of deep recession. Japan's share of U.S. steel consumption rose from 5.1 to 7.9 percent, an increase that contributed to sharply declining profit margins, plant closings, bankruptcies, dividend reductions, and layoffs in the United States.

MITI sought to create an international competitive advantage by helping the industry to rationalize its structure, by providing financial assistance for modernization, by fostering the development of advanced technologies, and by promoting and subsidizing the acquisition of raw materials.

In the field of research, for example, MITI promotes the development of new steelmaking processes by subsidizing joint government-industry research and development projects. It also grants funds to individual companies for their own R&D efforts. And in the field of raw materials acquisition, Japan's government not only built deep-water ports to accommodate large ore-carrying vessels, it also aided the fleet's construction. Then, the government made available loans for long-term overseas raw materials development projects and purchasing contracts. The result of these efforts is that resource-poor Japan can now procure coal and iron ore more cheaply than can U.S. steel firms which own huge reserves.

Japan's industrial promotion program became a model

for other governments throughout the world. In South Korea, the Philippines, Taiwan, Brazil, Mexico, and even Western Europe, one can find evidence of government protection, subsidy, planning, cartelization, and export promotion, as well as other policies the Japanese perfected in the postwar years. The third world steel that flooded into U.S. markets at such low prices in 1982 cost a great deal to produce if one takes into account the enormous capital costs it took to build modern third world mills.

A second competitive menace to American integrated steel producers was the growth of minimills. These mills represented a technological advance that the steel majors could not control. A minimill melts scrap in an electric furnace to make molten steel, which is then fed to finishing mills for the production of bars, rods, and wire. Because minimills don't need coke and coke ovens, iron ore, and blast furnaces, they are cheap to build. Equally important, they don't need to be located near supplies of coal and iron, or on transportation routes for carrying the raw materials. Minimills can be built wherever steel demand is great and supply is limited—in the growing Sunbelt, for example. These are often areas where industrial growth is recent and union strength feeble. As a result, the new mills pay less than half what integrated mills pay for labor.

At first integrated steel companies dismissed the minimills, believing that technological barriers would confine them to the low-quality, low-price part of the market, where profits were meager to begin with. This was a mistake. As happens in so many industries, the minimills' technology improved as their business expanded; each year that passes sees a wider product range, higher prices, and business growth. By 1983, minimills had gained half the market for rods and wire. Many integrated steelmakers gave up trying to compete with them.

The growth of both international and domestic competition hurt America's integrated steel producers on two fronts. First, it cost them sales. By 1983, foreign steelmakers and minimills combined to share 39 percent of the domestic market. Second, competition meant lower prices and profits. America's oligopolistic steel companies had kept prices artificially high for sixty years, but they can't do that anymore. If they refuse to cut prices when demand is slack, their customers can purchase steel on the world "spot" market, or from domestic minimills.

During the years 1968–1977, when imports hovered around 18 percent and minimills began to sprout throughout the land, America's integrated steel producers made profits of 6.7 percent. Viewed in one light, that was not so bad; Japan, that model of modern industrial success, averaged just 1.7 percent, and most European steel producers earned even less. But our steel companies function within our own business system, and in America, a corporation that earns only 6.7 percent profit will not be able to raise the capital it needs: the average rate of profits in the manufacturing sector is more than twice that.

American steelmakers were in a trap. Small profits made modernization bad business. But failure to modernize increased vulnerability to imports. Caught in a double bind, U.S. steel companies responded schizophrenically; they have sought protection from imports, allied themselves with foreign steel producers, demanded wage concessions from employees, initiated new experiments in labor-management cooperation, modernized some old facilities, shut down some modern ones, and diversified out of the steel industry altogether. But all along there has been one constant in these varied and contradictory strategies: an attempt to escape from the new competition.

U.S. STEEL IN A COMPETITIVE MARKET

One solution to the competitive menace is import restriction, and for fifteen years, U.S. Steel has led the industry's struggle for trade relief. In 1968, corporation representative R. Heath Larry went to Congress seeking relief from Japanese and European "dumping" of steel on American markets; the campaign paid off in the form of voluntary restraint agreements in 1969–1970. But these agreements fell by the wayside after 1972. When imports surged again in 1976, U.S. Steel led the industry in filing a new spate of dumping complaints.

This placed the Carter administration in an awkward position. It wanted to appease U.S. Steel and its congressional allies but feared that acting on the dumping complaints would jeopardize the president's efforts to promote free trade. The solution was the trigger-price mechanism, which set minimum prices for steel imports at the level of Japanese production and shipment costs. At the same time, Japanese producers agreed informally to limit steel shipments to the U.S. to six million tons annually.

When imports increased again in 1982, U.S. Steel's Chairman David Roderick led the steel companies in a third round of lobbying for import controls. The result was a trade agreement with the European economic community to limit steel shipments until 1985.

At the same time that they were campaigning for protection from foreign competition, most American steel producers began to shift their assets out of steel into industries that promised greater profitability. U.S. Steel, for example, nearly doubled its investment in nonsteel businesses between 1976 and 1979, while its steel assets increased just 13 percent.

When Roderick took the reins in 1979, he accelerated the diversification program, explaining "U.S. Steel is in business to make profits, not to make steel." In the fall of that year, he ordered the closing of thirteen U.S. Steel plants, eliminating 13,000 jobs. During the next three years, fifty more U.S. Steel facilities at thirteen different sites were closed down.

Even when steel profits surged to 13.3 percent in 1981, Roderick kept U.S. Steel moving on its headlong flight from the competitive steel industry. In December of 1981, he con-

cluded a deal to purchase the Marathon Oil Company for
$6.4 billion. The purchase added $3 billion to The Corporation's debt load and decreased chances for future steel modernization. Then in 1986, Roderick moved further into the
energy business by purchasing Texas Oil for $3 billion in U.S.
Steel stock.

While transforming U.S. Steel into a diversified business,
later renamed U.S.X., Roderick has simultaneously carried
out the second part of the program he had announced in
1979, "cracking down on labor." In March of 1983, reluctant
USWA local presidents approved concessions that saved the
company at least $3 billion in labor costs. But they could not
halt U.S. Steel's efforts to get out of steel. Just days after the
local presidents approved wage reductions, Chairman Roderick announced negotiations with the government-owned
British Steel Corporation to import slabs from Ravenscraig,
Scotland, for finishing at the Fairless Works in Philadelphia.
Had the plan been implemented, it would have eliminated
3000 jobs in Fairless's raw steelmaking departments.

Nine months later, the people of the Southeast Side learned
that they too were victims of Chairman Roderick's diversification strategy. On December 27, U.S. Steel announced major
reductions in its steelmaking operations, including the permanent shutdown of six facilities and a partial shutdown at
thirty others, South Works among them. Fifteen thousand
employees were laid off permanently, including 4000 who
were working on the day of Roderick's announcement, and
another 11,000 who had been furloughed and were hoping to
come back to work.

U.S. Steel shut down so much of its steelmaking capacity
because it was staggering under a double load—$1.5 billion
losses on steel operations in 1982–1983, plus its interest payments for the Marathon Oil purchase. Virtually drained of
capital, U.S. Steel adopted a policy of triage in its steel division. It would invest in steel only to protect important assets
or to fund its big money-makers. The Corporation's largest

mills, in Gary, Indiana, and Birmingham, Alabama, would be saved if at all possible. That's why Roderick's announcement included plans to build continuous casters at those two sites. Marginal facilities like South Works were left out in the cold.

U.S.X. is not alone in its flight from competition in the steel business. In the last two years, National Steel sold its Weirton mill to employees, Wheeling-Pittsburgh announced plans to import Brazilian slabs to finish in Pittsburgh, Kaiser closed its raw steelmaking departments in Fontana, California, and Bethlehem Steel reduced capacity 20 percent by closing facilities in Johnstown, Lackawanna, and Bethlehem. Overall, the integrated steelmakers closed down 199 facilities between 1974 and 1982.

There is even better evidence of the steelmakers' flight from competition, however, and that is their shifting stand on imports. In the past, the companies justified their demands for import protection on the ground that foreign producers practiced unfair trade. Each time the steelmen launched a new legislative campaign, they assured the Congress that American steel would prosper whenever true competition was restored. In the summer of 1983, they dropped that argument. Their new refrain was that competition must be interrupted until American steel could get back on its feet.

Bethlehem Steel led the industry's new push for protection, in the fall of 1983, filing a petition with the federal government asking for the imposition of quantitative quotas on the grounds that imports were destroying America's steel industry. For sixty years, America's steel producers gave lip service to the virtues of competition while maintaining a virtual domestic oligopoly. For twenty years more, they pledged allegiance to competition while calling for import restraints. Now by diversifying out of the steel industry, clamoring for import quotas, and merging with each other in order to close "duplicate" capacity, they are confirming in the strongest possible fashion what was already clear to J. P. Morgan back in

1901: competition is not compatible with a healthy steel industry, not in America, nor elsewhere in the world.

The American steel industry was both shrinking and changing profoundly. Between 1979 and 1984, the steel companies had closed more than 20 percent of their productive capacity and permanently laid off 40 percent of their work force—150,000 steelworkers.

As steel executives scrambled to change their game plans, as Wall Street analysts revised their forecasts, residents of the mill communities tried to come to terms with the grim realities of mass unemployment. For people to whom the workings of the steel industry had once been invisible, terms like "disinvestment," "the balance of trade," and "foreign competition" now took on palpable meaning: these were forces that could topple a steel mill.

The silent, empty mills, like gaping cavities, provoked disbelief, outrage, and fear in dozens of mill communities from Buffalo to Birmingham. Few places were more intensely shaken than the Calumet region of Illinois and Indiana, steel's heartland.

4

Dark Days

Wisconsin Steel sticks out like a big sore now. There's vandalism, and weeds growing up all around it. It really bothers me. My dad worked at Wisconsin. On summer nights, Mom and I would walk over the bridge and meet him. I can remember standing by the fence and seeing Dad walk out and feeling so excited. Now there are no men pouring out those gates every day. It's completely deserted. That's what hurts.

Patricia Masselli
The East Side

THE STEEL INDUSTRY'S decline set off an avalanche of economic dislocation in Southeast Chicago. Over 15,000 jobs were lost with the closing of Wisconsin Steel and the partial shutdown of South Works. Soon Republic Steel on the East Side had laid off half its 4000 employees. Smaller firms struggled to survive, and many failed.

Then steel-related businesses also began to collapse. The historic Pullman railcar factory closed its doors, idling 3000 workers. Illinois Slag and Ballast Company also went out of business. In nearby Indiana, dozens more firms closed, cutting off any hope steelworkers might have had of finding work across the state border. In the short span of three years, the Calumet region's economy was reduced to shambles. The impact on the people of the mill communities was immediate, and often devastating.

Carl Stezko, white male, mid-50s:

I worked at Wisconsin Steel for almost thirty years. I get a partial pension of $300 a month, that's all. No other benefits. Nothing. I had a hernia. The doctor said I could die if I didn't have an operation. I didn't have any hospitalization, no money to pay for it. I tried to get a green card [Medicaid] to pay for it, but they said sell your house and car if you want it. I couldn't do that. Finally, my doctor says if you can get into the hospital, I'll do the operation. So I lied to the hospital, just went in there and told them I had insurance. I never could have imagined doing such a thing.

I've been everyplace looking for a job—White Castle, Burger King, McDonald's, Sears, K Mart. I've been to hospitals and cemeteries. I went to Jays Potato Chips. They gave me a test and said, "You're overqualified." I said, "I'll tell you what, you said you're paying $5 an hour, well I'll work for $3." They still wouldn't take me. I'm a skilled electrician, plumber, a pipe fitter. But they ain't gonna hire a guy like me. I still go out every day and look.

My wife isn't healthy. She can't work. We have a two-flat, but the mortgage isn't paid off. I get $160 a month in rent on the other apartment. I'm paying $200 on the mortgage and $160 in gas bills. So you can't make ends meet. I only eat one meal a day. Food stamps turned me down. I don't know where to turn. I'm ashamed to ask for anything. I always swore I'd never go on pension— I'd work till the day I died.

I did go to the alderman for a year and a half trying

to get a job. I was begging, pleading. I saw him at least twenty times. They kept telling me, "You're at the top of the list." You know you get desperate: one day I approached him in the parking lot to ask about the job. The next time I saw him, he really went after me, just about spit on me cause I did that. You're never supposed to come up to him about something like that outside of his office. I just had to sit there and take it. I'm a big guy. Fifteen years ago, maybe I would have knocked him down. But when you got nothing, you've got to take that kind of stuff. Maybe the good Lord will come down and help me. I pray every day. That's all I have faith in anymore.

Mary Morgan, black female, early 50s:

I started in at South Works in 1973. I had two kids still at home and was just separated from my husband. He died a few months later.

I really liked that job. By me being a widow, I could support myself. I didn't have to go out and ask somebody for money. I didn't have to go on Aid. I could support my own self. That's very important to me.

I've been off work since January of '82. I haven't been able to find anything else. And all my benefits is ran out, even my little savings. My children help a little. I have six—all grown now. They're all unemployed. Three of them worked at one company that was sort of like the mill. It's all but closed down now. They had been going on unemployment and trying to find a job, but that has ran out now. I have my youngest son, my oldest daughter, and one little grandchild living with me. Altogether I have ten grandchildren. That's what makes it rough.

I've been looking for other jobs. I've been to Sweetheart, Tootsie Roll, Sure-Plus, Libby's, Soft Sheen. I've been to places to find something in the line of what maybe I could do. Cause, you see, some of these jobs you can't apply for them if you don't have the ability or education. Most of them just say they're not hiring. It gets discouraging.

I definitely blame Reagan. Because you know like they say, you're supposed to clean up your own backyard before you go and clean up somebody else's. And all this money he's got going for all these other things, like nuclear, he could be using that to put people back to work. I hope and pray—if I live—if they do get another president, that he'll do better than this one has been doing. Because he just don't care about women—he don't understand that we've got to live just like the men do. We've got to make a living.

I have very little hope—very, very little. I'm praying that I can find me a job somewhere. But if they don't open up something where peoples can get a job, it don't look very good at all. I guess they just want us all to dig a hole and get in it.

Victor Gonzalez, Hispanic male, early 50s:

I spent most of my life at Wisconsin Steel. I thought I was set. In four more years, I'd have had my thirty years and got my pension.

I'm a carpenter. I've tried everything to get a job. But you don't have the opportunity to prove to anyone what you can do. When you tell people you're a former steelworker, they won't hire you. I went down to the Job Service [Illinois Bureau of Employment Security] and they were going to send me out for an interview. But when I told the guy I'd worked for Wisconsin, he said, "Forget it, they won't want you."

Then I went to Florida to look for work because my wife's mother lives there. I got a job in the fields trimming trees for $2 an hour. Then I got into construction; I was hauling cement bricks for $4 an hour. The boss really liked me, but the job ended and there wasn't any more work. So we came back up here.

We had just moved from South Chicago to Dolton [a nearby suburb] the year before the mill closed. The mortgage payments were $310 a month and we couldn't handle them on top of all our other bills. Our unemployment ran out. We lost the house—and our car too. We went to live with our daughter in South Chicago. But that's hard. You feel like you're intruding. You wish you had a place of your own.

Our children are hurting too. Out of six, only one has a regular job. One daughter worked at South Works, another at Wisconsin; our son was at Wisconsin; one son-in-law was there, another at South Works. So it's the whole family.

So many people that I know, they just gave up. But I'm not giving up. Right now, I'm trying to get into construction. It's hard, though. I feel like I've been robbed —robbed of twenty-five, twenty-six years of my life really.

If the precipitous decline of the steel industry took even financial analysts by surprise, it's not hard to imagine how completely unawares it took the people of Southeast Chicago. The initial reaction was determined disbelief. "It's human nature," says Barbara Lavelle, former director of the Employee Counselling Center at South Works. "People don't want to give up what they know."

On the day Wisconsin Steel closed, Mary Garcia brought her dying husband home from the hospital. His reaction was typical. He'd worked at the Torrence Avenue mill for thirty-three years and he was convinced it would be back in operation before long. "He always said, 'That place is gonna open, they can't close such a big place,'" Mary recalls. "He couldn't talk so he'd write stuff down. He lasted eight months and he would always ask me about the mill—'What's the news?'"

This reluctance to face up to the extent of the devastation is understandable: mill work was all most people had ever known. "Steelworkers, especially men, think of work as the most important part of their life," notes Barbara Lavelle. "The job provided a structure; once that structure crumbles, people's personality crumbles."

With only seven years of schooling, Jessie Cruz didn't have too many options in life. But you didn't need any degrees to get a job in a steel mill. Under South Works' huffing smokestacks, he learned plumbing, carpentry, and electrical wiring, skills he practiced with pride. Now, he tries to keep busy with household chores, but he can't afford the materials to make needed repairs. He imagines that when other people see him, they're saying " 'You're nothing, you're nobody.' And that's the way I feel about myself."

Dorothy Gomez, a former security guard at Wisconsin, "just went crazy" when the mill closed. "If you don't have a job, you don't have a purpose in life," she declares vehemently. "I've worked all my life. I never collected a dime in compensation. So to be without a job! I had bottles of pills. I'm not kidding. I had pills under my pillow and I would think that one night I was gonna get up and end it all."

Unemployment of this sort does kill. According to Dr. Harvey Brenner of Johns Hopkins University, every 1 percent increase in unemployment results in a 4.1 percent increase in the rate of homicide, and a 1.9 percent increase in deaths due to heart attacks and cirrhosis.

While no mortality studies have been done in Southeast Chicago, impressions abound. When asked what is becoming of laid-off South Works employees, Barbara Lavelle responds that "some of them are dying. Workers often gather here and lately they talk of funerals. They have no hope. And when people give up hope, they do die."

There is talk of suicide, of sudden mysterious illness. Carl Stezko tells of a foreman who hung himself in the wake of the Wisconsin closing and of a younger worker also dead by his own hand. "I used to work with the kid. After the mill closed, he was about to lose his home. He took a gun to his head and blew his brains out."

Most people, of course, do not die. But many sink into depression and lethargy, unable to cope with the rapid changes in their lives. Depression is anger turned inward. "What can you do with your anger?" Joe Smetlack wonders. "Do you beat against a wall? If McCardle was here, I could show you what to do with it. If that Linde was here. . . ." But without such outlets for their frustration and rage, jobless workers most often internalize their pain. Victor Gonzalez' brother never missed a day of work during all his years at Wisconsin Steel. Now he just sits in his backyard all day long, drunk by the time evening comes.

People who lose confidence in their own worth often develop health problems. Vince Champaign, former social worker at a South Chicago clinic, noticed that when the layoffs started, a lot more men began coming through the center's doors, often with stress-related problems, such as chest pains and migraine headaches. And a survey of health providers in the region found over half reporting increases of patients with specific conditions related to unemployment and financial stress.

Ironically, just when health problems seem to be increasing, health coverage is disappearing. Access to quality comprehensive medical care has long been one of the most important bonuses of a mill job, but a 1983 survey of unemployed workers in the region's near south suburbs found that 69 percent no longer had any form of health coverage.

As with other forms of public assistance, those who own property can't qualify for Medicaid. They fear the city's only public hospital and are unfamiliar with the few clinic programs that might be able to help them. Left to face the spiraling costs of doctors, dentists, hospital stays, and medications without financial assistance, jobless workers react with panic or despair.

Medical coverage for Mary Garcia's husband, Pete, who was suffering from cancer, was cut off the day Wisconsin Steel shut down. After using up her savings, Mary was left to plead with a local hospital for the radiation treatments he desperately needed. When he died, there were more financial difficulties, since his life insurance policy benefits were still tied up in bankruptcy court with all the mill workers' other assets. There was no money for the funeral. "My kids come through with help," Mary remembers. "And there's a tavern on Torrence Ave. that made a benefit. With that money and the money from my children, I buried my husband."

Many jobless workers ignore basic health needs and rely on their prayers to protect them from serious emergencies. "I wouldn't even let the kids ride their bikes for fear they'd get hurt and need medical treatment," says Dorothy Gomez. And Mary Gonzalez explains that while she does have a green card, it doesn't cover dental care. "You just have to neglect your teeth and let them fall out."

The blows to physical and mental health are matched by the severity of the economic impact of industrial decline on the Southeast Side. According to a recent study of former South Works employees, median family income has been nearly halved from $23,000 annually to $12,000.

Few mill workers ever imagined that hunger would one day come to inhabit their households. Restaurant meals might be few and far between, but three meals a day on one's own kitchen table—that could be counted on. Now food is a question mark. In thousands of homes, unemployment compensation has long since run out. Some people have been able to get food stamps, but many more have been ruled ineligible because they own homes or cars; they can't qualify for public assistance for the same reason.

People who once scorned welfare and thought charity was what they did for somebody else now find themselves lining up at neighborhood food pantries for weekly distributions of cheese, butter, beans, or rice. Four years ago, there wasn't a major pantry on the Southeast Side; now there are ten. When a church group on the East Side got a truckload of bruised onions for its pantry, it took only twenty-four hours for word of mouth to spread the news and the onions to disappear. At Our Lady of Guadalupe in South Chicago, 15,000 pounds of cheese and butter were distributed in four hours.

Paying bills can pose even greater difficulties. "There are people out there collecting cans," says Mary Garcia of South Deering. "They're doing all kinds of things to bring in a little money to pay for their light or gas. You got to pay them bills; otherwise, they'll turn them off on you."

According to John Cronin, head of the East Side's St. Vincent dePaul Society, utility bills are the single greatest problem facing unemployed workers. "In the last months, we've had people come to us for six or seven gas shutoffs and a dozen electric shutoffs," he reports. "A lot of people have gotten to the point where they'll sell their food stamps to pay their gas bill, then go and get some food from the pantries."

Many people have serious problems absorbing such drastic changes in the way they live. The financial and emotional stress that job loss places on the family structure can leave it cracked and trembling. Domestic violence is on the increase. Social workers say that alcohol is largely to blame. Men who used to drink in bars now often have their whiskey at home; it's cheaper and they don't have to worry about holding their heads up high. Thomas Paprocki, a lawyer with the South Chicago Legal Clinic, explains that in many of his divorce cases, the physical abuse only began when the husband started drinking heavily in the wake of losing his job.

Heavy drinking does not always lead to violence, but it usually does create arguments and tensions. And even without alcohol, unemployment is a diligent gardener of bad feelings, digging up long-buried resentments and planting new grudges. Katherine Altobelli recalls the months after her husband was laid off as "the worst of my entire life. He was absolutely paranoid because he could not take care of his family. It's very hard on men's egos—in this community, in particular."

Like the Altobellis, Jimmy and Julia Torrez weathered a stormy period as they came to grips with the effects of unemployment. "Rejection was on his face," Julia remembers. "He felt, 'What good am I?' We were always fighting. There were constant arguments about money."

Although these marriages have survived, many others are giving way under the strain. In a community that prized marital stability and scorned divorce, a growing number of families are torn by conflict. "A lot of my buddies are separated or divorced," says Jimmy Torrez. "If I knew 200 guys from the mill, 160 of them are divorced."

Mexican-American families have been especially affected. "Many of the men have simply picked up and left, heading back to Texas or Mexico to look for work," says a local social worker. Sometimes, he notes, they send money back home, and sometimes they leave "so the lady can go on welfare." Occasionally, they disappear without a trace, driven off by their feelings of disgrace. "You must understand," says jobs counselor Ruth Hammer, "when you have a man who is used to supporting his family, it's devastating. 'No soy hombre— I'm not a man—I can't even support my family; they're better off without me.' "

When a parent loses a job, children lose also. "It had a big effect on our kids," says Jimmy Torrez. "My little girl is eight. She developed a peptic ulcer and was constantly getting stomachaches and headaches. It's hard to explain to them when they're so small."

Juan Chico was ten years old when Wisconsin Steel collapsed; his parents' marriage soon collapsed in its wake. "I was mad at Wisconsin Steel," he said three years later, "because I knew that's why my father was drinking and getting into lots of fights with my mother." Juan's younger brother couldn't cope with the conflict and had to be sent to live with a grandfather in Texas. Juan, however, has become more determined; he works hard in school and plans to study computers in college. His father is gone now and his mother has found a job in the post office. Juan likes sports but says he doesn't go out for any teams because he wants to be available to help his mother whenever she needs him.

Alice Gooch, principal of the Marsh Grammar School in Slag Valley, finds such attitudes on the rise among her students, the children of former mill workers: "They're very mature. It's 'I have to take care of myself.' They're extremely serious about things. It's not what you think of for children anymore in this neighborhood."

This is not the future that Southeast Side parents imagined for their children. Some have had to take their grown children back into their homes. "The only thing that saved me is my parents," says Ron Turner. "If I didn't live here, I'd be out on skid row, I know it."

Others have had to watch in frustration as their children search for work. Patricia Masselli has four jobless children: one is a navy veteran skilled in computers; of another, she notes, "There's not a lazy bone in his body." "Our two boys are machinists," says Thomas Kozel. "Where they used to work five days a week, now they're only working two. Our son-in-law's been out of work for a year and a half. We hoped our children would be more financially secure than us. It makes you despondent what's happening to them."

Few people in these neighborhoods have escaped the impact of unemployment, but women and blacks have been particularly stricken. Female steelworkers had the low positions on the seniority totem pole, and when layoffs started, they were the first to go. Many were single mothers who now face even greater problems than unemployed men. They don't have wives to go out and get jobs; and if they take any of the few low-paying jobs that are all that is available to them, they can't afford child care.

The impact on black steelworkers was even greater because the mills had been an even larger source of jobs for them. A study of former South Works employees found that far fewer blacks had found new jobs after being laid off from the mills than had their white counterparts.

Many blacks in the mills were the first generation of their families to attain financial security. But their tenuous hold on middle-class status melted away like snow on a sunny day, and they found themselves back on the economic margin. "I've had to change my life-style completely," says former Wisconsin worker Pete Jefferson. "I come from a Southern family. They always looked up to me because I'd done so well financially. I used to be the head of the family; now I'm just a member."

Steve Alexander says that what hurts most is the way that unemployment has driven a wedge among workers. They've lost the camaraderie that gave life its zest and they miss the friends they had. "We placed such a high value on relationships," Steve says. "Now I'm afraid to call people I knew. I avoided them when I went to pick up my sub pay. I'm afraid to find out what's happening with them. They're starting to lose the ability to hold on."

DOWN IN THE DUMPS

The sum of so much personal suffering is a community in trauma. "It just doesn't have the vibrance it used to," Jaime Gomez says of his old South Deering neighborhood. "If you see someone, they don't even want to talk. People just stay in their houses."

On the surface, these neighborhoods have deteriorated very little. Lawns are as well tended as a golf green; houses are newly painted or shingled. The reality is that unemployment has produced idle hands that search out every odd job at home and has made people anxious to keep the image of their neighborhood up. "In my neighborhood, there's very few working," says Henry Schlesinger. "The homes are well kept up because that's all they have to do. You'll see a few that say, 'The hell with it.' They'll let the houses go because they're down in the dumps. But neighbors will talk to them and get them to clean up."

Local business districts present a more obvious indicator of the region's economic fortunes. Once Torrence Avenue in South Deering featured a bustling row of taverns and restaurants directly across the street from a bustling steel mill. By 1983, many of the doors were locked or boarded up. Rose Alivojvodic runs a tavern just off Torrence on 104th Street. "It's bad here, real bad," she says. "At lunch time, it used to be so crowded in here, they'd sit on the radiator, on the pool table. Now I'm lucky if I can fill the bar stools."

Fewer stores have closed in Hegewisch or the East Side, but business is poor. Barbara Minster of the East Side chamber of commerce believes that local merchants are "hanging on, waiting for things to turn around."

And Commercial Avenue, the main shopping district of South Chicago, is steadily deteriorating. Once, Goldblatt's Department Store and Laumann's Clothiers anchored the avenue, drawing a stream of people from nearby neighborhoods. Now Laumann's has moved to the suburbs, and Goldblatt's is a dispirited mockery of its former self, a bargain-basement store of discounts and seconds.

Fear of crime is increasing as the street's character changes. Dr. Edward Lukas, who's practiced podiatry in South Chicago for thirty-five years, shuts his Commercial Avenue office at 2:30 in the afternoon because his patients are afraid to come any later. In between appointments, the doctor nervously peers out the window so he can keep an eye on his car parked behind the building. "You've got to watch these kids," he warns. "They'll strip your car in a minute."

Although police data do not indicate any marked increase in crime in the area in recent years, Dr. Lukas's concerns are widely shared. There is a strong public perception that the rising unemployment rate is sparking more crime. "It's really gotten bad around here," says Mary Gonzalez of her Bush neighborhood. "I've been robbed three times. You see people out there that used to work that have to steal now. They're selling drugs to make ends meet." Henry Schlesinger echoes this view: "Something had better break or you won't be able to walk the streets after dark around the East Side."

Much of the crime is committed by juveniles, and local youth workers believe the delinquency is related to the malaise that has afflicted teenagers since the mills began to decline. It was always taken for granted that there would be jobs waiting for these kids—decent jobs that required little in the way of prior experience, skills, or education.

Now the future is a blank. "There's a lot of aimlessness, hopelessness," says Vince Champaign. "There are also a lot of untimely deaths among the young—drinking, car accidents, violence." And Neil Bosanko, who has spent years working with South Chicago teens, finds that "they now feel, 'Why should I go to school when at the end, there's nothing.' "

With all these changes, however, community stability has only been bruised. There is little movement out of these neighborhoods. You can credit this to the strong attachment to community roots, as does Barbara Minster. "Whole families have lived in this area and they want to stay together," she points out. "They don't want to move all over the country. They like it where they are." Or you can credit it to simple economics: Who will buy these homes? Local realtors report it can take two or three years to sell the occasional house that does go on the market.

Many residents refuse to believe their neighborhoods will be drastically altered, even in the wake of industrial decline, but others point with trepidation to the only growth industry in all of Southeast Chicago: hazardous waste dumps.

Over the years its vast expanses of open land—and the porous clay that lines them—have made the Calumet region the prime receptacle for all manner of waste—human, industrial, and hazardous. "No one knows how many dumpers have operated on the Southeast Side," says the *Chicago Reporter*, an investigative journal. "Many filled their holes and left long before state and federal authorities began to keep count."

But what is known is worrisome enough. There are thirty-one EPA-designated land pollution control sites in the Southeast Chicago area, eleven of them concentrated within a territory the size of Chicago's O'Hare airport. There are hazardous landfills with ninety-foot-high hills of waste; there are sludge treatment facilities that perfume the air with the odor of excrement; and there are incinerators that burn, among other things, PCBs. In addition, illegal dumpers have littered the landscape with everything from discarded sofas to deadly chemicals.

The scope of the problem is immense, according to Dr. James Landing, professor of geography at the University of Illinois. "It makes no difference where you go in the Lake Calumet area," he says; "near you there's going to be some kind of waste disposal facility." There are currently 1140 acres in sanitary and hazardous landfill, with proposals for another 1000 acres still under review by regulatory agencies. This estimate doesn't include the two incineration plants, the industrial waste processing plant, the waste transfer plant, the two sludge drying operations, or any of the on-site disposal done by area industries.

Concerned citizens have a lengthy list of complaints against the dumps: increased truck traffic—one dump can bring an additional 500 trucks per day into the area; the smell—in summer, it can be overpowering, causing a spate of headaches and nausea; declining property values—each new dump threatens them further. And, perhaps most important, they fear the potential impact on human health —"My wife was worried the entire time she was pregnant," says David Devine of Hegewisch.

Almost in tandem with the decline of the steel industry,

waste firms have stepped up their pressure for permits to expand existing facilities or build new ones. The most recent proposal, from Waste Management, Inc., the region's most notorious dump landlord, would create a 289-acre hazardous waste site within blocks of South Deering's grammar school.

Residents worry that the proliferation of landfills is a sign of the Southeast Side's permanent abandonment as an industrial center. Dr. Landing sees good reason for their concern:

> The waste firms have propagandized everybody for years that you need a good network of hazardous waste operations to attract industry. But we have failed to uncover a single solitary example of that in the Lake Calumet area. If that argument is true, then this area should be attracting more industry than anywhere else because it has more hazardous waste facilities. In fact, it acts as a deterrent.

Southeast Siders also fear that the dumps are a symbol of the indifference—even contempt—with which outsiders view their neighborhoods. "You walk into a house you don't like and say, 'What a dump.' That's a very denigrating thing to say to a person—or a neighborhood," notes St. Kevin's Father Schopp. "To physically use it as one, it's an insult."

This is a community confronting change that is rapid and raw. While waste dumps and scrap heaps climb steadily upward, two massive steel mills are now only great iron deserts. "It's almost like the ground really is shifting under our feet," says one former mill worker as he gazes glumly at the tattered fence that once shielded Wisconsin Steel from all unauthorized intrusions.

LOOKING FOR JOBS

Probably no single aspect of the shifting economic order has produced a greater sense of disorientation than the drastic shrinkage of the local job market. Selma Wise, former director of the South Chicago Development Commission, believes that unemployed steelworkers are having trouble finding new jobs because they refuse to adjust to the realities of deindustrialization. "They don't want to accept the fact that the world has changed and they're going to have to work for less," she says, a trace of irritation obvious in her voice.

But the steelworkers themselves dispute her view, insisting that there simply aren't jobs to be found—at any wages. "I've been everywhere—to factories, retail stores, restaurants, hotels," says Jimmy Torrez, who has been out of work for over three years. "I once worked for $3.50 an hour. I'd do it again. I'll do anything—wash toilet bowls." Alfred Thomas, who spent seven years at South Works, agrees: "People are willing to do almost anything for a job. Men got kids; they got to do what they got to do." A recent study of former South Works employees offers support for these claims. It found that the current unemployment rate among mill workers who had been laid off over the last seven years was 46.3 percent.

The difficulty of finding work can be explained in part by the general weakness of the Calumet region's economy, but a second factor is that prospective employers are wary of ex-mill workers, who might bring with them a union tradition and high wage expectations. "I tell employers I'll take a job, even at $6 or $7 an hour," says Bob Harrington, once a mill foreman, "but they don't believe you. They see you worked at Wisconsin Steel and you can't get nothing. You start to think the world is against a Wisconsin steelworker."

The roadblocks are especially high for those over 40. They find it difficult to imagine gaining new skills; more importantly, they find it difficult to find employers who will hire anyone their age. One interviewer told 58-year-old Henry Schlesinger: "I'm gonna tell you right now, if I can't get fifteen years out of a person, I'm gonna tear the application up."

Those who have found jobs have already settled for a lot less. Jaime Gomez, a millwright with twenty-six years at Wisconsin, has a job in a small machine shop at half his former salary; there is no pension plan and no benefits. Another man, with thirty-four years as a Wisconsin mill hand, now works as a crossing guard for $3.50 an hour. Alfred Thomas went to work for a furniture manufacturing firm at $3.75 an hour. And a number of mill workers have become farm workers, earning little more than minimum wage; some work at truck farms nearby, while others have joined the ranks of the migrants who range from Wisconsin to Florida.

The growing desperation of this search for work breeds increased reliance on local politicians. The ability of the alderman to open the door to employment is legendary. Most steelworkers once scorned his system of political patronage, but lately they find themselves heading for his office with hat in hand. Some have found jobs through this route; others are told they're on a waiting list—and there they wait. Often, a jobless worker is asked to demonstrate political commitment to secure a placement. "I worked for the alderman because he promised me a job," says a young black man on layoff from South Works. "I never saw it. I'm still trying to get in touch with him. He won't even give me an interview now."

If the men of Southeast Chicago have found the doors of prospective employers slammed in their faces, their wives have encountered a far different reception. All over the mill neighborhoods, women have joined or rejoined the work force to support their families. They are secretaries, waitresses, clerks, and sales personnel, almost invariably at salaries far below what their husbands once made.

Their husbands' reactions are a mixture of relief and resentment. At a local community meeting on unemployment, every man in the room is out of work, while a number of the women have jobs. When the group's leader announces that he has applications for jobs with United Parcel Service, hands start to shoot up. "Only for women," he adds. Angry murmurs explode around the room. But several women confer with their spouses and then rise to take the forms.

Brian Kennedy expresses the ambivalence that many men feel: "I used to be embittered about girls working, but let's face it, a lot of people wouldn't make it if their wives wasn't working." Despite this recognition, there remains the sense of a world gone topsy-turvy: men are left to mind the children and make a pass at cooking dinner, while women leave early each morning to bring home the bacon. John Cronin suspects employers "want it this way. Change the worker from the husband to the wife and she's working for half as much. They got it made. It was probably planned, for all I know."

The arrival of this new sexual division of labor—with its attendant decline in family income—does not herald a new era of equality or progress for women, but it has helped women in these communities to discover new strengths and to grow in self-esteem. Attitudes within the family are changing as well. Jimmy Torrez says that when his kids ask if they can buy something, he tells them to ask their mother since she's the one bringing home the paycheck. And Juan Chico marvels at his mother's determination to get a good job after his father abandoned the family: "She worked so hard. I don't know how she did it."

What, then, is to become of the displaced industrial workers of the Southeast Side? Academic articles and TV shows alike proffer two alternatives: retraining or relocation. Neither has proven effective thus far.

According to conventional wisdom, the smokestack industries are doomed and their workers must be retrained in the skills our society requires today. The exact nature of these skills is seldom defined, but there is usually mention of computers or "high tech."

Southeast Chicago has a dismal lack of job retraining programs. A CETA program, set up on the heels of the Wisconsin closing, was more political than vocational in purpose; it enabled then-Mayor Byrne to make a gesture of support for the angry workers and it provided a few staff positions for supporters of the local alderman. But the skills it taught—welding and machining—were of little value in the region's depressed economy. When a young woman at a community meeting bemoaned the fact that her husband had been through the program but couldn't find a job, an older man near her burst out, "It's no wonder. I've been a welder for twenty-five years. I can weld anything put in front of me. And I've been out of work for three years." Jimmy Torrez's frustration with the program is typical of its graduates. "I went to that school—came in third in the class. I got a certificate in welding. When I went for welders' jobs, they told me I needed five years' experience. They said the diploma was just a piece of paper. The Illinois Job Service told me, 'Toilet paper is worth more than that.' "

By 1983, the CETA program had reorganized under the direction of the South Chicago Development Commission. Courses were retargeted to employment growth areas: building maintenance, auto parts sales, and electronics. The program improved record keeping and beefed up placement efforts. Nearly half the students who graduated from its ranks found jobs. Then, just as it seemed to be finding its bearings, the Reagan administration eliminated CETA and the local program died. There were 700 people on its waiting list.

In the absence of adequate public or nonprofit retraining efforts, many former mill workers seek out private programs, often at considerable personal cost. Mary Gonzalez, a 25-year-old mother of two children, worked the night shift at South Works and took courses by day to become a medical assistant. When she was laid off from the mill, she found a position as a medical assistant in a nearby hospital. Within months, she was laid off. Unable to find other health care work, she went back to school and got certified as an auto mechanic. But there have been no jobs in that field either. Today, Gonzalez would like to become a nurse, but she can't afford any more schooling. "I still owe for my other tuition," she explains. "The medical assistance program was $2500. And they never really help you find a job."

For steelworkers, job retraining isn't just a matter of learning a new skill; it's a matter of learning a new way of life. "There are few jobs anywhere that are like working in a mill," Steve Alexander says. Steelworkers become used to old clothes, to heat, to sweat. Most importantly, they are used to the easy camaraderie the mill fostered. Mill work allowed mill workers to be themselves. It required no pretenses and it allowed few; people knew you too well for too long, knew how you acted in a crisis, how you reacted when someone died before your eyes, how you responded to jokes and pranks. If you were having a bad day, you could curse a fellow worker or even yell at a foreman, secure in the knowledge that your friend and your job would still be there the next day.

Jobs that require suits and ties, deference to superiors, and polite smiles for customers and coworkers seem a million miles from the grime and gusto of a steel mill. "I got a job at Sears, but I just couldn't take being a salesman," says former mill worker Bob Harrington. "People aren't cut out for certain things."

Although it's too soon to pass any judgments on the success of retraining as a strategy for aiding displaced industrial workers, the paucity of efforts on the Southeast Side have left its unemployment problem virtually untouched. Relocation hasn't proven a viable solution either.

The most obvious question is: Where should workers go? The steel industry is in trouble throughout the United States; mill skills are not exactly in demand anywhere—except maybe Brazil or Korea. For those who have other crafts—carpentry, bricklaying, electronics—the prospects are only minimally brighter. The Sunbelt states, only recently considered a paradise of employment opportunity, have reached the saturation point. Those Southeast Siders who journey to Texas or

Florida find that jobs are scarce there and newcomers unwelcome. Most return home with nothing but frustration in their pockets.

The road more often traveled these days is the one to the local welfare office. The blue-collar workers' traditional aversion to welfare programs is being eroded by sheer necessity. "The guys are all on public aid," Ron Turner says of friends who worked at Wisconsin. "I didn't want to go. You figure you're mooching off the state. A lot of people wouldn't go. They were too proud to take it. But eventually everybody decided; one starts and then the next one."

Pride is being put away with the heavy clothes and thick-soled boots. "I'm not proud no more," says one East Side father. "Being proud don't feed your kids."

LAYING BLAME

There is an aura of mystery that attends any death, especially one that comes without warning. Suddenly, we are forced to meditate on what has always been taken for granted. "All of us, now that we're losing it, have more of a sense of what steel means to us," says Neil Bosanko, the son and grandson of South Works' employees.

Memories of the mill are the stuff of tavern talk these days. As with a deceased friend, its faults are all but forgotten, its virtues enshrined. "I really miss the place," says Bob Harrington. "It was fun. There wasn't a day that went by without something happening." Ron Turner speaks wistfully of the bonds among the workers: "I worked with some really nice people there. I wish I could work anywhere with people like that. There wasn't no prejudice; it was more like a family."

Then, hunched over coffee or beer, they try to unravel the mystery of steel's demise. Why did it happen? Whose fault is it anyway? Was it murder, or an act of fate?

There are those who steadfastly refuse to assign blame,

chalking up their lost jobs to the vagaries of the economy. Others believe the responsibility should be spread around. "No one person is to blame" is Patricia Masselli's view. "It's a whole combination—the individual worker, the unions, government, business; it's you and I."

Most people search for a more definite reason. They can't accept that this is all part of God's plan, nor are they willing to take the responsibility onto their own shoulders. The easiest target for their ire is "the government"—that vague entity that takes tax money and sets national policy.

"We paid heavy taxes all those years," fumes Joe Smetlack. "We were more or less supporting the government when they were having riots and the country was in turmoil in the 1960s. If it wasn't for us, the average working guy, the country would have gone to hell. Now, they're going to sell us out?"

The sense that our country's priorities have gone wildly awry pervades discussions on the Southeast Side. "I don't know how the government spends their money, what their priorities are," says Bob Harrington. "What disgusts me, the government sends $50 million to El Salvador to stop a revolution, but they don't got $40 million to spend in the old country to put steelworkers back to work."

The policies of the Reagan administration come under particular fire. "A lot of guys blame Reagan for letting the Japanese come over here and beat us at our own game," says one disgruntled worker, noting that it took the administration four years to curb steel imports. Others, like Maria Lourdes, are offended by the President's repeated attempts to minimize the extent of unemployment: "He is only for the rich people. I get so disgusted I don't even want to watch him anymore on the news."

But there's plenty of blame to go around—and it's not restricted to the powerful. Recent immigrants, virtually at the bottom of the economic totem pole, are also a frequent target of fire. "Immigrants are favored by the government," complains Jimmy Torrez, who says he was turned down for food stamps while "foreigners" were being approved. And Henry Schlesinger believes he was bypassed for a job in order to give preference to "immigrants." "I found out right then that if you wanted anything you had to speak some other language besides English, you had to be born in Haiti or Cuba. If you were born in this country, forget it. And if I sound bitter, I am."

Unions also come in for their share of bitterness. Resentment against the Progressive Steelworkers Union is especially strong. There's a sense that the union tried to get away with too much when the mill was going and did far too little once it closed down. "The union just sold us out completely," says one former Wisconsin worker. "Even to this day everybody can't figure out why they didn't try to do something."

Toward the USWA, feelings are more confused. Usually people aren't sure exactly what they think the union should have done; only that it should have done more. What it comes down to is that the mill workers had relied on their union for protection and it let them down. "The unions have become wholly inadequate," says Ken Wychocki, frustration evident in his voice. "They don't have the numbers anymore."

Steelworkers official Ed Sadlowski isn't sure that anger at the union is a bad thing. "Doesn't that indicate that they relate to the union more than they relate to the company?" he asks. It's the way that people will be very polite to a perfect stranger, he argues, then go home and fight with a husband or wife. "Why do you argue with those you love the most?" Union activist Rob Persons concurs, noting that it's always easier to blame the person (or institution) that's closer to you in the pecking order. "If I blame the guy that's more powerful than me, then the next logical question is what I want to do about it. And most of us don't feel we can do too much about the guy who's in a strong position."

Finally, although it's deeply buried beneath the surface on the Southeast Side, anger at the companies is there waiting to explode. "I blame International Harvester," says a former Wisconsin steelworker vehemently. "They were the ones that gave us the promises, then snatched everything out from under us in two hours' time." And another adds that "Harvester gained more out of this than anybody. Why they're not in jail, I just don't know. I guess you can't prosecute a big company."

U.S. Steel comes in for its share of hard knocks as well. John Ortiz spent sixteen years at South Works. Once he considered himself conservative; now he's just plain angry. "They don't care about me. They never did. They already got our blood. What else do they want?"

Although workers often profess ignorance of their employers' financial status or investment policies, nonetheless they blame the companies for allowing the mills to deteriorate. "They want to reap big profits, pay out a bonus on dividends, and not reinvest," asserts a veteran Wisconsin employee. "That's the way a house becomes a slum. You can build a brand new home, but if you don't paint it every few years, clean the gutters, then it starts rotting. That's the same thing they did in steel. They bled those mills for everything they could."

Trying to make sense of the past is only slightly less frustrating than trying to envision the future. Here, perhaps more than anywhere else, individual personalities and experiences come to bear. Those who are still at work, at local firms like Republic, General Mills, Ford; those who have marketable skills; those who can move easily into new situations—these are the people who can accept the demise of Southeast Chicago's industrial base with good grace. They can imagine a future for themselves, even for this community. "We've still got opportunities," says a buoyant William McLeod of the South Chicago chamber of commerce. "But steel isn't it. We have the raw materials to reindustrialize. All we need are ideas and entrepreneurs. And a good restaurant! We even have an idea for the restaurant. It would commemorate the steel industry—a combined museum and eatery. We were thinking of calling it The Blast Furnace."

To those who've lost mill jobs and can find no others, there is little ground for optimism. They face the future with deep unease. "I wonder sometimes what's gonna happen," Mary Garcia says fearfully. "I think about my kids who are out of jobs. What's gonna become of all of us? Nobody seems to know. Nobody gives you any answer."

Blas and Adrienne Paloma share a dark vision of what's ahead. Their voices run together as they describe it. "Our kids—I think they're gonna have a rough life. Employers will be taking more advantage of people. It'll be a throwaway society. They'll just use people up and throw them away. It'll eventually be down that road unless somebody straightens things out. And you won't have nobody fighting for you, either, because little by little, they're doing away with the unions. Once they do, they can really call the shots."

The chaos of people's own lives is reflected in their images of the community's fate. "If U.S. Steel closes, that's the end of this community," predicts Ken Wychocki. "It will become a disaster area, that's for sure." A former Wisconsin steelworker is equally apocalyptic in his forecast: "When unemployment compensation runs out, we're gonna have one big funeral around here. If they don't do something soon, this area is going to be the biggest slum in the United States."

The people of Southeast Chicago think of themselves as workers. By this they mean both that they work for a living and that they are the sort who dig in and get things done. "The solution here for everything has always been 'work harder,'" notes John Cronin. And Theresa Marzullo points out that people like her father who spent a lifetime at Wisconsin Steel always believed that "if you worked, you didn't have to worry."

Now the rules have changed: the hardest work is of no

avail; there is no work to do. Few understand this new game plan, according to union activist Alice Peurala:

> They're telling workers they've got to step back and do with less. What does that mean? Not having a car? Not being able to make the payments on their house? Not being able to send their kids to college? Not having any money for recreation? I thought that's what it was all about—to make the life of the worker decent and with dignity and the ability to enjoy the things of society like culture and recreation. Now they're saying we've taken too much from the corporations. To me, that's reversing the goddam ball of wax.

And in that reversal, the American Dream, as it was known here, seems hopelessly mangled. Steelworkers believed themselves secure in the ranks of middle America; now they've plummeted into something close to poverty. "The American Dream is going," insists Alicia Bodnar, wife of a former South Works employee. "The name of the game is to keep your head above water. You're going to survive this new depression. You're going to survive it. . . . Then you get mad and you think how the rich get richer and the middle class are just going down with the poor."

As they watch their world crumble, people look to the familiar institutions that have shielded and aided them—the union, the Democratic party, the churches. "Who's gonna help them now, really who?" asks Mary Garcia. Can local forces hope to have any impact on a problem that is international in scope?

Some Southeast Side citizens doubt that anything can help them. But a surprising number of people shun despair, though it forces itself upon them from time to time like an unwelcome guest. "Sure, I've got hope," says a former Wisconsin steelworker. "What else have we got?"

5

Local 65's Painful Dilemma

IN TIMES OF TROUBLE, the families of Southeast Chicago have looked to the United Steelworkers International Union of America for leadership, and the union has delivered. Over the course of forty years, steelworker wages rose from near the bottom of America's industrial work force to a place at the top: from the poverty of the Depression years to a middle-class standard of living. But wage increases were only part of the story. The union also negotiated substantial pension improvements, comprehensive health care programs, extended vacations, and paid personal holidays. The USWA even pioneered in the introduction of supplemental unemployment benefits which enabled steelworker families to weather economic recession without undue suffering. And finally there was job security: the seniority principles wrested from the companies by tough union bargainers enabled steelworkers to be pretty certain that once they had a job in the mill, they'd be able to keep it until retirement.

Over the decades, the USWA's ability to extract ever-improving wages, pensions, and benefits from some of the greatest industrial giants of the world's richest and strongest

119

nation gave the union an aura of invincibility. Whether or not steelworkers participated in their union's activities, they depended on it for protection.

Few in the steel towns understood that the mighty USWA was itself dependent—dependent on the continued prosperity of the American steel industry. And if they did understand that fact, it would have hardly seemed worth mentioning, for the steel corporations seemed as rich and permanent as America herself, surely a secure foundation on which to base a way of life.

But somehow, as the 1970s neared their end, that solid foundation began to shake. Not only did mass layoffs spread through the mill towns but strange news reports began to appear in the daily press—LTV buys Youngstown Sheet and Tube, Armco Steel becomes Armco Corp., U.S. Steel shuts the Campbell Works.

The USWA responded to the steel industry crisis by negotiating yet another benefit—a $400 per month payment to senior employees laid off when the mill department they worked in was shut down—and by lobbying the Congress for increased import restrictions. These efforts helped cushion the impact of the prolonged economic slump, but nonetheless, tremors continued to rock the foundations of America's steel communities—and to shake the confidence of union members in their organization's power.

In Southeast Chicago, it was Wisconsin Steel's sale and later shutdown that first focused community attention on the problems of the steel industry. But the failure of the Progressive Steelworkers Union fully to protect its members did not create a crisis of confidence for Southeast Siders: everyone knew that the PSWU did not win much that was not achieved first by the larger, and more powerful, USWA. Only when a second wave of mass layoffs swamped the steel industry during the recession of 1981–1982, did Southeast Siders begin to realize that the USWA itself was in crisis. Mill shutdowns became commonplace, and the union's plant-closing benefit proved inadequate to stop the hemorrhaging. Employment levels sank so low that the union-negotiated supplementary unemployment benefit funds were drained. Steel company demands for wage and work rule concessions proved irresistible, and local unions found themselves in a competition to underbid each other in a desperate attempt to save jobs no matter what the cost to union principle or labor solidarity.

For the people of Southeast Chicago, the failure of the USWA's traditional bargaining strategies to cope with the steel industry's abrupt collapse was symbolized by the decline of U.S. Steel's great South Chicago Works. In the early 1980s, U.S. Steel announced that South Works' survival was in jeopardy. Soon afterward, the corporation announced plans to build an ultra-modern rail mill that would assure South Works' future. Then the company said it could only afford to build the mill if USWA Local 65 agreed to make work rule concessions. This was followed by demands for much greater union give-backs.

The story of how Southeast Siders, and especially members of the USWA's Local 65, responded to U.S. Steel's ever-escalating demands reveals how difficult it is for workers and their unions to develop effective strategies in the new age of international economic competition.

Prologue to the Rail Mill Saga

In July of 1982, U.S. Steel announced that it would not build a new rail mill that would guarantee South Works' survival unless members of Local 65 of the USWA agreed to relax work rules that had long governed labor relations in the mill. With great reluctance, and only after strong prompting by their International officers, Local 65 members agreed to this first round of company demands. But that was not the end of the union's problems, for U.S. Steel did not build the rail mill.

For the next eighteen months, as U.S. Steel's demands for concessions escalated, the unionists' attitude developed into a bitter mixture of fury at the company's failure to deliver on its promise, disappointment with the USWA's perceived lack of leadership, and passive resignation about the future. An interview conducted with one of Local 65's leaders in the fall of 1983 brought out the membership's attitudes quite vividly:

Bill Bloom is frustrated and angry. As a local union officer, it's his job to make sure that South Works' management respects the contractual rights of union members. And he can't do it. While 6000 Local 65 members languish on layoff, management has begun an unprecedented campaign to reduce its labor costs. Under the new regime, steelworkers are being ordered to work sixty-hour weeks to save the company the expense of rehiring laid-off employees, they're being ordered to double up on jobs so that their buddies can be let go, and they're getting pink slips themselves as management hires outside firms to perform skilled and unskilled tasks that unionized steelworkers have always done.

"Right now, in my opinion, we in the union are not helping our people at all," Bill complains. "They see the jobs getting contracted out, they see the layoffs, and they wonder, 'What am I paying dues for?' "

In 1982, Bill served on Local 65's bargaining committee during negotiations over management's demands for work rule concessions for the proposed rail mill. "At the time I thought it was the best thing to do," he says of the union's agreement to concessions. "I realize now it was a mistake. I would never do it again. Not even if I knew they were going to build the fucking thing. I would not give them the satisfaction. Cause they allowed us to be embarrassed in front of our own people. Every facility U.S. Steel ever threatened to close down, they've closed down. So what's the big fucking deal to get two years of life?"

Bill is also unhappy about the national wage concessions approved by the USWA in March of 1983. "Before, we could tell our senior members, 'You get thirteen weeks extended vacation because of the union.' We can't say that anymore. We don't get vacation bonus anymore. A lot of the things that we could point to, we can't anymore, because we've given it up."

Bill is angry both at U.S. Steel and at his union's leadership. "For the last ten years, the International has tried to work things out with the boss on a friendly basis, while the company's stuck it in our ass. The people involved in the labor movement forty years ago have to be turning over in their graves because of what's happening. The world is crumbling around us and nothing is being done. We're back where we were forty years ago. The company's using slave tactics."

Bill believes the fight is over. "There's no future for this plant here. South Works is modern, but all of it is uncompetitive. Why would they build a rail mill that's uncompetitive?"

Despite the fact that South Works' decline has shattered Bill's dream of a career in the labor movement, he does not believe he can fault management's decision. "For years, they had been losing money on steelmaking. Why not take money from a losing business? Look, I work for a corporation. I'm not going to blame them. Who the hell am I to tell them, 'Keep your plant open'? But I do have a right to voice an opinion if you're going to continuously fuck me, take dollars out of my pocket."

Shortly after this interview was conducted, U.S. Steel announced that it would build the rail mill only if Local 65 agreed to a whole new set of concessions. This time, the union said "enough is enough." Then he, and the entire Southeast Side, waited to see if U.S. Steel would follow through on its threat to cancel plans for the rail mill and shut South Works down completely.

Although Bill Bloom's anger at the company and the union and his resignation about the future were typical of Local 65 members, they were hard for people outside the labor movement to understand. Take the issue of concessions. American steel companies have been losing ground to imported steel ever since 1959. The public asked: How could steelworkers at South Works reject demands that they relinquish some of their previous gains now that U.S. Steel no longer dominates the marketplace?

Or take the question of union leadership. Why did steelworkers in Southeast Chicago blame International union officers in Pittsburgh for poor leadership instead of devising their own plan to save their mill? Why did the USWA leave Local 65 on its own to deal with the mammoth U.S. Steel Corporation?

The answers to these questions lie partially in the particularities of U.S. Steel's behavior in the Rail Mill saga, behavior which outraged not only steelworkers, but public officials, the press, and the local business community as well. But a fuller understanding of the union's actions requires that we delve into history: the decision of members of Local 65 to make a final stand in defiance of their employer's threats and their International union's conciliatory policy was conditioned by a collective memory of how poorly the steel companies treated employees in the days before there were unions, of how fierce were the struggles to organize the USWA, and of how their union changed in the years after it won the organizing campaigns.

THE NONUNION ERA

It was no accident that working conditions in turn-of-the-century steel mills were brutal: steelmasters believed that their immigrant workmen were racially inferior and could not be harmed by working twelve-hour days and seven-day weeks—indeed, keeping the men usefully employed would deprive the Devil of idle hands.

Steelworkers were less convinced that employment under such harsh conditions constituted good fortune: quite often they quit and left for their homelands. Emigration back to impoverished, overpopulated Eastern Europe persisted at high levels.

But in 1914, war broke out in Europe. Emigration was closed off, and service in the United States Army gave many immigrant steelworkers a sense of citizenship. Five years later, in 1919, Southeast Chicago's mill workers astonished the worlds of labor and management by initiating a nationwide strike for union recognition and the abolition of the twelve-hour day.

U.S. Steel and the harsh Chicago winter crushed that strike, but in its wake, the company launched an effort at labor reform. The twelve-hour day was jettisoned, and new stock sharing and pension plans were introduced to tie employees more closely to the fortunes of their company.

The press praised U.S. Steel's "benevolent paternalism" in the 1920s, a decade when big business dominated Washington's halls of power. But in steel towns like South Chicago, the paeans to corporate enlightenment rang hollow. Steelworkers deeply resented their enforced dependence on foremen for jobs and promotions, and the company's "enlightened" pay policies kept them just a layoff or an injury away from poverty. Nevertheless, their crushing defeat at U.S. Steel's hands in 1919 and the threat of blacklisting stifled their protest. An uneasy peace settled on the mill communities, but images of the horrendous work conditions in the U.S. Steel mills of the nonunion era became part of the collective memory of Southeast Chicago. More than half a century later, they would color unionists' reactions to U.S. Steel's demands for concessions to make the proposed rail mill cost-competitive.

STEELWORKERS REBEL

When the Great Depression brought mass joblessness to South Chicago, the steelworkers' grievances mounted rapidly. In these circumstances, the foreman's control of hiring and firing gave him the power to allow a steelworker to earn a living or to sink into destitution. A spirit of sullen anger permeated Southeast Chicago, waiting only for a spark to touch off rebellion.

Congressional passage of the National Industrial Recovery Act in 1933, which gave workers the right to organize and bargain collectively, was the sign for which steelworkers were looking. They immediately began to organize. Their first efforts were directed at taking over company-initiated employee representation plans (ERPs) established in 1933 to forestall the organization of independent trade unions. The campaign to organize South Works is particularly celebrated in the annals of labor history because it was there that an employee named George Patterson took control of the ERP sponsored by U.S. Steel and led it into the Steel Workers Organizing Committee (SWOC) organized by John L. Lewis of the Committee of Industrial Organizations (CIO) in 1936.

Local leaders like George Patterson affiliated with SWOC, an organization controlled by outsiders, because they knew they could never organize unions on their own. The CIO poured hundreds of thousands of dollars into the steel organizing campaign, and hundreds of prounion workers went on SWOC staff. They were an army the companies could not discharge.

U.S. Steel mightily resisted unionization. The company's espionage system hounded workers, creating fear and dissension among men who found their every move anticipated. Many workers suspected of union sympathies were fired and became dependent on SWOC support. And as 1936 gave way to 1937, the union still did not have one contract with U.S. Steel to show for its years of organizing efforts.

And then, in the depth of the winter of 1936–1937, history took an unexpected turn. Myron Taylor, chairman of the board of U.S. Steel, decided to abandon The Corporation's thirty-five-year war against organized labor. He and John L. Lewis of the CIO began a series of secret meetings to discuss alternatives to the long, bloody, and costly strike that both had been preparing to fight.

On March 1, 1937, they shocked the nation by announcing a historic agreement: U.S. Steel would recognize SWOC as the bargaining agent for its members.

Jubilant steelworkers believed that U.S. Steel's capitulation meant the triumph of unionism in the entire industry. But it was not to be that easy.

The Little Steel companies were steeped in antiunion ideology and they were not about to abandon their antiunion principles. In the spring of 1937, one of the bloodiest and most bitter battles of the entire decade erupted on the streets of Southeast Chicago.

THE LITTLE STEEL STRIKE

The steel companies that made up Little Steel traditionally followed U.S. Steel's lead, but when it came to recognizing SWOC, they broke the pattern.

Tom Mercer Girdler, the superintendent of Jones and Laughlin's Aliquippa Works from 1920 to 1929, and Republic Steel's chairman of the board throughout the 1930s and 1940s, has come to symbolize Little Steel's management. Girdler's labor policies at Republic's East Side plant were much tougher than those prevailing at U.S. Steel's nearby South Works. For example, during Girdler's reign, Republic employees had to report to the mill gates six mornings per week but were given just two or three days of work: anyone taking "outside employment" was fired. On Girdler's orders, Republic's police force of 370 men possessed 552 pistols, 64 rifles, 245 shotguns, 143 gas guns, and 232 nightsticks.

While SWOC organizers tried to take advantage of the victory at U.S. Steel, Girdler devised a strategy to repulse the union tide by provoking a premature strike. After he instituted mass layoffs at two Republic mills, and then locked workers out of one of the mills altogether, SWOC leaders were forced to set the strike date: May 26, 1937. When striking workers began walking out of Republic's East Side plant, it became clear that Republic's security forces had organized more thoroughly than SWOC had done. Union efforts to set up "mass picketing" in front of the main gate were thwarted by the industrial department of Chicago's police force, which had been retained by Girdler months before for a hefty "tip." Furthermore, Girdler had arranged for a thousand Republic employees to bed themselves down inside the mill, ready to resume production the next day.

The unionists' only hope was to set up a picket line strong enough to give workers inside the plant confidence that the union could win. But the Chicago police would allow only six picketers per gate. In utter frustration, SWOC called for a mass protest rally on Memorial Day.

When 1000 men and women began marching to the mill gate on May 30, they were ordered to disperse. As discouraged march leaders turned to leave, someone in the crowd threw a tree branch toward the police. A patrolman fired his pistol in the air. Within the next fifteen seconds, policemen fired 200 shots toward the fleeing strikers.

Ten marchers were shot to death. Thirty received gunshot wounds that left them permanently disabled, twenty-eight required hospitalization for cuts and bruises, and thirty more received emergency medical treatment. Not one policeman had been shot.

In the wake of the violence, discouraged strikers began going back to the mill. By the end of June, only a hard-core group of 500 strikers remained—not enough to hurt Republic Steel, but a significant drain on SWOC's coffers. As SWOC slowly reduced its strike support, Local 1033 members began to quarrel among themselves; they threw in the towel on November 3.

Ultimately, unionism came to Republic Steel, but victory came as much through the courts and the political process as through struggle on the industrial battlefield. Although Chicago's law officers and courts gave Republic strikers little satisfaction, the federal legal apparatus was not as forgiving of Tom Girdler's tactics. On October 18, 1938, the National Labor Relations Board ruled that the labor spies, the beatings of union organizers, and the incitement to violence all constituted illegal interference with SWOC's right to organize. This ruling was upheld in the federal courts.

At the same time as the courts were outlawing the tactics of the Little Steel companies, changing economic conditions were undermining their antiunion zeal. War orders from Europe were fueling a boom in the American economy, and after the horror of the Depression, no businessman wanted to miss out on the feast. Furthermore, the Roosevelt administration did not want corporate antiunionism to impede preparations for war.

When SWOC launched its second campaign to organize Little Steel, late in 1940, it met quite a different response from that of three years earlier. It was Tom Girdler's turn to throw in the towel. By November 7, 1941, Republic, Bethlehem, Youngstown, and Inland had all granted SWOC recognition. After twenty-two years, South Chicago steelworkers finally could bargain collectively with their employers. The days of corporate dictatorship, benevolent or otherwise, were gone.

The labor struggles of the 1930s left an ambiguous legacy in South Chicago. Among prounion families, stories of labor spies and vicious policemen created an abiding anger against the steel companies; the hall where Local 65 members assembled to discuss the rail mill concessions bears the name of one of the victims of the Memorial Day massacre. But among the families of the Wisconsin Steel workers and the "loyal" employees of Republic Steel, who shunned the CIO out of conviction, fear of the boss, or distrust of outsiders, the bitter struggles of the 1930s taught a different lesson—not that unions are bad, but that union-management conflict is dangerous and to be avoided.

Fifty years afterward, Southeast Chicago would remain divided between those motivated by anger at the steel companies and those intent on avoiding conflict. The divisions would even be found within the ranks of Local 65 and would complicate that union's efforts to avert the shutdown of U.S. Steel's South Works.

BIRTH OF THE USWA

Local activists and national SWOC leaders had learned different lessons from the struggles of the Depression years. For men like George Patterson in South Chicago, the local union was an instrument of battle in an ongoing war.

But in SWOC headquarters in Pittsburgh, President Philip Murray and his mentor, John L. Lewis, had learned that labor could not win an all-out war unless it had help from sympathetic government officials; and furthermore, that so long as employers remained bitterly antiunion, organizing victories by themselves would yield meager fruit. The only way to gain employer acceptance and retain government support, Murray and Lewis concluded, was for SWOC to guarantee that its locals would act moderately, live up to their collective bargaining agreements, and, above all, eschew the wildcat strikes that infuriated corporate executives. And this meant that SWOC would have to have substantial control of its locals' actions. Over time, the local-national differences in viewpoint were to produce a serious rift; a permanent duality was developing within the ranks of steelworker unionists.

Once organization was achieved, local militants wanted to run their own affairs. One of their goals was to "square accounts" with the bosses who had "kicked them around" for so long. Another was to boost SWOC's prestige with those employees who had not signed union cards. The result was frequent wildcat strikes and breakdowns in collective bargaining.

Into this chaos, International union officers attempted to bring order. They tried to convince management that settling grievances promptly and granting the union shop would improve both worker morale and plant efficiency; at the same time, they "educated" local union officers to trust management. Those local leaders who couldn't change their ways were removed.

After the Little Steel companies entered the union fold in 1941–1942, SWOC formalized its structure as an international labor union. Phillip Murray presented to the delegates of the United Steelworkers of America founding convention a constitution which reflected the centralized nature of collective bargaining in the steel industry. All power was centered in the hands of the International president, who could "appoint, direct, suspend, or remove such organizers, representatives, agents and employees as he may deem necessary." Moreover, only the president could authorize strikes, and he was a party to all the locals' collective bargaining agreements.

The story of George Patterson illustrates the power International officers exerted in the new organization. Patterson appeared to have a good chance to be elected director of the USWA's largest region, District 31, when he announced his candidacy in 1944. But then he was drafted into the army, despite the fact that all union staff members were eligible for deferments. Patterson always believed that he was inducted only because his opponent, union official Joe Germano, did not send the army verification of his exempt status. At any rate, Patterson learned he'd lost the election while stationed in India. Years later, USWA president David MacDonald admitted that he had sent Joe Germano 10,000 extra ballots.

The fate of George Patterson produced a strong distrust of their International leaders among some of the Southeast Side's strongest unionists. In the 1980s, the remnants of that distrust would handicap USWA efforts to forge a united response to the steel companies' concession demands.

Although the cooperative relationships pursued by International union officers brought significant wage and benefit gains, labor-management relations in the mills of American steel towns continued on their confrontational course throughout the postwar era, and steelworkers still had to work in authoritarian workplaces. Conflict over foremen's favoritism, disputed piece rates, and excessive absenteeism became a part of the mill, a familiar, chronic, controlled tension.

Over the years, as International union officers pursued their strategy of labor-management cooperation, while shop-floor conflicts persisted on the local level, a schism developed in the USWA. Edward Sadlowski's rise from the ranks of South Works' Local 65 to the status of challenger for the presidency of the Steelworkers International union in 1977, dramatized most clearly the continuing conflict within the USWA.

THE RISE AND FALL OF STEELWORKER INSURGENCY

Sadlowski came from an old South Chicago family; his grandfather started working at South Works in 1890 and remained there until 1914; his father, Ed Sr., worked at Inland Steel in East Chicago for nearly thirty years. When Ed Sadlowski, Jr., entered South Works in 1956, he was already steeped in the lore of Calumet-area unionism, and he threw himself into the political life of Local 65 with wholehearted enthusiasm. By the time he was 24, in 1964, he had put together a coalition of militant unionists from diverse ethnic backgrounds; his slate, including three Poles, a Mexican, two blacks, and a Serb, captured the Local 65 presidency in an amazing upset.

Sadlowski tried to reinforce the local membership's gut anger at U.S. Steel with knowledge of the heritage of their union's struggle. He collected and reprinted dozens of articles about the 1919 strike, the SWOC organizing campaign, and the Memorial Day massacre and distributed those reprints to classrooms filled with union activists. In 1968, after Sadlowski had served two terms as Local 65's President, district director Joe Germano appointed him to the International staff, thereby hoping to tactfully eliminate a potential challenger. But it didn't work. While serving as an International representative, Sadlowski defied his union's pro-Vietnam War stance by introducing antiwar resolutions at local union meetings. Then, in 1973, he announced his candidacy for District 31's directorship.

After thirty-one years as district director, Germano was stepping down. He named Sam Evett, who had served as his right-hand man for decades, the "official family's" candidate. Challenging Evett would be an uphill battle. As the organization's candidate, he had the support of nearly all the International representatives on District 31's staff, plus campaign funding from USWA leaders in Pittsburgh.

But Sadlowski's campaigners proceeded to outorganize their opponents. Using sophisticated public relations techniques, they established their theme: the International union's neglect of the rank and file. The slogan "Elect a Steelworker" reminded unionists that Sam Evett had never worked in a mill. At a time when popular journalists were proclaiming the birth of the affluent working class, Sadlowski's literature portrayed a different mill town society: "The next time you sit down to a meal of warmed-over macaroni, think of Sam Evett. He's eating steak."

The leadership's response was to portray Sadlowski's forces as the outsiders. Sadlowski's own loyalty to the union was even called into question because he had accepted campaign contributions from East Coast liberals.

Sadlowski narrowly lost that election, but when he filed a complaint with the federal labor department, charging that the "official family" had stolen the election, Sam Evett agreed to a rerun. The second time Sadlowski won by a 2–1 margin.

Sadlowski's victory made him a national celebrity. Reporters from all over the country came to Southeast Chicago to interview the working-class rebel, and steelworkers throughout the country began to call District 31's new director to ask him to run for International president.

Reluctantly, Sadlowski agreed. Organizing a national campaign was an awesome task for the insurgents, who adopted the name Steelworkers Fight Back. While hundreds of full-time, paid International staff representatives campaigned for Lloyd McBride, Steelworkers Fight Back had to ferret out supporters in far-off places, some of them foreign to the traditions and practice of steel unionism.

Sadlowski relied on the same appeal that had worked in his district election. He called for the democratization of the USWA constitution so that the rank-and-file steelworkers could regain control of their destiny.

In the basic steel locals, Fight Back won 52 percent of the vote. But by 1977, the USWA was no longer composed overwhelmingly of steelworkers. When it came time to tally the vote, the International's strength in nonsteel locals overwhelmed the Fight Back majorities in basic steel. McBride won the race by a 57–43 margin, and Fight Back efforts to overturn the election on the basis of alleged vote fraud in Quebec and the South were not successful.

Although Sadlowski's defeat did not usher in a new day of labor-management harmony in the mills, or local-International harmony in the union, steelworkers' militancy *was* eroding. Bill Bloom attributes the change to the peaceful bargaining climate of the decades following the 1959 strike: "There was really no deliberation or hard bargaining. Both sides wanted to stay away from a war. So we lost our reasoning about what the union is all about, and we lost an idea of where we're coming from."

Alice Peurala, who was elected Local 65 president in 1979, thinks the USWA's constitution is partly to blame for the decline of local union militancy. "Union members never had a right to vote on the basic labor agreement. And before 1974, we never had a right to strike over the local contract. The whole mechanism of the union worked against local militancy."

During Peurala's term as Local 65's president, 1979–1982, membership participation in union affairs increased dramatically, but Peruala was swimming against a swelling tide. Twenty years of peaceful bargaining and rapid wage gains had sapped Local 65's militancy. At the same time, steelworkers had another reason to adopt a more conciliatory attitude toward the company—fear.

By the spring of 1982, when Peurala came up for reelection, employment at South Works was down to 4000, the number 8 blast furnace had been shut for a year, and rumors abounded that the mill would be closed. Peruala's opponents charged that were she reelected, her tough bargaining tactics would push U.S. Steel management to shut down South Works.

Peurala's chief challenger, Donald Stazak, was more closely identified with management than candidates for union office usually are. During the late 1970s, Stazak organized union lobbying efforts on behalf of the steel companies' import restriction program. Management paid his lost time. As he walked through the mill, urging unionists to write letters to their congressmen on behalf of the legislation U.S. Steel was pressing, Stazak became well known as a "nice guy" and a "company man."

Stazak won by the slim margin of thirty-seven votes, in a three-way race.

And so the stage was set for the rail mill saga.

As it stood on the threshold of its ultimate challenge, Local 65 was rich in problems. The union was split between militant and cautious factions, each with deep roots in history. Nor did long-standing local-International differences strengthen the unionists' ability to stand up to U.S. Steel. But Local 65 had created a tradition of solidarity, a knowledge that workers had stood together in common struggle not only to organize South Works but to civilize it. That tradition would be put to the test in the rail mill saga.

THE RAIL MILL SAGA: ACT I

The days of Donald Stazak's presidency proved to be excruciating for South Works employees. In the very first month of his term, U.S. Steel laid off 3000 steelworkers. Matters soon got worse.

When U.S. Steel announced plans to build an ultramodern rail mill at South Works in 1981, the news was greeted with great joy, for Southeast Siders had begun to worry about their mill's fate. But soon the story of U.S. Steel's plan to build a rail mill became a bitter saga for the people of Chicago. The trouble began in 1982, when corporate executives announced that U.S. Steel was having second thoughts about whether it could operate a rail mill profitably. For the mill to be competitive, the company would need help from the union in reducing labor costs, and from the state of Illinois in eliminating a tax on rails produced in the state but shipped elsewhere.

Concessions seemed to be the order of the day in the steel

industry. For more than a decade, U.S. Steel had been blaming imports for the decline of American steel, but suddenly Chairman Roderick took aim at a different villain: union wage rates.

In response, USWA president Lloyd McBride went to work convincing his members that lower labor costs were essential to revitalizing the steel industry.

At South Works, the company wanted massive changes in work rules throughout the mill. The hardest to swallow would have abolished craft lines. One proposal was to combine the tasks of millwrights, electricians, and welders. Another would have destroyed the traditional prohibition against skilled workers doing production. Both proposals were aimed at a problem about which the company had long complained: maintenance workers don't work continuously. By combining three crafts and merging production and maintenance jobs, the company hoped to eliminate "nonproductive" time.

Just in case the mass layoffs of the past three years were not sufficient to force Local 65's acceptance, U.S. Steel heaped on other pressures. The company halted repair work on the big number 8 blast furnace and announced plans to give greater importance to its Gary Works at the expense of South Works. Next, boats began loading ore at the South Works slip for delivery to Gary. The message was clear: South Works was in jeopardy.

It seemed that Local 65 had to make concessions. Nevertheless, on July 16, the local bargaining committee rejected U.S. Steel's demands. Their defiance was more than a refusal to make material sacrifices; their fundamental motivation was anger at their bosses—and a sense of honor. Ike Mezo, one of the ten elected grievers, explained: "The guy who's been in the mill any length of time doesn't want to go against tradition. He cares about the next generation."

But the bargaining committee's rejection of U.S. Steel's demands was just the first round in the South Works drama,

for neither Donald Stazak nor USWA president Lloyd McBride
wanted to fight U.S. Steel or to risk losing the rail mill. After
national concession bargaining broke down on July 30, Stazak
asked McBride to send his assistant to South Chicago.

Suddenly, U.S. Steel began to bargain. The company
dropped its demands to change work rules throughout South
Works, retaining just a few points relating to the rail mill.
Local 65 negotiators agreed to these proposals in return for
strengthened seniority rules.

Even these moderate concessions, which would have affected only a few dozen skilled workers in the rail mill, provoked heated controversy between militant and cautious union
members. But in the end, the leadership of Don Stazak and
his superiors in the International hierarchy prevailed; Local
65 members swallowed their pride and granted U.S. Steel the
changes it claimed to need.

The USWA then went to work to make sure that U.S.
Steel's other demand was met. Illinois Governor James
Thompson wasn't happy about the idea of giving the giant
corporation a tax break, but in the face of the local unions'
acceptance of work rule concessions, he finally did sign a bill
repealing the rail tax.

But despite all the union's conciliatory efforts, nothing
improved. When the economic recovery began late in the fall
of 1982, employment at South Works remained pitifully small.
The rail mill equipment hadn't been installed; the repairs to
the blast furnace were not completed.

In the midst of these difficult local negotiations, the steel
companies' drive for national wage concessions could only
look like an added insult. With President McBride supporting
the company's demand for wage cuts, most steelworkers had
resigned themselves to limited concessions. However, the
agreement reached by the U.S. Steel-led Coordinated Steel
Companies and President McBride on November 1, 1982,
would have cost steelworkers more than $10,000 apiece over

four years and would have ended the principle of cost-of-living protection.

After local union presidents rejected those terms, it appeared that a strike was inevitable. But late in the winter of 1983, U.S. Steel changed its approach and the USWA agreed to a compromise. The monetary concessions of March 1, 1983, were large—$1.25 per hour during the first year—but the principle of cost-of-living protection was saved. Furthermore, the companies had promised to reinvest their cost savings in the steel industry, thereby halting the broad inroads that imported steel had been making in steel employment.

Then, just a few days later, Chairman Roderick announced plans to import slabs from Scotland rather than modernize steel production at the Fairless Works, and steelworker anger boiled over. At U.S. Steel's stockholders meeting in Chicago on May 2, 1983, angry steelworkers marched outside while USWA president Lloyd McBride went on national television to charge U.S. Steel with betraying its pledge to use concession savings for modernization.

Inside the stockholders meeting, however, Local 65 president Donald Stazak had a different kind of meeting with Chairman Roderick. Stazak recounts: "Roderick told me, 'Don, if you can get anything done with [Illinois attorney general] Neil Hartigan as far as environmental relief, do it by all means.' And then I got a call from Bill Miller, the vice president of labor relations, and he asked me to come to Pittsburgh. So I met him and his lawyer, and they said to me, 'Don, if you can get this thing done, three months after you get it done, we'll start building our rail mill.' "

In response to the company's requests, the USWA began collecting its considerable political debts. The "rail mill" luncheon held at Local 65's union hall on August 11 was a big-time affair, with Senators Percy and Dixon, Alderman Vrdolyak, and Congressman Savage in attendance. But the star of the afternoon was Attorney General Neil Hartigan, who unveiled a plan to give U.S. Steel $33 million in city and state revenue in order to defray the company's costs in meeting pollution standards at the Gary Works if the company would agree to build the rail mill.

U.S. Steel did not leap to accept Hartigan's proposal. Instead, on August 12, the company announced it would reevaluate its plans for the rail mill in light of deteriorating market conditions. Not surprisingly, Donald Stazak felt that he'd been had.

By then, the rail mill saga had been dragging on for a year, and workers inside the mill were growing restless as conditions deteriorated. Jim Fish, a twenty-eight-year veteran, reported in October of 1983:

> There's been a definite change in people's feeling in the last year. They don't have too much confidence in the union, they feel like it sold them down the river. The union leaders made a mistake granting all those concessions. Jobs have been eliminated. Rather than rehire people, they're working us overtime. I worked sixteen hours yesterday. I was just supposed to work til 9 o'clock, and then they told me I had to stay til 2 in the morning. Then I came home and I was hungry, so I ate, and went to bed, and I had to get up at 7 o'clock. I feel very depressed. People recognize that things aren't going to improve any more in the mill. They're just hoping the mill won't close. They bought homes and cars, so they're just trying to hold in there.

Although Don Stazak knows that his advocacy of concessions has brought him the scorn and anger of many union members, he doesn't regret what he did.

> Realistically, we know that U.S. Steel is going to close some plants down whatever concessions we give them. But at

least I know that if they close that plant down, I can go to bed and say I tried. I'd hate like hell to say, 'Go to hell, U.S. Steel, I'm not giving anything,' and then if they close the plant down, I got to think, 'Well, Jesus, they meant it. I should have done something.' At least I know I showed some willingness to work with them. But at the same time, I'm not going to bend down and hold my ankles for them to take whatever they want. I still have some integrity. If the bottom line is they're going to close it, then by god, I don't feel guilty. At least I tried.

Not everyone at Local 65 was content to wait for U.S. Steel's decision. The unemployment committee proposed a campaign to challenge U.S. Steel's apparent abandonment of the rail mill. Committee chairman Ike Mezo called on President Stazak to mobilize union members and community residents in support of government intervention to save South Works.

Stazak declined. Forty years of reliance on the International for leadership in dealing with the big companies militated against that approach. Twenty years of labor peace had weakened the tradition of membership participation. Four years of layoffs and rumors of shutdown had propelled into the local's presidency a man who believed in working with the company, not fighting it.

But even if President Stazak had agreed to mobilize a campaign to save South Works, formidable barriers would have remained. One was ideological: most unionists and community residents believed that companies are in business to make profits and will invest wherever they can get the best return. On what grounds could Local 65 challenge a decision not to build the rail mill after the company projected it would not be profitable? Furthermore, Local 65's ties to the community were weak. There were formal ties to the political leaders, to be sure, but not to the church unemployment committees, community organizations, or even nearby labor unions. Building a local alliance after years of isolation would not have been easy for any union leader.

And so Local 65 waited for U.S. Steel to make its decision. Despite all the blood and sweat expended in the task of union building, U.S. Steel was still calling the shots.

THE RAIL MILL SAGA: ACT II

The final phase of the rail mill drama began on November 10, 1983, when U.S. Steel's vice president for steel operations, Thomas Graham, announced that South Works would no longer be an integrated mill; the blast furnace, basic oxygen furnaces, continuous caster, and plate, rod, and bar mills would remain closed permanently. Furthermore, U.S. Steel would build the rail mill only if certain conditions were met. The state of Illinois would have to agree to give South Works an energy tax credit based on its being part of the new enterprise zone. A low-cost $40 million UDAG loan would have to be granted by the federal government, at the city of Chicago's request. The $33 million Hartigan plan to subsidize U.S. Steel's pollution expenses at Gary Works would have to be approved by the state of Illinois. And the city of Chicago would have to excuse U.S. Steel from paying a "head tax" on South Works employees.

Worst of all, Local 65 would have to agree to additional work rule concessions, not only at the rail mill but in the entire facility, before the corporation would finally build the mill.

U.S. Steel's demands went far beyond the original proposal Local 65 had rejected the year before. Now the company wanted the right to hire outside contractors to do maintenance work, while 300 to 500 Local 65 craftsmen would be eliminated. And to take advantage of cheap electric rates on weekends and late at night, U.S. Steel demanded the right to

work employees ten hours per day and weekends without
paying premium wages. To top it off, incentive pay would be
eliminated for most jobs. This not only would substantially
reduce the earnings of the men who elected to do hard and
dangerous jobs because they wanted the extra income, it also
would have violated the national basic labor agreement to
which the company and union were party.

Local officers had been saying for months that Local 65
would make no more concessions before the rail mill was built,
and they kept their word. On November 14, they flatly rejected U.S. Steel's new demands. President Stazak's statement
to the press painstakingly chronicled the union's efforts to
accommodate the company's demands. "U.S. Steel . . . con-
tinues to lie, connive, and threaten us for more and more
concessions without giving any guarantee that the Rail Mill
will ever be built. A stand must be taken against the abuses
U.S. Steel continuously attempts to heap upon the workers
and the community. We are willing to take that stand."

When Chicagoans watched the TV news that evening,
they saw stories about how U.S. Steel's demands had escalated
while its plans for the rail mill were scaled down; the disaf-
fection of political leaders who had tried to help the corporation was widely reported. The *Chicago Sun-Times* editorialized:
"There seems to be no end to U.S. Steel's hunger for new
concessions from workers and all levels of government before
it builds its long-postponed rail mill at its South Chicago Works.
No wonder many people suspect that the company has no
intention of going ahead with the project." If U.S. Steel hoped
to orchestrate public pressure on Local 65, its plans had failed.

Nor did the USWA International leadership come to the
support of the company's pleas for more concessions. Lynn
Williams, who had recently taken over as the USWA's acting
president, knew how hard Don Stazak had tried to accommodate U.S. Steel, and he also knew how strong rank-and-
file opposition to further concessions had grown. "We're opposed to any more wage concessions in the steel industry,"

Williams said. "The locals have been on their own until now. We intend to coordinate activities and offer support services."

The question remained: Would U.S. Steel go ahead with the rail mill in the face of Local 65's refusal to make more concessions?

The answer came on December 27: not only was U.S. Steel permanently shutting most of South Works, the rail mill was also dead. Only the number 4 electric furnace and beam mill would remain, employing 800 men; 300 maintenance workers would be eliminated.

U.S. Steel blamed the closing on the union. In full-page ads in Chicago's daily newspapers, the company charged that "USS committed that if we were made labor competitive, we would build a process-competitive rail mill. We asked for the Union's answer by year end, and on 12/21/83, the UNION REJECTED THE COMPANY'S PROPOSAL IN EVERY MAJOR ASPECT. USS, THEREFORE, HAS CANCELLED PLANS TO BUILD THE RAIL MILL, AND THE DECISION IS NOW FINAL. . . . WE BELIEVE THE COMPANY, THE COMMUNITY, THE TAX BASE, OUR YOUNGER EMPLOYEES, AND FUTURE JOB OPPORTUNITIES ARE ALL POORER FOR THE UNION'S DECISION."

The union's reaction was understandably angry. "Blaming the union is a terrible insult to all who have tried so hard to meet the original demands of U.S. Steel," Don Stazak responded.

Steelworkers interviewed by the national media as they left the mill after U.S. Steel's decision was announced backed their union's stand. Young and old, black, Hispanic, and white, they spoke with one voice: they'd made concessions before without result; "enough is enough."

Somewhat more surprising was the support local political figures gave to the union's stand. Rob Mier, Chicago's commissioner of economic development, said that U.S. Steel's demands "basically asked the people to vote to give up their jobs. . . ." Attorney General Hartigan vowed to force U.S.

Steel to install $33 million worth of pollution equipment at its Gary Works. And Chicago congressman Dan Rostenkowski threatened: "[U.S. Steel] is going to come back to Rostenkowski [for help in gaining tax relief]. And Rostenkowski's going to be an awful, awful quiet man for a long time."

For Local 65 the rail mill drama ended on a different note from the one on which it began. At first, local union officials were caught in a vise, with a determined employer, angry local activists, unsympathetic International union leaders, and hostile editorial writers squeezing from every direction. At the end, Local 65 had friends on all sides; it was U.S. Steel that was isolated. The turnaround was extraordinary, explicable only by the arrogance with which the corporation pursued its ever-changing interests.

Despite the fact that U.S. Steel was universally blamed for the rail mill tragedy, the episode was a terrible defeat for the USWA. Union leaders had put their prestige on the line twice, first by counseling concessions, and then by marshalling political support, and still had been unable to prevent South Works' closing. U.S. Steel, on the other hand, had put Local 65 members through more than two years of intense anxiety about their future, extracted costly wage concessions and precedent-shattering work rule changes, turned unionist bitterly against unionist, and weakened the membership's confidence in their union—and then the giant corporation walked away from the mill, leaving steelworkers impotent in their fury. Clearly, labor's power had declined on the Southeast Side.

The USWA's traumatic defeat in Southeast Chicago was not an isolated instance. During the steel industry's protracted depression, the rail mill saga was repeated—with variations of course—throughout America's steel towns, from the Mon Valley in Pennsylvania to Pittsburg, California. For more than forty years, the union had combined three ingredients—strong organization, anger at the steel companies, and workers' solidarity—into a powerful amalgam that had won comfortable wages and job security for steelworkers. Sophisticated negotiating tactics had even enabled USWA leaders to provide their members with contract benefits that cushioned the ups and downs of our nation's business cycles.

But when the American steel industry lost its leading position in the world's steel markets, steelworkers discovered the limits of their union's hard-won power. The unemployment supplements won by the USWA proved inadequate in the face of massive, sustained job loss, and the weakened union was in no position to extract greater benefits from employers.

As steel's crisis deepened in the fall of 1983, the USWA leaders recognized that they had to move beyond their traditional collective bargaining strategies. More than ever before, the union immersed itself in political campaigns that promised to shore up the collapsing industry.

But politics, Southeast Chicago style, is a very different sort of game. When local politicians turned their attention to the closing of Wisconsin Steel, and to the subsequent saga of the South Works rail mill, they didn't speak of national mobilizations to save the steel industry. They had other fish to fry.

6

The Limits of Clout

IT WAS PROBABLY inevitable that politics would play a major role in the drama of economic decline that rocked Southeast Chicago. For politics is never far from anyone's doorstep in these communities. At a minimum, it rings your bell every two years at election time to request your vote for the Democratic party's candidates. More often, it turns up with a petition to be signed, or tickets to be bought. It has myriad ways to remind you of its importance to the smooth functioning of your life, requiring that you go through the appropriate channels to get a trash can replaced or a sidewalk repaired. "If you have a problem, go see Eddie [Alderman Ed Vrdolyak]. Whatever it is, he can take care of it," says a local resident, summing up the prevailing wisdom of politics in the tenth ward of the city of Chicago.

It came as no surprise, then, that as local labor unions floundered in their attempts to save the mills, Southeast Side residents looked to their political leaders for rescue. From the earliest days of the Wisconsin Steel closure, politics quickly moved to center stage, and though it would occasionally disappear into the wings, it was to remain a key player in all that

147

followed. In the course of these events, the limits of clout would be dramatically revealed.

A NIGHT TO REMEMBER

On Wednesday, April 16, 1980, a chilly spring evening in Southeast Chicago, nearly three weeks after the closing of Wisconsin Steel, the streets outside St. Kevin's church are jammed with cars, and hundreds of people stream through the scarred wooden doors of the parish hall. The attraction is a meeting called by the South Deering Improvement Association (SDIA) to quiz local politicians about the mill's sudden shutdown. Although the gathering has been billed as a community forum, the bulk of those who crowd into the hall are the Wisconsin steelworkers themselves. They have had no information from their employer or their union since the closing. The only news they've gotten has come from their banks: their last paychecks have bounced.

The air in the room is thick with cigarette smoke, tension, and anger. By the time the meeting starts, it is almost impossible to move in any direction; bodies press in on each other like fans at a championship game. But this is no game.

The evening's chairman, SDIA president Andy Scanlon, is a Republican shoe salesman with little in his experience to prepare him to face such a throng. Unable to imagine a gavel sufficiently large to command attention, he has opted instead for a whistle which hangs from a chain around his neck. Perched atop a table at the front of the hall, he blows it strenuously and the meeting begins.

Nearly every politician within a ten-mile radius has shown up to voice outrage over the Wisconsin shutdown and promise support to the hapless workers. But there is only one official who might have some real news about their fate—Alderman Ed Vrdolyak—and there's no sign of him. Not only is Vrdolyak the most powerful politician on the Southeast Side, he is also the attorney for the Progressive Steelworkers Union. The feeling toward him is not kind: he damn well better know what's going down.

For a while it looks as though both Vrdolyak and PSWU president Tony Roque are going to pass up this engagement, and the crowd gets more and more restless. Shouts of "Where's Eddie?" begin to echo around the hall. Andy Scanlon gets more and more anxious; the shrill screech of his whistle repeatedly cuts through the air. Then there's a disturbance near the door, and the room erupts into hoots, boos, and catcalls. The alderman has arrived.

Edward R. Vrdolyak strides across the front of the room, with Tony Roque and the rest of his entourage in tow. A path is made for him as readily as the Red Sea once parted its waves. Resentful whispers note his deep tan, which rumor has it was acquired at a Florida golf outing.

Undaunted by the shouting crowd, Vrdolyak peels off his expensively cut jacket, rolls up his shirtsleeves, and leaps on top of the table, all in a single motion. He reaches over his head, grasps a ceiling pipe with both hands, and leans intently toward the angry assemblage. At first he has to talk over the yells, but within a minute or two, the noise dies down. Begrudgingly, the men in the windbreakers listen to the man in the shiny suit. By turns his voice is angry and cajoling; his tone, at once unabashed and familiar. He projects a sense of weary determination.

"I've been talking to everyone, including the president, the mayor, and the governor," he tells them. "I want to get the mill open as soon as possible and get your back pay. . . ." He goes after Envirodyne for going into the Wisconsin purchase with "bullshit and bubblegum—they didn't have a dime," and hints that Harvester might want to come back to operate the mill. He scolds the crowd like a benevolent but irritated parent—"Don't you know I'm out there working my butt off for you? How could you doubt me?" Most important, he predicts that the plant will soon be reopened.

In five minutes or so, it's all over—and the boos have turned to cheers. There is immense relief: Eddie is going to take care of things. Now everyone can go home. Andy Scanlon puts away his whistle and the hall quickly empties.

The next day's headlines tell the story—and foretell the stories of many more meetings to come: "Vrdolyak sees reopening of Wisconsin Steel plant" (*Chicago Sun-Times*); "Wisc. Meeting Calms Worried Steelworkers" (*Daily Calumet*). Hope is kept alive.

"I've seen scores of politicians and I don't think I've ever seen one turn a negative situation around as quickly and effectively as Ed did that night," Kevin Fitzgibbons, then an aide to the district's congressman, will recall three years later. "If you got thirty speech writers together, they couldn't have written a better speech than he gave off the cuff. It was an extraordinary performance."

But what happens when the curtain falls and the applause dies down? Eddie Vrdolyak carried the day—or the night— at St. Kevin's. But it was a short-term triumph. In the long term, it becomes clear that reopening a steel mill in a depressed economic situation is not the same thing as renewing a liquor license or repaving a street.

THE MACHINE

It is, however, precisely the ability to take care of such elementary business as stoplights and street signs, liquor licenses and carnival permits, trash pickup and the delivery of services that had made the Chicago Machine, also known as the Regular Democratic Organization, the stuff of legends.

To some political experts, the machine brand of politics seems little more than a creaky anachronism. To others, it is an ethical mark of Cain, denoting these communities where pragmatism has triumphed over principle. But for many Chicagoans, like those of the Southeast Side, "the Machine" is simply a fact of life, as much a part of their neighborhoods as the churches or schools.

In the old immigrant communities of late-nineteenth-century America, machine politics was a crude exchange of a vote for food, drink, or money. It worked best among those who were desperate for a helping hand and ignorant of the political process. Half a century later, such practices were obsolete. Desperation was no longer a political factor, ignorance of politics no longer commonplace. A new system of machine politics emerged—one that relied on the provision of jobs for a few, the provision of services for the majority, and a network of personal contacts linking the two.

But the new system did not eliminate the corruption for which the old Boss Tweed form of machine politics had been so notorious. A local TV station recently reported that in the past ten years, 250 public servants, including 40 elected officials, policemen, and election judges, were convicted of crimes in Chicago. The number who were indicted or under investigation is probably too high to tally.

While control of jobs—in both the public and private sectors—remains the lifeblood of machine politics, in recent years, the Regular Organization has increasingly come to function as a mediator between bureaucracies and the individual citizen. Such mediation is a growing component of machine politics wherever it is practiced; as our society becomes more complex, politicians have discovered that helping constitutents cope with red tape and runarounds has a high payoff at the ballot box. It is particularly important in working-class communities, however, where people often lack the confidence to fend for themselves or the personal connections to get strings pulled for them.

This version of machine politics has found one of its great practitioners in Ed Vrdolyak.

Born in South Chicago in 1937, Edward R. Vrdolyak has

spent most of his life in its schools, churches, taverns, and meeting halls. After graduating from the University of Chicago Law School, Vrdolyak set up a practice on his home turf, specializing in personal injury law. He began to make money the way he did everything—fast. He also began to gather around him the people who would help him crack the tenth ward political power structure.

In 1967, he tested the strength of his organization, backing an independent challenger to the incumbent machine alderman. The challenger won. In 1968, Vrdolyak beat the same machine politician for the post of Democratic committeeman. "I remember the first time he ran," says former East Sider Bill Bork. "All of a sudden there were signs everywhere that just said 'ERV.' I didn't know what they meant, but they sure made you sit up and take notice."

People have been taking notice ever since.

By the early 1970s, Eddie had solidified his position in the tenth ward. He was both alderman and committeeman, a political honcho who could dispense favors and command loyalty. From this base, he began to make his moves on City Hall.

In those years, Chicago's City Council members were a bland bunch, a collective fairy godmother for Mayor Daley's every wish. The council's somnolence was shattered only by the occasional outbursts of its few anti-Machine aldermen. It wasn't long before the newcomer from the tenth ward was stirring up trouble.

Vrdolyak helped organize the City Council "coffee rebellion," so called because its participants opted for backroom negotiations, which could net them greater political influence, rather than the reformers' public protests. When Eddie and his friends settled back down into the ranks of the Machine faithful, he had become the chairman of the council's prestigious building and zoning committee, complete with private office and staff.

In the ensuing years, Ed Vrdolyak proved a formidable

figure in the power struggles that racked the Machine, especially after Mayor Daley's death. His father's steel mill tavern had provided invaluable schooling for the rough and tumble world of Chicago politics. Never one to shirk a fight, Eddie always seemed happiest when the gloves were off and the old bare-knuckled battling was under way.

The alderman's free-wheeling style and high-powered deals have generated controversy, however, and the whiff of scandal has lingered around the tenth ward wunderkind for much of his career. The Chicago media have tended to look askance at questionable financial practices, run-ins with the IRS, and unsavory associates. *Tribune* columnist Mike Royko, the city's premier journalist, has been one of the alderman's bluntest critics. "When it comes to swindles," he wrote in a 1983 column, "Eddie Vrdolyak has always been the most broad-minded and fair of men. He doesn't care what your race, creed, ethnic origin or political affiliations are. . . . If you got it, he'll try to grab it."

Despite such sharp blows to his public image, Ed Vrdolyak continued to amass both money and power, ascending to the chairmanship of the Cook County Democratic party in 1982. Then, with the election of an avowed reformer, Harold Washington, as Chicago's mayor in 1983, his stock hit an all-time high. The tenth ward impresario orchestrated a city council bloc that was all Machine and all white. It had the votes to control the council, but not to override the mayor's vetoes. The battle was joined and Eddie Vrdolyak was right at the center—just where he always wanted to be.

With all his citywide notoriety, Alderman Vrdolyak did not forget the necessity of maintaining his own base. "He realizes the importance of helping and he's very hardworking," says Kevin Fitzgibbons. "He still gives personal attention to the problems of people in his ward."

The alderman holds office hours every week; as many as fifty people will line up in his waiting room hoping for an audience. They are there for every imaginable reason: a kid in trouble with the law; problems with a building inspector; welfare checks cut off; hassles with immigration papers. Many will get the help they need; almost all will feel that a serious effort has been made on their behalf.

The rewards for Alderman Vrdolyak have been considerable. He has the cooperation of most major institutions in the area—churches, taverns, small businesses, sports teams. In addition, he has the devotion of a solid core of stalwarts who have been with him for years. "You've got people who would walk through a blast furnace for him," Fitzgibbons says.

It makes for a potent force at election time when all the chits are called in. "When you go out in opposition to Eddie, you're not just asking people to vote against Vrdolyak, but against their next-door neighbor, the precinct captain, or their brother-in-law who works in the police department," observes Rob Persons, who spent a lot of hours knocking on doors for opponents of the Regulars' slate.

And if such loyalty—whether given freely or as payment in kind—isn't sufficient to ensure victory, the alderman's critics claim he has other means of garnering support. They charge that his career has been bolstered by his exploitation of the racial fears of his white constituents. In 1968, when he ran for committeeman, he overcame his political anonymity by leaping into the front ranks of the fierce antibusing battles: "I will do everything in my power to oppose the busing plan. It is headed straight to a commune setup and I believe it therefore defies the American way of life," he said at the time.

In his 1971 campaign for alderman, the young lawyer was accused of introducing a tactic that critics charge has recurred over the years. According to his opponent John Buchanan, "in the black areas, I was called a racist and in white neighborhoods, I was an integrationist."

Alderman Vrdolyak has denied charges that he tries to foster racial antagonism. There's little doubt, however, that many people on the Southeast Side see pulling a lever for Ed

Vrdolyak as a vote for keeping blacks out of their neighborhood.

Despite his seeming invulnerability, Ed Vrdolyak's reign
has not gone unchallenged. One source of steadfast opposition began with the Steelworkers Fight Back campaign of Ed
Sadlowski. Clem Balanoff, a former mill worker and Fight
Back strategist, was convinced that the steelworker insurgents
had to shift the USWA's allegiance from the Regular Democrats and toward independent candidates—candidates who
would have the interests of the workers at heart. He mapped
a challenge to Vrdolyak's candidate for state representative;
Clem's wife, Miriam, was the Fight Back standard-bearer.

A graduate of the University of Chicago Law School, Balanoff had little experience in the world of door-knocking and
speech-making. A small middle-aged woman with carefully
tended hair, she seemed more suited to a high school class-
room than the clash of politics in a steel town. But what she
lacked in pizzazz, Balanoff made up in persistence. In 1976,
she waged an aggressive campaign and lost by just 376 votes.
In 1978, she tried again and won. Her victory was the product
both of a spirited grass roots campaign that stressed issues
like utility reform, and of a special system of weighted voting.

In office, Balanoff tirelessly advocated legislation to require prior notification of plant closings and to ban hazardous
waste dumps; she was also an unyielding adversary of Alderman Vrdolyak. But she wasn't able to develop a base of
support that could measure up to the Regulars at the polls.
The Fight Back group never managed to elect any other
candidates, and in 1982, when the weighted ballot system was
eliminated, Miriam Balanoff was defeated by a wide margin.

A second source of opposition to Ed Vrdolyak came from
the growing black population in Southeast Chicago. The bat-
tleground was the second congressional district, including most
of the seventh and tenth wards, as well as portions of several
largely black wards.

In the 1970s, it was represented by Congressman Morgan Murphy, a close ally of Alderman Vrdolyak's. Charming, Irish, and well-connected (he was one of Mayor Daley's few close friends), Murphy was the quintessential Chicago politician. But in 1980, in poor health and with a district that had become almost 70 percent black, he decided not to run again.

Into the void stepped Gus Savage, a short, intense black man with a freckled face and a gift of gab. Savage had a colorful history as a civil rights activist, newspaper publisher, and losing candidate. A longtime critic of machine politics, he was outspoken, untroubled by controversy, and sharp-tongued with the press and public. He was also an indefatigable self-promoter and a wily political operator.

In the Democratic primary election, Alderman Vrdolyak backed a little known black high school principal, but he was no match for Gus's zeal. On March 18, 1980, Savage won the Democratic nomination to the U.S. Congress, virtually a certified ticket to Washington, D.C. His election was an indication of the growing influence and independence of Southeast Side blacks.

Once in Congress, Savage had a hard time translating his rabble-rousing style into an effective legislative presence. He continued to play the role of the outsider, leading marches and giving rhetoric-charged speeches. Thus, it came as no surprise that when the *Chicago Sun-Times* surveyed the attendance records of local congressmen, Gus Savage was at the bottom of the list. Sitting down isn't his style.

The opposition forces have demonstrated that the Machine can be beaten; they have yet to show that it can be supplanted. Thus the wars continue. Even when the collapse of Wisconsin Steel warned Southeast Siders that their community's very existence was in danger, the armies of the Machine and the insurgents continued to struggle for political dominance. Those hostilities would become hopelessly entangled with the efforts to rescue the mill and provide new jobs for the displaced steelworkers.

BROKEN PROMISES

In the early days after Wisconsin Steel shut down in the spring of 1980, few people wanted to see the loss as total. And so there began a long and tortured effort to restore Wisconsin Steel to life.

Within days of the closing, Jim Morrill, Wisconsin's plant manager, went to the union and proposed that together they devise a plan to keep the mill rolling. PSWU president Tony Roque was prepared to make drastic wage and work rule concessions. Like Morrill, he knew that the huge inventory locked within the mill's gate was of far less value than the finished steel products into which it could be transformed. And both men also knew that if the mill remained shuttered for long, it could take months to get it in shape to run again.

In no time flat, Chase killed the plan. On March 28, the banking giant had secured the mill's inventory and seized its payroll accounts. It wanted to avoid getting tied up in bankruptcy court battles that could go on for years before it collected the money it was owed. So Chase hauled out the raw inventory as fast as possible, even though that meant losing the millions of additional dollars it could have made on the finished products.

In the following months, a skeleton crew kept the coke oven and furnaces alive, while Jim Morrill plunged into another effort to rescue the mill.

During the summer of 1980, Morrill got a call from Thomas Fleming, a Philadelphia businessman who had helped arrange the original deal between Harvester and Envirodyne. Fleming was intrigued by a federal "set-aside" program for minority businesses, which required companies with government contracts to make a portion of their purchases from minority-owned suppliers. There was no minority-owned company in all of the steel industry; if one could be set up, it would have an enviable edge.

Fleming had already lined up potential investors for the

plan. He enlisted Morrill to prepare an analysis demonstrating the feasibility of keeping Wisconsin in operation. Then he found a black man to head up the incipient firm, fellow Philadelphian Walt Palmer. By September, Walt Palmer Industries had filed a proposal in federal bankruptcy court to purchase Wisconsin Steel for $52 million.

Walt Palmer was an unlikely choice for the job. A former civil rights activist, Palmer had an academic record that included a law degree and management courses, but his experience in the business world was minimal, and of steelmaking he knew nothing. Palmer did have considerable brains and immense bravado, however. He saw the purchase of Wisconsin Steel as another crusade, an extension of the marches and sit-ins he had once led. And he attacked it with the same zeal.

In a whirlwind of activity, the Palmer group set about securing financing through the New York investment banking firm of Drexel Burnham Lambert. They got the firm to issue what South Chicago banker Jim Fitch called a "noncommittal commitment letter" indicating it would try to raise $90 million in new investment dollars to make the mill a viable operation. But before it would proceed, Drexel wanted assurances that the Economic Development Administration would come up with the $35 million in loan guarantees unused by Envirodyne and that the agency would surrender the first lien it held on the mill.

Meanwhile, local union and political leaders bought into the Palmer plan in a big way. Tony Roque and Ed Vrdolyak began using their influence to help promote the idea. Whether or not they honestly believed in its feasibility is impossible to say. But people were looking to them for a solution and Walt Palmer was the only one at hand.

For his part, Palmer had not completely forsaken his activist past. Instead of relying on the behind-the-scenes negotiations common to conventional corporate moguls, he went public from the start. Clearly, he knew the value of publicity as a form of political pressure. He gleaned endorsements from prominent blacks, such as the Rev. Jessie Jackson and the Rev. Leon Sullivan. He was featured in newspaper interviews ranging from *The Daily Calumet* to *The Wall Street Journal*. And he met with Chicago's top decision-makers, including the mayor.

"I've got a dream I want the people of Chicago to share," Palmer told *The Daily Calumet*. And in those still-hopeful days, people on the Southeast Side of Chicago were only too ready to share in any dream that might bring back their mill.

The EDA was more skeptical, however. Although its public pronouncements were noncommittal, in private meetings the agency consistently expressed doubts about Palmer's plan. After taking a $55 million bath on Envirodyne, EDA officials were not enthusiastic about selling the mill to another company without money. To surrender its lien on the mill would expose the agency to the loss of the last bit of security it had to show for its millions. And to guarantee an additional loan merely on Drexel Burnham Lambert's promise to try to raise money, that was too much to ask.

By fall, another factor had entered into the negotiations — the impending presidential elections. Chicago politicians repeatedly sent messages to the White House that failure to aid Wisconsin could cost President Carter tens of thousands of votes.

On October 6, over 1000 Wisconsin steelworkers gathered at the Auditorium Theater in downtown Chicago for a membership meeting of the Progressive Steelworkers Union, chaired by Tony Roque. Walt Palmer was the featured attraction; his speech presented his plan to save the mill as a virtual fait accompli. But it was Alderman Vrdolyak and his special guest, Mayor Jane Byrne, who stole the show.

Mayor Byrne announced that the mill would soon be back in operation. "You'll all have turkeys on your tables for Thanksgiving," workers recall her promising. That promise might have seemed empty had Byrne not stressed her powerful allies, asserting that she had "received a pledge from

the White House that you can count on the company reopening." It was like manna to those lost in the desert; workers left the meeting with tears of joy in their eyes.

This gathering, with its revivalist fervor, may have been
a last-ditch attempt to stampede the EDA into supporting the
Palmer plan. Or it may have simply been a callous ploy to
buy time till the November election. It's likely, though, that
Vrdolyak and Byrne knew by that time that the Palmer deal
had little chance. They had been privy to the EDA discussions
with Palmer in which the agency made clear its skepticism
about his plan.

Soon, it was over. As mysteriously as he had appeared,
Walt Palmer faded from the headlines. On October 12, the
Sun-Times printed excerpts from an EDA letter to Palmer
pointing out the flaws in his plan. The *Chicago Tribune* carried
a piece asserting that the mill might reopen, but not anytime
soon and not under Walt Palmer.

What began as tragedy ended as farce. Or so it seemed
on October 13, the day of Walt Palmer's final appearance in
the Wisconsin Steel story. That morning a UPI story went
out over the wires announcing that the Wisconsin Steel deal
had been consummated. It landed in the *Chicago Defender*,
the city's black-owned daily, under the headline "Walt Palmer
now owns $52 million steel mill." Local radio stations began
broadcasting news of the sale and hopes soared once again.
The next day UPI issued its corrections and the last brief
flicker of faith in Walt Palmer sputtered out.

But things could not be left in such a doleful peace—
there was still an election looming. In late October, Mayor
Byrne jumped back into the headlines on Wisconsin Steel.
Acknowledging that Palmer was no longer in the picture, she
announced that HUD would immediately provide $10 million
to reopen the mill for coke oven repairs, putting 500 people
back to work. President Carter himself would join her in
Chicago to make the formal announcement.

Excitement surged again. EDA consultant Peter Bohn recalls sitting in a Calumet City bar with banker Jim Fitch and then-Congressman Morgan Murphy on the Thursday before the election, anxiously awaiting a call to inform them that HUD had granted the final approval for the $10 million. It didn't come. When Bohn called HUD the next day, officials there told him that a letter had been sent to the mayor in July informing her that the HUD money couldn't be used for mill maintenance. When Bohn confronted Byrne's aides with this information, they acknowledged receiving the letter but claimed that the mayor never saw it.

Election day came and went. Carter's announcement wasn't made; the money didn't materialize; the mill didn't open.

On November 27, Thanksgiving Day, 1980, a ragged band of Wisconsin Steel workers marched in front of Jane Byrne's posh Gold Coast apartment high-rise. They knew that politicians can forget promises almost as fast as they make them. They wanted the mayor to know that workers have longer memories.

While politicians battled for the allegiance of the displaced workers, legions of lawyers were doing daily battle in U.S. bankruptcy court over the carcass of Wisconsin Steel. Estimates of the mill's total debt ranged from $90 million to almost $150 million.

In the early months after the closing, the bankruptcy court judge regularly allocated funds from the company's frozen assets to keep the furnaces alive in the hopes of a speedy sale. To bank the furnaces and let the coke oven go down would have resulted in damages in excess of $50 million—adding to the already mammoth start-up costs for a new owner. As the winter months wore on, however, no buyer materialized and the creditors were clamoring for a settlement.

Finally, the judge could hold out no longer. In January 1981, he ordered the mill sold—for scrap if necessary. In a last-ditch effort to salvage its $55 million investment, the EDA purchased the mill, still hoping to sell it intact to someone who wanted to make steel. But with the steel industry sinking into crisis—and steel markets at an all-time low—the prospects were bleak.

The creditors crowding into bankruptcy court ranged from the Wisconsin steelworkers who were owed back pay, special unemployment and plant-closing benefits, and workers' compensation settlements, to small suppliers who totaled in the hundreds, to International Harvester and Chase Manhattan Bank who claimed they were owed more than the assets they had already seized. Chase and Harvester were the most aggressive in their demands. The claims of the workers seemed to be at the bottom of the list.

But then, the steelworkers scored a small victory over the banking Goliath. Chase had been resolute in its refusal to release the payroll accounts it had seized, claiming that secured lenders had priority over company employees. However, when the bank's plans to haul out its captive inventory were thwarted by picket lines at the mill's gates, it headed for the negotiating table and agreed to reimburse the workers for three-fourths of their bounced paychecks.

Taking on Harvester, however, proved a lot more complicated; the stakes were a lot higher—the pensions of thousands of active and retired Wisconsin steelworkers.

Despite its zeal to unload its pension liabilities through the sale of Wisconsin Steel to Envirodyne, Harvester had never completely turned over control of the pension fund assets to the Envirodyne Holding Company. As it turned out, the fund was short over $80 million: Harvester had owed it $60 million, a liability passed on to Envirodyne as part of the mill's purchase price; then the Holding Company failed to make an additional $25 million in contributions. After the shutdown, both companies disclaimed any responsibility for pension payouts.

The federal Pension Benefit Guaranty Corporation (PBGC), established by Congress to protect workers in the event of bankruptcies, had to step in. The agency took control of what pension fund assets there were and began paying benefits to all workers eligible under normal retirement rules. When the assets ran out, the government would be on the hook for years to come; it was the largest payout in PBGC history.

Nevertheless, Wisconsin steelworkers received less than their union contracts stipulated. Provisions of ERISA, the pension act, place limits on what PBGC can pay the pensioners of bankrupt firms. Men with twenty years in the mill are receiving just $200 monthly, 40 percent of what they would have gotten had the pension plan been fully funded when the mill shut down.

The PBGC was no happier with the situation than Wisconsin workers. In 1981, the agency made good on a threat it had made to Harvester years earlier by filing suit in federal court, seeking a judgment that the sale to Envirodyne was a sham transaction and that Harvester remained liable for the pensions. The case will be in litigation for years.

Among politicians on the Southeast Side, the shuttered mill remained a source of controversy. In the wake of the Palmer affair, Tony Roque and Ed Vrdolyak settled into an uneasy silence. Roque would occasionally comment on some issue of back pay or pensions; Vrdolyak would occasionally allude to his search for a buyer for the mill. But the fanfare of the early months was gone.

Gradually, Gus Savage and Miriam Balanoff began to take on the mantle of the champions of the jobless workers. Almost from the day the mill closed, Vrdolyak tried to close ranks, excluding these two foes and playing up their impotence. At the St. Kevin's meeting in mid-April, he'd told the crowd he'd "do Gus Savage's laundry if he or anyone else gets the money to reopen this mill." A few weeks later, at a mass membership meeting of the PSWU, he lashed out at Balanoff, claiming she was "not doing a thing for Wisconsin Steel."

In fact, both Savage and Balanoff were very active on behalf of the Wisconsin Steel workers, but their emphasis was not on reopening the mill. Savage drew on the tradition he knew best; he kept on marching, gaining valuable publicity for the workers' plight. When rank-and-file Wisconsin unionists demonstrated in front of Harvester headquarters in downtown Chicago, Savage was in their ranks, insisting that "you must be in the streets when agitation is needed." A year later, when jobless Wisconsin workers went to Washington to plead their case, Savage made the trip arrangements and led them in picketing the White House. Behind the scenes, Savage worked to pressure the PBGC to cut red tape and speed up pension payouts. "Gus Savage was the only son-of-a-gun politician who tried to help us," insists Joe Smetlack.

Miriam Balanoff was also trying to help, but she took a different tack. Although she frequently appeared at rallies in support of the jobless workers and quietly aided the organization of anti-Roque PSWU members, Balanoff saw her primary mission as challenging the promises of those who held out hope for reopening the mill. "In the early years, it was not a popular stance," Kevin Fitzgibbons says of Balanoff's oft-stated conviction that the mill would not reopen. "But as time wore on, Balanoff won respect for her consistency and her foresight."

The bickering and the battling went on for nearly three years. During that time, Gus Savage was reelected to the United States Congress, Miriam Balanoff lost her seat in the Illinois General Assembly, and Ed Vrdolyak continued to declare that a buyer would be found for Wisconsin Steel.

Then in the winter of 1983, Eddie Vrdolyak found himself in the midst of a hotly contested mayoral primary. The alderman had tied his fortunes to the reelection of Mayor Byrne. Neither of her opponents—Richard Daley and Harold Washington—had much love for Eddie, and both were tough enough to take him on.

But people on the Southeast Side did not exactly have

fond memories of Jane Byrne. Much of the bitterness over the failure to reopen Wisconsin Steel had settled on her head; three years after the Auditorium Theater gathering, workers would derisively recall her promise of Thanksgiving turkeys. Carrying the day for the mayor would not be easy.

Then, out of the blue, after hundreds of prospective buyers had toured the mill and refused its blandishments, after much of the machinery had been sold, after hopes had just about been buried—there came the Ore to Steel Corporation (OTS) with a plan to buy Wisconsin Steel.

By this time, the EDA was desperate to unload the rusting hulk on Torrence Avenue; almost any offer would have been a godsend. In all the years since the shutdown, only two firms had been seriously interested—American Spring Wire of Cleveland and Stelco of Canada—and both had retreated in the face of shrinking steel markets. If OTS could come up with a $350,000 deposit and a reasonable financing plan, the EDA was more than willing to sign on the dotted line.

But, once again, a rush of premature publicity was unleashed before either cash or plan was on the table. This time there was no Walt Palmer to go out front with the ball; Ed Vrdolyak had to carry it himself.

On January 12, Alderman Vrdolyak announced that the EDA had given its approval and was about to sell the mill to OTS for $7 million. "I know they are drawing up the final papers right now and that something could be done in the next few days, perhaps even tomorrow," he told *The Daily Calumet*.

But tomorrow brought a different story. EDA spokesmen insisted they lacked sufficient information to proceed with the OTS deal. "I'm just sorry this has gotten out and has gone as far as it has," the agency's public relations officer told *The Cal* on January 13. "Everything is really very preliminary."

Meanwhile, the newspaper began its own investigation of the OTS Corporation. The findings cast further doubt on the proposed sale.

The Daily Calumet revealed that the main financial architect of the plan, one Sam Tartaglione, was president of a firm whose previous experience consisted of the development of homes and apartments in and around Hackensack, New Jersey. Moreover, Mr. Tartaglione was under investigation by the federal government for his part in a mob-related loan kickback scheme. The paper also discovered that OTS president Edward Van Dornik, who claimed to be head of a California-based chemical company, was not listed in that state's corporate directories, nor was the company.

Equally questionable were OTS's plans for restarting the mill. The firm was touting a revolutionary new production process that would enable it to put 2000 people back to work within a year. But *The Cal*'s investigation turned up nothing but skepticism about the economic feasibility of such an operation. And the mill's on-site caretaker reported that while other prospective buyers had made repeated visits to the aging facility, OTS's sole analysis had consisted of a two-hour drive-through tour.

But none of these revelations was sufficient to deter Ed Vrdolyak and Tony Roque from promoting the OTS deal. As Roque explained it: "They're saying this guy from OTS is a con man. So what? Who cares what anybody is if they can make a plan work. These guys in big corporations, to me they're the biggest con men in the world, for crissake. . . . I don't know of anybody in this country that didn't make millions without stealing or hurting some people."

Things were left hanging for several weeks. Then, with a February 22 election date looming, Vrdolyak and OTS were back in the headlines. On February 16, the alderman released a letter from OTS claiming that the EDA had agreed to the sale and that a contract was in the mail to the agency to clinch the deal.

Vrdolyak vehemently denied accusations that the timing of the letter was designed to prop up Jane Byrne's sagging campaign, insisting he didn't care who got credit for reopening the mill. Nonetheless, the letter stressed how helpful the alderman had been in cutting red tape and arranging meetings with city officials. And while OTS officials disavowed any interest in the outcome of Chicago's mayoral election, they did emphasize that "Mayor Byrne did pledge to do all she can to make it work."

Once again, the EDA told a different story. The next day, agency officials stated that while there was an "agreement in principle" with OTS, nothing concrete had been settled. They were still waiting to see OTS's draft contract, which was to detail the specifics of its offer. And there the matter rested, with Alderman Vrdolyak and OTS continuing to insist that the necessary documents were tied up in the mail and that everything would be arranged in a matter of days.

Thus Election Day passed. Jane Byrne carried the tenth ward, but she lost the city. Ed Vrdolyak and his organization were in trouble.

The EDA never did receive the OTS contract. Within weeks of the election, the enigmatic firm had faded from the headlines. It reappeared briefly nine months later when Alderman Vrdolyak produced a letter from the firm to the city of Chicago—sent via his office—requesting a $15 million municipal loan to cement an agreement it was about to sign with the EDA. Wearily, EDA officials denied the claim, saying they hadn't heard from OTS since June and were no closer to an agreement than they'd ever been.

On January 25, 1984, the U.S. Economic Development Administration signed a pact with the Cuyahoga Wrecking Corporation of Great Neck, New York, to begin the dismantling of Wisconsin Steel. The agreement temporarily spared the number 6 mill—the pride of the place—in a last-ditch hope that a buyer could be found to convert it to a minimill. But a Cuyahoga spokesman deemed the prospect "not very likely."

With the rambling structure consigned to the scrap heap, the taxpayers have lost over $50 million, the politicians have lost the biggest pawn they ever played with, and the workers have lost a very big piece of their lives.

POLITICS AND THE USWA

Alderman Vrdolyak had been a central figure in the aftermath of the Wisconsin Steel shutdown, but he played no public role in the efforts to save South Works from a similar fate. Vrdolyak's absence reflected the fact that USWA's Local 65 was not part of the tenth ward organization the way the PSWU had been under Tony Roque; indeed, for most of the years Vrdolyak has ruled the Southeast Side, he has been opposed by Local 65's leadership.

More importantly, the steelworkers' union exercised its political muscle primarily through the city- and statewide Democratic party organizations, rather than through the tenth ward. Given the centralized nature of the USWA's organizational structure, it really could not have been any other way: the union had many locals scattered throughout the city of Chicago and the state of Illinois, and high-ranking union officials wanted to exercise the locals' power in concerted fashion.

And so they did. During the reign of District Director Joe Germano, the USWA was a major ally of Mayor Daley, and a dominant force in the Illinois Democratic party. Even when Mayor Daley died, and the Machine began to splinter, the USWA remained a key player. When the American steel industry began its cascade into crisis in the beginning of the 1980s, it seemed that the USWA still packed a mighty political punch.

Its first major move came in 1981, when Ronald Reagan assumed the presidency. The steel companies were clamoring for changes in federal tax laws to provide cash desperately needed for modernization, and congressional Democrats were unsure how to respond. Dan Rostenkowski, the chairman of the House Budget Committee, was a stalwart in the Chicago machine, and a good friend of the USWA. He helped swing House Democrats behind the steel companies' tax bill.

After U.S. Steel used its tax cut windfall to buy Marathon Oil, it asked Local 65 for help in financing the rail mill. Carl Alessi, the USWA's political strategist for Illinois, used his influence in Springfield to get the state tax removed on rails shipped out of Illinois. And when that didn't suffice, Alessi brought in Attorney General Neil Hartigan, who proposed providing U.S. Steel with $33 million additional aid.

But as the closure of South Works loomed ever larger, these tactics proved futile. Politicians and trade unionists were making all the right plays, but they just couldn't score. They were in a different ball game now, and the old rules no longer applied. As long as America's economy was expanding, politicians could respond to the union's legislative goals without undue cost to their reputations as public servants, and above all, without challenging the interests of the powerful corporations.

But by the 1980s, the economy was slumping, foreign imports were flooding American markets, and corporations were receiving rave reviews on Wall Street every time they shut down "excess capacity." Carl Alessi could lobby legislators to get public subsidies for U.S. Steel's proposed rail mill; whom could he lobby after the company walked away?

Gradually, machine politicians settled into uneasy silence as the massive mill on Lake Michigan sank into an eerie stillness. But every month, as new layoff notices arrived in workers' paychecks, desperation grew, and factions within the union began to call for more drastic action. In response, the USWA started to forge new political alliances and to experiment with tactics that never would have been dreamed of just five years earlier.

It was a new breed of politician who responded to the dilemmas posed by the South Works closure. Illinois attorney general Neil Hartigan was an Organization Democrat with a flare for publicity and a streak of independence. Rumored to be planning a run for governor, he was quick to respond to the union's pleas for help in saving South Works. And Mayor Harold Washington, locked in a fierce feud with Ed Vrdolyak, also had good reason to act on behalf of the alderman's constituents. Moreover, these two top Democratic officeholders in Illinois both would have found it hard to stand idly by in the face of the loss of one of the state's major employers.

Thus, in the spring of 1984, Attorney General Hartigan joined the USWA in a suit to gain a temporary injunction preventing U.S. Steel from beginning to tear down portions of South Works. Then the attorney general, the mayor's Office of Economic Development, and the USWA agreed to fund a study of the mill U.S. Steel had just abandoned, to determine the feasibility of resuming operations under new ownership. Implicit in the lawsuit and the study lay the daring notion that the city might one day have to exercise its right of eminent domain and take the mill from U.S. Steel.

That the politicians and USWA were discussing eminent domain was astonishing, but there is a difference between discussing a radical idea and actually implementing it in the face of opposition from our society's dominant economic institutions. Without explanation, the city of Chicago withdrew from the project, and plans to follow up the preliminary feasibility study were shelved.

The USWA has been called selfish by U.S. Steel and archaic by the press. But it has held fast to its basic purpose—defending the livelihood of its members. And it has insisted that the politicians who once clamored for its support must join it now that bold strategies are required to halt industrial decline.

Although the union's efforts to enlist political support for saving South Works never got very far, when one compares them to the earlier political machinations to save Wisconsin Steel, they suggest that workers and their allies have learned important lessons. But Chicagoans are still a long way away from developing a strategy for reversing the process of industrial disinvestment—and on the Southeast Side itself, the leadership vacuum makes that basic economic issue all the harder to confront.

THE LEADERSHIP VACUUM

Despite—or perhaps because of—the immense economic dislocation they've suffered, Southeast Siders have been reluctant to unsettle the political order. Some people carefully absolve their elected officials of blame. "I'm sure Eddie is doing the best he can," says a South Deering tavern owner. "But what can he do? His hands are tied. It's a national problem."

This is the lesson that many people have drawn from Southeast Chicago's plight: the power of the Machine is no longer what it was. There are now forces—the federal government and corporations, chief among them—against which the clout of Eddie Vrdolyak cannot prevail.

Critics of the Machine see in the current crisis no more than its normal failings writ large. By its very nature, they argue, the Machine views everything through the lens of its own self-interest. Unlike a single politician who may rise above his or her own narrow concerns for some larger good, the Machine is an organism that knows no right or wrong save its own perpetuation. Thus, even in the midst of Wisconsin Steel's deepest trauma, greed and ambition continued to dictate the Regulars' actions. "I'd like to put up a plaque on every one of these abandoned mills saying, 'This is a monument to what machine politics has wrought in Southeast Chicago,'" says one angry community activist.

This would-be plaque-hanger, and others like him, did

not expect the Democratic Organization to triumph over the forces of international competition single-handedly. What angers them is the machine politicians' failure to admit just how serious the situation is. As one local industry after another shut its doors, the politicians simply shut their eyes, as if they felt that to acknowledge the depth of the economic problem would be to admit the limits of their own power.

So they close their eyes and mouths and abet the region's decline by their silence. They don't aggressively seek retraining programs, community development funds, or new social welfare programs to address the changing needs. And they don't risk innovative activities that challenge corporate decision making. "Vrdolyak just doesn't want to admit that *his* ward is having problems with unemployment," Katherine Altobelli suggests.

This is the world that clout built. But its politicians are no longer on top of the world. Growing bitterness over the Wisconsin Steel fiasco, the waste dumps, and the economic decay have combined to cut into Ed Vrdolyak's support. "I used to always vote for him," says former Wisconsin steelworker Ron Turner, "but I wouldn't help him at all now."

Nonetheless, Alderman Vrdolyak is still on top for now. He's got two high cards. The first is access to employment—and here, hard times only strengthen his hand. Jobless workers are drawn to the tenth ward headquarters as if it were a magnet.

His second card is racial tension. Wisconsin Steel veteran Steve Jarzyna believes that the racial fears of whites provide a political buffer for the alderman. "The city is getting more and more polarized. If it wasn't for that, he might have been hurt a lot more."

On April 14, 1980, just a few weeks after the gates of Wisconsin Steel slammed shut, a *Daily Calumet* editorial pleaded for a strong community response to the closing: "We need a committee—composed of city and state politicians, chamber

of commerce presidents, civic leaders, union officials, and
other community representatives. . . . Unless the community
comes together to present a united front," the editorial said
with ominous prescience, "the temptation might be strong to
simply liquidate the mill." "Where," it asked urgently, "are
our leaders?"

That united front was never formed. Instead, politicians
turned the mill into another weapon in the ward's ongoing
battles. But as the traditional political leaders demonstrated
their inability to face up to the awesome catastrophe unfolding around them, new leadership began to emerge to take
up the *The Daily Cal*'s call for community action.

7

Down But Not Out

HAVING TURNED to their unions and their political organizations with such limited results, some Southeast Siders began to feel they had no one else to turn to but themselves. Their response, however, was not the dramatic protest that has occurred in other steel communities, such as Youngstown, Ohio, or McKeesport, Pennsylvania. For Southeast Chicago had a very different history and tradition to draw on in charting a new course.

Unlike many steel towns, Southeast Chicago is very much part of a major metropolitan area. While mill workers were able to mark off their home turf to some extent, they were never able to escape the unwanted attention of Chicago's civic leaders. In the late nineteenth century, with equal measures of genuine concern and elitist contempt, a portion of Chicago's upper class raised a hue and cry about the filthy conditions in which the immigrant mill workers lived. Their complaint was partially against the unscrupulous landlords who failed to maintain their properties, but it was also against what the blue bloods viewed as the ignorance and dirtiness of the immigrants themselves.

By the 1930s, living conditions had improved and the steel neighborhoods were no longer objects of derision. But the onset of steel union organizing once again shifted citywide attention toward the Southeast Side. Headlines in the major dailies told of anarchy, communism, and mob rule. And once again, the communities in the shadow of the mills were branded as un-American.

The 1950s witnessed a single-minded trek into middle-class respectability, and relief from the prying eyes of the city. But the legacy of the scorn once heaped on these neighborhoods is a deep unease with social protest. "Don't make a scandal, don't stir up trouble—that's the rule," social worker Ruth Hammer explains. Community residents take great pride in their status as law-abiding citizens.

Today, despite the drastic change in its fortunes, Southeast Chicago remains largely invisible to the rest of the city. And in some respects, its residents prefer it that way. They would rather be anonymous than notorious.

Thus, the weight of convention—not lack of imagination—imposes severe constraints on community response to the mill closings. Furthermore, although union and political leaders have been unable to stem the flow of jobs out of the Calumet region, some have been quick to try to discredit anyone initiating new strategies for concerted action.

So it is that the emergence of a new leadership has been a haphazard process, uneven in its development, unsure in its course. However, over the last few years, a number of groups have begun to inch their way into action—with some unlikely new faces at the helm. They have chosen diverse strategies, worked with different constituencies. But they have all shared one overriding problem: how to address the reality of deindustrialization. It is the steel companies' disinvestment that has caused the community's decline. But how does a community group take on an international steel corporation? The trap of futility waits at either end: if an organization challenges U.S. Steel, its efforts may seem no more than empty rhetoric; if it focuses on a manageable local issue, such as activities for youth, its efforts may seem irrelevant.

It is also true, however, that all these groups share one great strength: a common heritage of solidarity and charity. It is a legacy of mill work bonds, of union struggles, of religious traditions, of ethnic ties. They use it now to confound the experts who imagined them helpless victims or ready accomplices in their assigned fate.

A FOURTH FORCE

Leo Mahon, pastor of St. Victor's Church in Calumet City, a blue-collar suburb just outside the border of Southeast Chicago, is not the sort of activist priest who frequents picket lines or protest marches. Father Leo prefers to get things done on his own steam—with a little help from the Lord.

But neither is he a conventional clergyman. In the 1950s, Mahon was a young turk fighting for a greater emphasis on neighborhood needs in the Chicago archdiocese. Then he went off to Panama, where his work among the poor caused consternation in certain circles: he was tailed by the CIA, almost jailed by the military, and threatened with death by he knows not whom.

When Father Mahon returned to the States in 1976, he settled in at St. Victor's, a placid parish about as far from the turmoil of Central America as one could imagine. But in just a few years' time, Leo Mahon would find that he had simply moved from the eye of one storm to the vortex of another.

In the spring of 1980, the Wisconsin Steel closure still seemed like an aberration, and perhaps a temporary one at that. The mill, it was widely believed, would soon reopen. The economy would rebound. Wisconsin steelworkers wanted a champion, someone who could help them through the hard times and plead their cause to the higher authorities. One group of workers turned to Mahon for help.

At about the same time, Mahon was contacted by a fellow priest who had just come back from Youngstown, Ohio, then in the throes of a battle to save its own steel industry from extinction. The message from Youngstown was dramatic: the problem was not one or two isolated mills, but a major crisis that would rock the entire steel industry. Prompted by this admonition and the sight of a shuttered mill in his own community, Mahon sprang into action.

That summer, Father Mahon convened an ecumenical gathering of Calumet region clergy and lay leaders to discuss joint action on the industrial crisis. Foreseeing drastic job loss and community destabilization if the steel companies continued their pattern of large-scale layoffs, over 100 conference participants called for the formation of a church-based organization to address steel policy in the region. The Calumet Community Religious Conference (CCRC) was born.

The CCRC saw itself as a "fourth force" that could provide a voice for the community in dealing with management, labor, and government representatives. Although a number of its participants were sympathetic to the labor movement, CCRC was determined to avoid "taking sides" between the unions and the companies. It wanted to project an image of conciliation, even daring to imagine that the steel companies would welcome its initiative and join in its dialogue.

While lacking a defined strategy or program, CCRC was powered by a fervent sense of mission. Not only were its leaders deeply concerned about the personal havoc job loss was creating in their community, they also believed that the steel industry's demise would be disastrous for the economic health of the region and the security of the nation.

But Mahon knew that without a solid base of support in the churches, the clergy would be no more than voices crying in the wilderness. So, CCRC staff launched an ambitious program to establish core groups in every local parish and congregation.

Before long, however, it became clear that the idea of calling the steel companies to account strained the credulity even of those who believed firmly in the possibility of miracles. Father Dennis Geaney, who was involved with CCRC from its earliest days, saw a great gap between Leo Mahon's vision and the pragmatism of local church members. "To deal with the closings of steel mills when everybody knows the decisions are made at Chase Manhattan Bank and U.S. Steel headquarters in Pittsburgh," Geaney says, appeared sheer "futility to the ordinary person who works in a store or whose husband works in the mill."

As the staff made the rounds of local churches, the gap Father Geaney described came to seem an unbridgeable chasm. Parish meetings featured low turnout and high skepticism. These were people who had watched the steel companies exhibit impersonal ruthlessness in the name of economic necessity. In the past, the union had relied on strikes—or the threat of them—as leverage. But what leverage did the churches have to bring a steel giant to the negotiating table? Without leverage, protest did seem futile.

The biggest blow to Mahon's hopes came in the winter of 1981 at a meeting to establish a CCRC branch at his own parish. Despite the pastor's great personal popularity and prestige, only forty people showed up—and most of them expressed the same kind of doubts that had been heard at other parish gatherings. It was hard to miss the message, Mahon acknowledges: "We learned that we were in no way ready for this crisis. There's no way this parish, as strong as it is, can look at U.S. Steel and do anything."

But Leo Mahon did not abandon hope, or his organization. The CCRC spent most of 1982 going back to the drawing board. By 1983, the organization had taken on a new face: its goals were the same, but its short-term strategy had changed markedly. It began setting up parish-based committees that would focus on pastoral care and liturgical renewal on their home base. If these groups take on issues of economics or social justice, it will likely be those that are safely within their reach.

Dealing with deindustrialization is down the road. First, Mahon explains, "we're going to have to develop vocation people—people who want to serve the world." Federation is the second piece of the strategy. Once the core leadership is formed in each parish, the committees would join together to take on larger issues. "Without that kind of federation," Mahon believes, "you're just struggling with a huge problem and you end up giving people sacks of flour."

SACKS OF FLOUR

"If I've ever met a saint, it's Lolly Rodriquez," says John Cronin of the human dynamo who powers the St. Vincent dePaul Society at St. George's parish on the East Side. A volunteer organization committed to aiding the poor and needy, it works best in an area in which impoverishment is the plight of a very few, since its human and material resources are limited. Once the East Side was such a community. Today, it is not.

Lolly and her husband, Bob, seem unlikely leaders of an organization to aid the needy. Simply put, they are the needy. After spending twenty years as a grain trimmer on the docks of South Chicago, Bob hasn't worked steadily for the past three years. Since his unemployment compensation ran out, the Rodriquezes have supported themselves and their twelve children on their small savings, the income from odd jobs, and a modest foster care allotment.

As part of their work with the society, Bob and Lolly run a food pantry out of the parish hall on a periodic basis and out of their home on a daily basis. Bob explains how their kitchen and sagging porch have become a magnet for the hungry:

> People know that we help people, so they bring food here every day. Last week we had the corn deal: one day we got three dozen ears of corn from one guy; the next day, three cases from another guy; in one week we must have had twenty-five dozen ears of corn dropped off here. . . . We don't need to store the food. We get it today and get rid of it today. People come by word of mouth. Once they find us, they're here on the porch every day waiting to get the food.

When they hold a distribution at the church hall, the response is overwhelming. "We usually feed about 500 people there," Lolly says, "but often there's more. A couple of times we've had 1000 people at that little bitty church without any advertisement."

Farther down Ewing Avenue on the East Side is St. Francis deSales Church, where John Cronin heads a St. Vincent dePaul group which ministers to a growing number of jobless in the parish. Cronin, a retired schoolteacher, is a genial man who wears a look of perennial surprise, as though life had just whispered some great secret in his ear. But John can also get his Irish up—as he does when speaking of the reluctance of some religious leaders to acknowledge how desperate the situation of the unemployed has become. "You almost have to scream at them, 'Unemployment *is* a problem,' " he laments.

Still, the contents of the poor box in the back of the church —about $70 per week —are the society's primary source of income. And, the religious connection is vital to its purpose. "There's a spiritual dimension for us," Cronin explains. "It's an honor to serve our Savior."

The work of the society isn't limited to food pantries: John says they will respond to any request for assistance—no one is turned away. But, he notes, there are still many people who are too proud to ask for help. One family lost their home because they didn't want to admit they couldn't keep up the mortgage payments. By the time a relative called the society, it was too late; the eviction papers had been issued.

The efforts of Bob and Lolly Rodriquez, of John Cronin, and of many others like them, form a bedrock response to the Southeast Side's economic crisis. These are essentially self-help programs, run without the intervention of outside agencies. The kind of personal charity that sustains them derives from a religious tradition that preaches the virtues of the Good Samaritan and from a community tradition of neighborliness. Once it was as simple as bringing a pot of soup next door during an illness. Now, when the health of the entire community is jeopardized, the response is more structured, but the impulse is the same.

No one has tried to quantify this work—how many people are served each week, at what income level, in what area of need. Such tallying is better left to the bureaucracies. Those who are involved are all too aware of the limits of their programs: they know there are many needy people they cannot serve. But they also know firsthand the value of their work. They don't need statistics to measure their contributions. It's true, as Father Mahon points out, that you don't want to just end up handing out sacks of flour, but that may be a good place to begin.

ORGANIZING THE UNEMPLOYED

Ken Wychocki is a burly man with a bristly mustache, slicked-back dark hair, and intelligent eyes behind thick glasses. He speaks with the air of a person who believes his opinions should count for something. "I think U.S. Steel owes this community something. Cause you wipe that mill out and you aren't just wiping out eight or nine hundred jobs, you're wiping out a whole lot more."

Wychocki, an electrician who spent twenty-eight of his forty-six years at South Works, is part of a small band of local residents who make up the East Side Clergy Unemployment Committee. The committee had its origins in 1982, when George Schopp, then associate pastor at St. Francis, began interviewing parishioners to identify their major concerns. With the assistance of a local community organizer, he also set about identifying those lay people who could be trained to help revitalize the parish's social and spiritual life.

It didn't take long for Schopp to assemble a core group of twenty people who helped him conduct over 500 interviews. Within a few months' time, they'd found that unemployment topped almost everyone's list of concerns. The Unemployment Committee was formed to help give public expression to the painful stories the interviewers had heard in living rooms all over the East Side.

As its first activity, the Unemployment Committee organized a public meeting for jobless workers. The gathering was a big success, drawing over 150 people on a cold January night. On the East Side, where pride tends to keep problems locked up inside homes or heads, the simple sharing of distress provided a surge of energy. "There were so many people there who just looked around and said, 'My God, them too? They all got their problems too?'" Wychocki recalls.

But the mandate of the meeting surprised its organizers. "We thought people would want to do something about utility bills," explains Therese Costello, one of the committee's most hardworking members. "But what really had them upset was all the problems they were having with the unemployment compensation bureaucracy." The unemployment office was too far away; the staff treated people rudely; there were endless snafus in getting benefits. By the end of the evening, it was decided: the Unemployment Committee should try to improve the compensation system.

Costello, the mother of three children and wife of a laid-off steelworker, plunged into the campaign to have an outpost of the Bureau of Employment Security established in their own neighborhood, where it could be closely monitored. It took a lot of table-pounding at meetings with state personnel, but within a few months, the group had won a decisive victory. The BES began operating out of an East Side union hall one day each week. It was a big morale booster for the young organization. Father Schopp believes the intense experiences crowded into that first year—planning meetings, devising strategy, confronting government officials—gave participants a new sense of their own abilities:

> It comes right out of their tradition of faith—love of neighbor and love of God as the first commandment. . . . But in our neighborhood, there's strong political under-pinnings: When you needed something, you went to the tenth ward office and hoped they would be able to honor your request, but you always owed. What this committee has done for people is that they find their problem doesn't have to mean to go to someone for a favor. They find there are things they can do on their own.

Then, just as the committee seemed to be taking off, its efforts were brought up short. Father Schopp was transferred to another parish.

Undeterred, the group decided to continue its work under other auspices. It affiliated with a network of East Side clergy and became part of the United Neighborhood Organization (UNO), Southeast Chicago's largest community organization.

Founded in 1980 by Mary Gonzalez, a former social worker, and her husband, Greg Galuzzo, a veteran community organizer, UNO was quick to make its mark in Southeast Chicago through dramatic protest actions and a flair for garnering media coverage. In short order, it won a new community mental health clinic, improvement of school facilities, and a reduction in train fares. In the process, it developed a committed and effective core of community leaders.

Beneath its flamboyance, however, UNO was a thoughtful and serious organization, determined to bring increased power to local residents. It was this commitment, more than its protests, that set it on a collision course with the local political powers. In the fall of 1981, *The Daily Calumet* printed a scathing denunciation of the group authored by a prominent Mexican leader whose agency is heavily dependent on city funding. Other friends of the tenth ward Regulars followed suit.

Such attacks had little impact where it counted. UNO was beginning to build a solid base in local churches. Clergy and lay leaders alike knew its staff and its approach; they believed their parishes were strengthened by the leadership training and social action it fostered. At the same time, UNO was shifting its tactics, replacing showy public protests with the slow, undramatic work of creating parish committees.

By December of 1983, when UNO held its annual convention, that work had borne fruit. At a religious service to open the event, the altar was crowded with over a dozen priests and the church was thronged with over 500 people. Father Thomas Cima told those assembled: "In a world of bad news, we here tonight are a real sign of hope. . . . Under our skins, which are black, white, and brown, we are truly brothers and sisters."

UNO organizers believe that this combination of religious vision and practical organizing skills will enable the group to confront the Southeast Side's most glaring problems: unemployment, crime, and waste dumps. But as Southeast Siders cling to the hope that their community can recover, UNO's most important function may be its ability to keep alive a sense of possibility; in the midst of massive economic and social insecurity, its activities provide spiritual sustenance.

THE SMALL BUSINESS RESPONSE

Jim Fitch is a man of ideas—the sort of dreamer who spins out plans and schemes almost without pause. But Fitch is also a man of action, with a practical bent that has made him one of the Southeast Side's most successful entrepreneurs. As president of the South Chicago Community Bank, he has long been a leading light at the chamber of commerce. When the region's economy began to founder, it was only logical that Fitch would emerge at the forefront of the small business response to the crisis.

To spearhead the effort, he founded and funded a new organization—the Southeast Chicago Development Commission (SCDCom) in January of 1982. In its short life, SCDCom has carved out a course of judicious boosterism. Although its former executive director, Selma Wise, describes it as an "activist" organization, protest in the UNO mold is as alien to its operation as booze at a Temperance Union banquet.

Instead, Jim Fitch functions firmly within the given political and economic framework. He uses his ties with the Regular Democrats to win their backing for his various economic brainchildren, and the Regulars can point to SCDCom as their response to economic decline.

SCDCom's point of departure is the conviction that steel's fate is beyond its ken. "Whatever happens to the mills happens to the mills, and we cannot intervene," Wise insists. It tries instead to focus on new directions for the region's economy.

The group's first campaign was for the passage of a state "enterprise zone"—a measure to give tax breaks to businesses that expand or locate in certain designated areas. The idea quickly took hold in Southeast Chicago. Although they knew little of the specifics of the proposal, people saw it as a means of luring new industry to their community. Before long, the term was on everybody's lips—a sweet sliver of hope. SCDCom persuaded local Democratic politicians to support the bill and, after a round of compromises with the Republican governor, the measure was signed into law in 1983.

Opponents of the idea expressed skepticism about its potential for community revitalization, pointing out that the law did not require a business to employ local residents or even to create jobs in order to qualify for the tax breaks. And once the Southeast Side was designated an official enterprise zone a few months later, a more fundamental problem became evident: tax breaks could not lure new firms to a community experiencing industrial flight.

As faith in the enterprise zone faded, Jim Fitch's wheels started to turn again. His next campaign was strikingly bold. For years, a group of prominent Chicago businessmen had labored to have their city designated the site of the 1992 World's Fair. In the spring of 1983, the fair's Paris-based oversight committee granted the approval. But all was not rosy: The proposed site—a piece of lakefront property just south of the Loop business district—had drawn criticism from environmental groups.

Then Jim Fitch jumped into the picture. He proposed that the fair's site be shifted to Southeast Chicago, where the millions to be spent on infrastructure could have more lasting benefit; after the event, the land could be developed as an industrial park. SCDCom set about trying to influence the mayor and the city council to make the change. But after a brief and bloodless battle, the old boys' network prevailed and the city's stamp of approval was given to the downtown site.

SCDCom's big plans have come to little. These days the group is contenting itself with a more modest agenda: sidewalk repair and facade improvement on the Commercial Avenue business strip, technical assistance to medium-size industries in the area, and identification of sites for new industrial ventures.

Critics charge that Fitch and his allies alternate between wild-eyed schemes that have no chance of success and Band-

Aid programs that have no impact on the hemorrhaging economy. And they point to the group's close ties with the Regular Democrats as evidence of its unwillingness to recognize that the old ways no longer work in Southeast Chicago. But, for now, SCDCom is the only organization to go beyond the traditionalism of local chambers of commerce and chart a more aggressive course of revitalization. In this respect, it represents the most enlightened elements in the local business community—and those most likely to stick with the community in its darkest hour.

DUMPING THE DUMPS

Seated at the kitchen table of her cramped South Deering apartment in the summer of 1983, Mary Ellen Montes, a petite, dark-haired mother of three children, described the course of events that led to her arrest after she joined over half a dozen other local residents in blocking the entrance of a nearby hazardous waste dump.

By that time, Montes was already a leader in one of the Southeast Side's most infamous organizations—Irondalers Against the Chemical Threat (I-ACT). She was quoted in newspapers and featured on TV clips. But only two years before, she'd been a political novice who hadn't been active in any group since her days in the Girl Scouts. The daughter of popular community figure Petra Rodriquez, Montes says that she had "always had this feeling of wanting to help in some way if I could make things better for people by working with them," but she never had an outlet for these sentiments.

Then, in 1982, Montes learned about a proposal for a 289-acre toxic dump within blocks of South Deering's grammar school. The developer of the project, Waste Management, Inc. (WMI), already operated two 100-foot toxic mountains that are among the area's most notorious landfills.

And the site for its latest venture was already contaminated with heavy metals that were leaking into underground water supplies. Mary Ellen Montes had found her cause:

> You think about your children or your parents. I feel at my age, I'm perfectly healthy. But little children, they're really affected by it and you don't know what's going to happen to them. I know how badly it smells right now with what we have. If they put this new one through, those fumes are going to come, and what they're going to carry with them, we don't know. You can't risk that.

But WMI had friends in powerful places. That summer, Alderman Vrdolyak had sent a letter to the zoning board of appeals in support of the project. It read in part: "In view of the efforts and commitment being made by Waste Management on behalf of the . . . communities, I wish to inform this Board that I do not oppose this application for special use." Taking on the waste firm and its allies would be no easy task.

I-ACT started with a meeting in Montes's living room, but it soon grew to a core group of 40 activists who could turn out 200 to 400 people for spirited public meetings. As members learned more about the extent of the hazardous waste problem in their community, they became more passionate in their opposition to this latest—and closest—encroachment.

WMI was deaf to their demands. Despite massive public meetings in opposition to the dump, the company refused even to meet with I-ACT representatives. In desperation, the group turned to more drastic measures: it decided to prevent dump trucks from entering WMI's nearby landfill in Burnham. Twice they took to the streets to block traffic, forming a human chain across the entrance. The second time, they were hauled away in police wagons. And that was how Mary Ellen Montes came to be awaiting trial.

Although UNO provided staff assistance to get I-ACT off the ground, the group has basically been a volunteer operation. It has operated informally, without officers or structure, held together by the fervor it has generated. Montes is its unofficial leader by virtue of her granitelike resolve, impressive grasp of the dump data, and ready eloquence.

WMI withstood the storm of controversy that I-ACT evoked, quietly moving ahead with its permit requests and construction plans. But Mary Ellen is convinced that the landfill will never be built. WMI, she notes, "really think we're going to die down. But they have a surprise coming, because we're not. We're willing to do anything to stop them."

In Hegewisch, four miles south of South Deering, Jim and Gail Foley sit in the living room of their modern ranch-style home, with their two small children orbiting around them. The Foleys are part of a network of Hegewisch residents, some of whom have been fighting against landfills in their community since 1976. This movement's greatest resource has been *The Hegewisch News*, a community weekly with a circulation of 2000. In the main, the paper concentrates on news of local graduations, weddings, and church activities, but it has kept news about waste facilities among its front page stories for years. And its crusading publisher hasn't hesitated to lay the blame for the waste firms' greedy expansionism on Alderman Vrdolyak's doorstep.

In the summer of 1983, Jim and Gail Foley are involved in a pitched battle to prevent the burning of PCBs at a chemical treatment plant halfway between Hegewisch and South Deering. Despite their organizing a public hearing attended by 300 residents—nearly all opposed to the plan—and orchestrating a high-visibility pressure campaign, it is a battle they will lose. By fall, all legal recourse is gone, all the necessary permits have been issued, and the burning begins. Within a matter of weeks, the leakage local residents feared occurs: two railroad workers at the site are sprayed with the chemical as they unload it from railcars; an unknown quantity seeps into the ground.

The Foleys believe the greatest hope for halting the expansion of waste dumps in their area is involvement in politics. They are hesitant to criticize Alderman Vrdolyak for his dealings with dump owners, arguing that it's important to keep all lines of communication open. Jim says that so far he's found the alderman a cooperative ally in their efforts. And Gail notes that while politicians may have been too generous with waste firms in the past, "you have to give them the benefit of the doubt and assume they felt they were aiding the welfare of the community."

Susan Juracich makes no such assumption. A 25-year-old Hegewisch resident who cut her teeth on antidump battles while still in her teens, Juracich takes a jaded view of the tenth ward Regulars. She believes their occasional gestures of support for her cause are empty, while their support for the waste companies has had disastrous results. The hearing on the proposed WMI landfill in South Deering still sticks in her mind. "We were there in the courtroom just pouring our hearts out about why we didn't want that dump," she recalls. "And then they get up and read a letter from Vrdolyak about what a great thing it is."

I-ACT activists share the view that their community has been betrayed by the Regular Democrats' cooperation with the dump firms. Noting the role of a South Deering precinct captain in promoting the WMI proposal, Petra Rodriquez points out that "he has a job in the Department of Sanitation; one of his daughters works at the Department of Human Services; his other daughter works at the gym here. So, you see, he's bought. It's too late for him."

But their most disappointing experience with their elected representatives came when they persuaded Alderman Vrdolyak to accompany I-ACT leadership on a visit to the landfill site. Mary Ellen Montes recalls the conversation that took place on a cold winter day on that contested terrain:

> I started out saying you could see the housing on 109th Street, you could see the CHA housing, you could see the school. He said, "Gee, I didn't realize it was that close. How close is that—a mile?" I said, "A mile??? We're talking about one block, one city block.". . . So, I said, "So, you're not going to allow this to happen, are you?" He said, "Oh, no, that's not what I said. I said I think it looks too close. I'll have to go back and reconsider. I'll let you guys know what I think in three days." It's August now. He never got back to us.

On the evening of August 24, 1983, in the same church basement in which the Wisconsin Steel workers gathered after their mill closed down, another meeting is taking place. The political picture has changed some in the intervening three years. This meeting is organized by I-ACT. Chicago's recently elected mayor, Harold Washington, already locked in combat with Eddie Vrdolyak, has agreed to respond to the group's demand that he help stop the WMI dump.

St. Kevin's pastor, Father George Schopp, stands near the door, warmly greeting the scores of people—white, black, and Hispanic—who pour into the hall. Alderman Vrdolyak is nowhere in sight, but he has lawyers in three-piece suits and precinct captains in windbreakers uneasily lining the back wall of the hall. When the room is filled, over 500 people are on hand.

Mary Ellen Montes gavels the meeting to order. Once again people have come together to demand information from their public officials. But tonight it is Montes who displays confidence and control—and the crowd is right with her. Mayor Washington reveals that his staff have found that, under the former mayor, the permit for the South Deering site was issued by the city's zoning department without going through the proper procedures. After promising a thorough investigation, he pledges to work with local residents to halt the landfill and receives a standing ovation. But, as he turns to leave amidst the applause, Montes moves in quickly, insisting that the mayor respond specifically to I-ACT's five demands. As they are read, he agrees to each one; then the hall again erupts into cheers and the night is over.

As people leave St. Kevin's, the mood is upbeat. They are both more jaded and more hopeful than the crowd that left back in April of 1980. They now know more clearly the limits of politicians' promises. But they also know that they have an organization that can try to hold officials to their word.

And the mayor keeps his word. He initiates an ordinance to ban temporarily the construction of new waste dumps until tough new standards for buffer zones and waterwell safeguards can be developed. In 1985, that ordinance is still in effect, and Waste Management, Inc., is still prohibited from building its South Deering dump.

WISCONSIN WORKERS ORGANIZE

After thirty years on the scarfing docks at Wisconsin Steel, burning defects out of steel billets, Frank Lumpkin's face is worn and his body stooped. In the lively political world of the Progressive Steelworkers Union (PSWU), Lumpkin, a softspoken black man, was a marginal figure, part of a militant group that tried to bring the CIO into the mill. But in the wake of the shutdown, Frank Lumpkin soon emerged as the leading actor of the Wisconsin Steel story.

PSWU president Tony Roque didn't formally abdicate that position; he simply disappeared from view. As frightened steelworkers looked for answers and leadership, Roque was hard to reach on the phone and unavailable for comment to the press. A few weeks after the closing, Eddie Vrdolyak took to the pages of *The Daily Calumet* to offer an explanation for his friend's behavior:

> ... his silence on these matters should not be interpreted as evidence of inactivity among the union leadership; rather it is illustrative of the union's concern that ongoing negotiations and talks being conducted to save the affected jobs may be jeopardized by the giving of inopportune or premature public statements.

Later, Roque would offer his own account in simpler language. "We didn't know what the hell was going on and which direction to take. . . . I was on the phone constantly. . . . It took us about three weeks before we could say anything."

Those were three long weeks. During that time, workers learned that their last paychecks had bounced, their hospitalization coverage would be cut off, and their supplemental unemployment benefits (SUB pay) had vanished.

And during that time, Frank Lumpkin and his longtime allies formed the Wisconsin Steelworkers Save Our Jobs Committee. Stranded in the dark with everyone else, they began their own quest for information. Save Our Jobs members made the rounds of the offices of elected officials and government agencies. Sometimes they were met with rudeness, sometimes with a polite runaround. But gradually they gathered the facts. And those were disastrous.

When the mill closed, its employees lost everything except the portion of their pensions protected by the PBGC. Gone were pension supplements, special early retirement pensions, supplemental unemployment benefits, hospitalization, severance pay, and vacation pay. Altogether, union members lost $29.2 million in benefits guaranteed by their contract, an average of about $10,000 per worker.

Steelworkers had earned these benefits in long years in the mill, but now there was no one from whom to collect. Wisconsin Steel's assets were frozen in bankruptcy court, with scores of creditors lining up for their share. Envirodyne Industries had no legal obligation for the mill's debts: it was the EDC Holding Company that owned the mill, and the Holding Company had no other assets. And at that time, International Harvester was also disclaiming any liability: not only had the Holding Company assumed all its obligations to mill employees at the time of the 1977 sale, but the PSWU, in the person of Tony Roque, had signed an agreement absolving Harvester of responsibility for the benefits should Envirodyne fail.

When the union's executive board and membership realized what Roque had done, anger against him grew. After those first weeks of low visibility, Tony decided to ride out the storm. He called two membership meetings at downtown auditoriums (at a cost of thousands of dollars to the union's beleaguered treasury), took an active role in promoting the ill-fated Palmer deal, and was closely involved in negotiations over mill maintenance. It was Roque who made the deal with Chase Manhattan to allow the inventory to be taken out of the mill in exchange for a portion of the workers' last weeks' pay. And the PSWU president filed a lawsuit against Harvester to recoup the pension benefits he'd waived in 1977.

Angry Save Our Jobs members charge that even these activities were suspect. They contend that Roque used his position to violate seniority provisions, basing his decisions about who would work on maintenance crews on favoritism and the payment of kickbacks. They charge that he sent out postcards for a membership vote on the Chase deal but did not wait for the returns to come in before he signed on the dotted line. And they note that both in bankruptcy court and in the lawsuit that he filed, Roque and his legal allies have been but halfhearted advocates for the workers' concerns; the pension suit has gone nowhere.

By 1981, the PSWU had faded, and the Save Our Jobs Committee owned the field. Now it was Lumpkin to whom reporters and union members turned for answers. The group's office on Commercial Avenue, donated by Miriam Balanoff, was open day and night for workers needing reassurance or advice. Where Roque scorned mass protests ("I been around this business a long time. Marches do shit—that's what marches do"), Lumpkin thrived on them. Save Our Jobs marched to Harvester headquarters, to the State House in Springfield, and to the steps of the Capitol in Washington, D.C. The group demanded that the mill be reopened and that workers be paid all the benefits owed them.

Eventually, Lumpkin realized that survival needs were becoming primary for jobless workers. So the Save Our Jobs Committee established its own food pantry. Every other Monday night, the committee meets to report on progress and answer questions about the status of efforts to reopen or raze the mill. Afterwards free food is distributed to the 75 to 100 people, mostly black and Hispanic, who attend. Although there is no requirement that workers come to the meeting in order to get the food, it is assumed that they will.

As much as the food pantry helps sustain laid-off steelworkers, it's not enough to put them back on their feet, and Lumpkin knows it. So Save Our Jobs has filed its own lawsuit to try to recover the benefits due the workers. Tom Geoghegan, a partner in one of the city's labor law firms, filed a class action suit in behalf of all former PSWU members charging that Harvester's sale of the mill to Envirodyne was a sham transaction, and that the agreement Roque signed in 1977 was invalid, in part because the PSWU's executive board had not approved it. It calls on Harvester to pay the benefits to which workers were entitled under the PSWU contract.

Many former Wisconsin workers have pinned high hopes on this suit, imagining it will restore to them every penny they're owed. Joe Smetlack is already making plans: "If we ever get a settlement from Harvester, I'll go into business for myself. I don't want to work for anybody again, not if I can help it. . . . What if we don't get the settlement? That's a good question."

But although there will be some disappointments no matter what the outcome, if Lumpkin and Geoghegan succeed in winning even a portion of the disputed benefits, they will be heroes in many mill workers' eyes. Smetlack gets misty-eyed thinking of it: "If they do right by us, how grateful could we be to them? Lumpkin has probably had all kinds of threats, but if they manage to get anything for us, how could we thank them? I'll kiss their feet."

Frank Lumpkin wanted more than to be a hero, though. He wanted to see Wisconsin Steel reopen. To this end, he has worked with the Midwest Center for Labor Research to demonstrate the feasibility of a government takeover of the Torrence Avenue facility. And he has given support to political candidates like Congressmen Charles Hayes and Gus Savage and Mayor Harold Washington in the hope that they would advocate this cause.

At the same time, Save Our Jobs has lobbied for the extension of unemployment insurance benefits and for the expansion of food pantries. It has helped to establish national committees of the unemployed and it has marched for jobs in Washington, D.C., with labor unions and community groups.

Lumpkin's advocacy of political candidates and broader causes has cost the SOJC some supporters. There is a sizable number of former Wisconsin workers who shun its militant rhetoric and are fearful of its alliances and tactics. Daniel Vitas was one of the group's most active members in its early days, but now he's withdrawn from its ranks. "It's being exploited by the politicians," he charges, "and it's gotten involved in too many other causes."

The Save Our Jobs Committee has worked without pause for over three years. Whenever the EDA, Harvester, the PSWU, local politicians, or the bankruptcy court have made a move, its members have been there—demanding information and protesting any potential malfeasance. It has operated on a worn shoestring of a budget: Florencio Ortega gave over $1000 of his own money to get the lawsuit off the ground because he felt, while he had his pension to fall back on, other workers had nothing. There have also been small contributions from area businesses (which have grown even smaller over the years) and grass-roots fund-raisers, such as dinners and parties, with donated food and drink. Through it all, Frank Lumpkin's dogged determination has kept something akin to hope alive.

MARCHING TO THE MILL GATE

Organizing is bred into Ike Mezo's bones. The son of a union activist, Ike started organizing for Ed Sadlowski's district director campaign as soon as he hired on at South Works in 1974. When he was laid off from the plate mill in 1981, he kept right on organizing, becoming the cochairman of the Local 65 unemployment committee.

Ike is also something of a loner. He listens to everyone, but keeps his own counsel. Local 65 has been a hotbed for radical organizations of every stripe; Ike worked with all of them, but he didn't join any.

Alice Peurala created the unemployment committee during her term as Local 65's president, and she encouraged laid-off members to stay involved with their union. Her successor, Don Stazak, had more traditional ideas, however. Believing that most of these workers would never be called back, he left Ike and the unemployment committee pretty much on their own.

But Mezo struggled to keep the link with Local 65's leadership. To do otherwise, he believed, would have ensured the committee's marginality. Other activists disagreed, convinced that President Stazak would never support the kind of vigorous organizing campaign needed to save the mill. Every weekly committee meeting was filled with disputes between allies and opponents of Stazak's rule. Since Mezo believed

that only a united union, employed and unemployed together, could mobilize community and church backing for a
serious fight over the mill's future, he tried to mediate the
constant conflicts. It was a lonely task.

At 11 A.M. on a rainy Wednesday morning, November
23, 1983—the day before Thanksgiving—an American flag
and a coffin bearing the sign "U.S. Steel South Works" led a
march of 150 steelworkers out of the Local 65 hall and into
the streets of South Chicago. Down the block, in front of
Roma's Restaurant, they were joined by 100 former Wisconsin
steelworkers carrying signs reading "International Harvester:
We Want Justice." The flashing blue lights of a Chicago police
car led the marchers down Commercial Avenue, where cu-
rious shoppers and storekeepers stared and occasionally
shouted encouragement. The campaign of Local 65's unemployment committee to build community support for a
government takeover of South Works had begun.

In front of the mill's 87th Street gate, once the main
entrance to the plant, Rev. Josea Ivory, Mezo's cochairman
on the committee, told how U.S. Steel had deserted the mill.
As TV cameras caught yet another sad story of Thanksgiving
in Southeast Chicago, two of the marchers, Dan McCarthy
and Joe Francisco, reminisced about another march to steel
mill gates—that of Memorial Day, 1937, when Joe's brother
was killed by Chicago policemen. "During the Depression,"
Dan said, "only poor people lived in South Chicago. The rich
lived by the country club. The steel companies want it to be
like that again."

Leaders of the unemployment committee explained their
program for South Works: They wanted the government to
repeal the tax write-offs companies receive when they shut
down plants, they wanted a government program to rebuild
America's infrastructure, and they wanted the federal government to take over and modernize their mill.

Then, as the marchers resumed their slow journey through the dilapidated streets of Millgate, a big black limousine with license plates reading "U.S. 1" pulled up beside Frank Lumpkin, and Congressman Charles Hayes stepped out. Hayes, who represents a nearby district where many black steelworkers live, told the crowd: "I'm here to say that companies like U.S. Steel have a responsibility to the community. They can't just pick up and leave." To the cheers of the assembled, Hayes promised to convene congressional hearings on the decline of the steel industry in Southeast Chicago.

When Hayes finished, Don Stazak limped to the front of the crowd and took the bullhorn. Stazak had been suffering from gout and depression and he got out of his sickbed to address the marchers. He summoned up energy to pledge Local 65's support to the unemployment committee and to thank Reverend Ivory and Ike Mezo for keeping the members united in support of the union. For a moment, all were joined in a bond of solidarity, and then the march resumed, past the *taquerias* and cheap clothing stores of South Chicago.

Back at the union hall, Ike Mezo had mixed feelings about the march. It was good bringing laid-off workers from Wisconsin Steel and South Works together before the media, good to bask in a feeling of unity. But so many people didn't march! In the weeks leading up to the demonstration, members of the unemployment committee called 1000 laid-off workers and distributed thousands of leaflets at welfare offices, churches, and health centers. After all that work, the response seemed meager. And so much remained to be done.

The Local 65 unemployment committee changed members and leaders several times over the following two years. Although its drastic program for reviving the steel industry received little attention at first, the committee continued to act as a friendly prod on the USWA leadership, nudging it into actions that it otherwise might never have considered or risked: it was the unemployment committee's proposal that prodded the International union and the city of Chicago to study the feasibility of finding new ownership for the old South Works mill.

MAKING A DIFFERENCE

If the Southeast Side is to survive as a stable, secure place to live and work, much more remains to be done than these diverse groups can possibly accomplish.

This fundamental fact may make all of these organizations' actions seem thoroughly quixotic, more akin to tilting at windmills than to rescuing steel mills. Does it make any difference if these groups continue to exist? Don't they just raise hopes that will soon be dashed? Wouldn't all these people be better off packing their bags and heading for the Sunbelt?

It's true that some of the groups will quickly fade from the scene, unable to hold on to any sense of possibility as the once-mighty mills are demolished. But it's also true that some groups will grow, as they deepen their resolve to resist the destruction of their community.

There is something obdurate on the streets of the Southeast Side. People know what matters to them and they hang on to it. As Father Schopp sees it, there's a determination not so much to fight as to go on:

> Sometimes you read studies that say this is a dying community; it makes it sound like rigor mortis has set in and the body's rotting. Southeast Chicago has changed. . . . but people are still living here. Friendships continue to happen; marriages continue to be celebrated; babies continue to be baptized. The measure can't just be economic.

This determination is the anchor for all the organizing efforts; it gives them weight and meaning, transforming them from quixotic protests into symbols of the community's will to survive.

But these community organizations serve practical as well as symbolic purposes. They strengthen bonds among people, now that work bonds are gone. They build up the self-confidence that unemployment tears down. And perhaps most importantly, they act as a spur for larger efforts. They stimulate the USWA and local governmental units to take new directions and test new ideas. And their efforts can ripple around the nation, letting other victims of deindustrialization know that they don't simply have to give up or move on.

Still, even the most successful organizers do not expect to alter the national policies that dictate their community's decline. Addressing the fundamental problem of corporate disinvestment in the U.S. steel industry would require major policy initiatives and a political strategy to implement them. Whether or not such changes are possible in a nation now dominated by free-market thinking is the question on which the fate of Southeast Chicago hangs.

8

Saving Steel

THE FATE OF Southeast Chicago, like that of hundreds of other communities across the United States, is thoroughly enmeshed in a web of global economic competition, partisan political rivalries, and public policy controversies. Local efforts to revive sagging economies inevitably crash against this fundamental reality: small-scale revitalization is not possible without major shifts in these larger forces.

Yet almost from the first steel mill closing, there has been a sense of the inevitable clouding all discussions about the industrial crisis confronting our nation. Throughout the worst years of the steel industry's rapid decline, from 1982 to 1985, industry critics ignored the devastating impact of the grossly overvalued dollar on the steel companies and their customers. Instead, they pointed to the specter of the iron hand of the market, as a deadly grip against which there can be no useful protest and from which there can be no reprieve.

Policy analysts of widely divergent political orientations found common ground in the view that the steel industry could not or should not be saved. Most saw its demise as intimately linked with the decline of our entire durable goods manufacturing sector: the death of the smokestack industries

202

became a commonplace of public discourse. Some believed
that no matter what America did, it could no longer compete
as an industrial power against the low-wage countries of the
third world. Others held that unless the steel industry could
stand on its own, it did not deserve to survive. In this Dar-
winian economic model, the fittest would emerge, trim and
tough from the harrowing rigors of economic competition.

Underlying these views were two unexamined premises.
The first was that the economic environment of the early
1980s—the strong dollar, high interest rates, huge budget
deficits, and surging imports—was a fair test of the viability
of America's steel industry. The second was that a sound
manufacturing sector is no longer essential to the future of
the United States as a stable, secure, and just society—that
our nation can continue to progress, indeed thrive, without
its basic industry, or with a greatly shrunken industrial sector.

Both premises were false. The temporary economic problems of the early 1980s made it impossible for U.S. steelmakers to compete, thus seriously exaggerating the industry's
backwardness.

And the future prosperity of our nation will be endangered if we allow our industrial strength to wither. Moreover,
it is both possible and necessary to revitalize America's steel
industry. By doing so, we would also strengthen the entire
durable goods manufacturing sector, for which cheap, high
quality steel is essential.

A program to revive steel would require large public expenditures and substantial change in the way America formulates its economic policies. Such a program would evoke
howls of protest from free-market ideologues and devotees
of high technology.

Failing to act, however, could pose a threat to the security
and stability of our nation. We risk enormous losses in human
and material resources if we continue to evade this challenge.
Perhaps most importantly, we risk the weakening of the democratic tradition that is fundamental to our political system.

America has long prided itself on being the land of opportunity, moving toward a progressively wider sharing of the fruits of economic prosperity and a greater participation in national life. The creation of a large middle class was seen as a bulwark of national stability and a backbone of democracy. Now that backbone has been cracked. The middle is falling out of the American labor force.

In the postwar years, the manufacturing sector provided the most reliable guarantee of a long-term, relatively well-paying job for those without specialized education or extraordinary ambition. But between 1979 and 1984, 5.1 million Americans lost their jobs, many permanently. Of these, only 3.1 million had found work by January 1984, and almost half earned less in their new jobs. Workers in the primary metal industry were even more drastically affected. In 1984, over half were still unemployed and 40 percent of those who had found employment reported a greater than 20 percent decline in income.

Moreover, the much-ballyhooed alternatives of high technology and high finance have failed to generate more than a fraction of the jobs needed to supplant lost manufacturing employment. These industries have produced a patina of prosperity, especially in some of our major urban centers where young professionals congregate, but they have not reached into the heart of the American work force. Their demand for labor is limited, and most of the jobs they do generate require a high level of education and skill. It is the service sector, not microchips and computers, that offers displaced Americans the most likely source of reemployment.

According to a study by the AFL-CIO, by 1990, 72 percent of all jobs will be in the service sector if present trends continue unabated. This tallies with a Bureau of Labor Statistics report that of the top ten occupations expected to experience job growth, seven are in the low-skilled service sector. These jobs—like nurse's aide, security guard, orderly, salesclerk, and food worker—tend to require little education and pay low wages. Economist Barry Bluestone estimates that the average production worker earns $370 a week, compared to $248 a week earned by the average service worker. In addition, jobs in the service sector provide few benefits.

For forty years, manufacturing jobs, with their relatively high wages, good benefits, and pension plans—all tied to years of service—produced a remarkably stable and reasonably satisfied work force. Even the dirtiest and most dangerous of jobs never went begging for applicants. Service jobs, by contrast, have a notoriously high turnover rate. They tend to produce a wandering work force, ever in search of a slightly better opportunity. And they tend to produce chronically dissatisfied workers, because they fail to measure up to the promise of what employment in America is supposed to be all about.

Not only does the loss of a manufacturing sector threaten middle-class Americans but it also closes the door on opportunities for lower-income citizens. For many decades, industrial jobs have provided one of the surest routes out of poverty. It is no coincidence that discussions of a permanent "underclass" in our nation began to enter into public discourse at the same time that our industrial base began to shrink. More people are remaining poor because there are fewer entry-level jobs that provide sufficient economic incentive and job security to enable those who lack higher education and work experience to become integrated into the work force.

This decline in the standard of living of middle Americans and in opportunity for lower-income Americans is occurring in tandem with a decline in the influence of labor unions in American life. Manufacturing firms claim that it is union wages and work rules that have created their problems—and that unions must be eliminated or weakened if industry is to survive. Employers in other sectors of the economy point to the problems of manufacturing as an excuse to keep unions out of their workplaces.

Yet, according to Harvard economists Richard Freeman

and James Medoff, labor unions have set the standard for the wages of all working people, not just those in unions. As they have been weakened, the bargaining posture of individual workers has been greatly weakened as well. Not only are workers once again finding themselves without basic protections against arbitrary firing or favoritism, but all workers are finding that their real purchasing power is shrinking.

The result of this loss of stature, income, and opportunity for middle- and lower-income Americans has been a sharp increase in social instability as well as a growing disillusionment with American ideals: "I'm 54 years old, and until 1982, I was a proud man," wrote a former auto worker to his union newspaper. "Now I have become a beggar with no dignity or pride. . . . Today I go to county welfare to beg for assistance. . . . Does anyone honestly care that people are losing everything they worked years to get? That they are trying to sell their homes for almost nothing on a depressed market? Or that families are breaking up? I swear to God, no one cares."

This letter suggests the social cost of the dislocation that has occurred as a result of plant closures and industrial job loss. One study of displaced workers, by Sidney Cobb and Stanislav Karl, found a suicide rate "thirty times the expected number." Using national data for the years 1940–1973, Dr. Harvey Brenner of Johns Hopkins University calculated that every 1 percent increase in the total unemployment rate sustained over a six-year period was associated with 37,000 more deaths (including 20,000 cardiovascular deaths, 650 homicides, and 500 deaths from cirrhosis of the liver), as well as 4000 admissions to state mental hospitals and 3300 admissions to state prisons. The effect on families has already been documented in Chapter 4—violence, divorce, and trauma.

The economic consequence of industrial decline can be totaled in government budgets. In Southeast Chicago, thousands of former taxpayers are now on relief; thousands of consumers have nothing to spend. The decline in tax revenues imposes a heavy burden on the treasuries of local, state, and federal governments, precipitating new service cutbacks, new layoffs, and added unemployment and welfare expenditures in a dismal downward spiral. The layoffs of 15,000 steelworkers during the years 1979–1983 cost $444 million annually in lost tax revenues, and another $163 million in unemployment insurance and food stamps. Who bears the burden of all this? Not the steel companies, but the American taxpayers.

The problem is intensified because plant closings create social problems different from those which earlier welfare policies were developed to address. There is a growing bitterness among displaced workers who now find that they do not meet the eligibility requirements of welfare programs to which their taxes have long contributed.

There is an urgent need for new, publicly supported programs to aid these workers. At a minimum, such an approach should encompass:

- an early warning system to alert workers and communities to potential plant closings;

- technical assistance and loan programs to allow worker or community groups to buy out operations and run them on a cost-effective basis;

- company-supported shutdown funds to provide assistance in retraining and/or relocation;

- continuation of health care coverage;

- mortgage assistance to ensure that people don't lose their homes;

- more flexible criteria for income support programs.

Ironically, the need for new social programs is growing at precisely the moment that the federal government is massively cutting back all social spending and attempting to shift the responsibility onto local governmental units. Yet, the local areas where the needs are greatest are the very ones undergoing large-scale losses in tax revenues. It is all but impossible for them to initiate and fund the needed programs on their own.

Economic dislocation, social trauma, and dwindling resources are combining to undermine a basic unit of American society—our communities. Ever since the Puritans founded the Massachusetts Bay Colony, the ideal of community has been central to American culture, a counterweight to this country's restless individualism. Even as millions of Americans have joined the exodus to the atomized life of suburbia or taken up the nomadic existence of the modern corporate employee, more still have felt the need to sink roots into their home turf.

Economic stability is critical for sustained community life; thus it is that many of our most enduring communities have been linked to a major workplace. This is true not just of renowned industrial areas like Southeast Chicago or Youngstown. Even the most bucolic of small towns can often be found to shelter a granary, a meat-packing plant, or an auto parts factory.

Nor is the concern for community life limited to small towns and midsize cities. For the decline of our industrial base is intimately related to the much-bemoaned decline of our larger central cities. The loss of industrial tax revenues and industrial jobs that provided an alternative to welfare has contributed to the decay of large stretches of urban landscape. This crisis has served to break down the remaining bonds of community and associational life that survived even in many of our larger cities, and it is fostering a growth in crime and other antisocial behavior that creates intense racial and class antagonism.

The preservation of communities is a matter of conserving basic human and material resources. Today, giant steel mills stand abandoned, their equipment left to rust or to await the wrecker's ball. Smaller industrial concerns will follow them into oblivion, though often no one will bother to tear them down because there are no uses for the land profitable enough to justify the costs of demolition. Moreover, people are sitting idle, longing to work, but without work to do. And the social infrastructure of communities—small businesses, schools, police and firefighting forces—is deteriorating as well.

This is a waste of resources at once tragic and unnecessary—the product of economic decisions made without consideration of their social consequences.

American democracy has always suffered from the inadequate linkages between political and economic life. It was Thomas Jefferson who first recognized that economic security was necessary if each individual was to participate in the democratic process. However, it was not until the New Deal that American policy consciously acknowledged that the nation's stability and democratic heritage would be endangered if the government failed to take an activist role in steering economic decisions.

In the decades since the New Deal, the gains won by the labor movement, the support provided by programs such as Social Security, and the growth in labor market participation have all combined to enhance the possibilities for political participation. But the insecurity created by plant closings, mass joblessness, attacks on labor unions, and cuts in social security benefits is undermining the gains we have made. In Southeast Chicago, people who have worked all their lives have to walk hat in hand to the alderman's office and beg for part-time jobs. When they get jobs, they have to toe management's line: the proud assertiveness of their years in the mill has become but a mocking memory.

Children in grade school have to prepare themselves for the economic competition to come, and that means they have no time to play or to pursue interests that lack a foreseeable payoff. Older children are dropping out of school because they don't believe a high school diploma will help them get a job. This is not the best education for citizenship in a democratic society.

Healthy communities are also essential to the proper functioning of political democracy. The dense layering of social experiences and the bonds of trust and familiarity that grow in strong communities equip residents with the confidence and knowledge they need for active involvement in social decision making. Furthermore, economists Jeff Faux and Gar Alperovitz argue, the decentralized structure of local governments facilitates popular participation, while more centralized institutions make it all but impossible.

If our concept of governance is one in which people form their opinions through the media and cast their votes accordingly, then the loss of community is of small consequence. But if it is one in which an active and informed electorate seeks to participate fully in the nation's life, and where people can delegate their authority to those whom they trust, the survival of communities is essential.

The loss of America's industrial base represents a grave threat to the social and economic fabric of our nation. Thus the plight of basic industry cannot be evaded or shut out. The real issue is not whether the free market can be preserved, or whether high technology can solve all our problems. Rather it is whether our leaders will face up to the immense complexity of the problems before them and to the comprehensive solutions those problems demand.

A PROGRAM TO SAVE AMERICAN STEEL

The arguments of free marketeers and high-tech prophets that the decline of basic manufacturing industries was all but inevitable have not been completely victorious, however. Indeed, government leaders have made a number of halfhearted attempts to save the nation's industrial base. Their actions were motivated as much by political calculations as by an assessment of the social costs involved: the steel- and auto-producing states have many electoral votes, after all. But motivations were less important than policies: both Democratic and Republican administrations acted, and both have failed.

The federal government has been intervening to halt steel's decline ever since 1977, when the Carter administration initiated two programs—loan guarantees for small steel companies and a mechanism to keep out subsidized steel imports. Four years later, Congress adopted industry proposals to reduce the steel companies' tax burden. Finally, in 1984, the Reagan administration adopted a program to limit steel imports through "voluntary" export agreements with steel-producing nations.

Thus, in a seven-year period, the federal government initiated three separate, piecemeal programs to halt the decline of America's steel industry. Unfortunately, none worked.

For instance, by the time the Economic Development Administration began to implement the Carter loan guarantee program, in 1979, the Federal Reserve Board was instituting a restrictive monetary policy that dried up steel markets. Wisconsin Steel was one of the beneficiaries and victims of the self-defeating federal policy. Government would have done as well had it had poured $50 million into a hole in the ground.

Another instance of self-contradicting federal action occurred in 1981, when the Congress passed the Tax Reform Act. That bill gave the steel companies the cash flow they said they needed to modernize, but they did not do so because the recession triggered in late 1981 by the Reagan-Volcker monetary policy shrank steel markets, while illegally subsidized imports flooded into the U.S. in defiance of trade laws.

The Reagan import restriction program is similarly flawed. For one thing, its announced goal was to reduce steel imports to 18.3 percent of total U.S. steel consumption, but by the time Reagan administration trade officials had completed their negotiations with foreign competitors, the actual figure was closer to 22 percent. And even that higher figure did not actually reflect the amount of imported steel flowing into this country at the expense of domestic steelmakers. For most of 1985, imports captured more than 26 percent of the market. But even if the VRA's had achieved their announced targets, they would have failed to meet their announced goals—enabling steelmakers to modernize for global competition. It's true that quotas would have raised steel prices, but there is little reason to think that steel companies would have modernized enough to match the efficiency of the best foreign mills. Consider what happened during the years 1968–1978, when steel imports to the United States averaged 18 percent—approximately the same level the Reagan plan targeted. As we noted in Chapter 3, because demand for steel was increasing slowly during those years, steel companies averaged just 7 percent profits, well below the rate for American manufacturing as a whole.

The steel companies *did* plow a large portion of their profits into modernization projects—like the continuous casters at South Works and Wisconsin Steel—but at a 7 percent rate of return, they could not justify sufficient investment to fully modernize these mills. By the end of the decade, America had many partially modern mills, and none that were world class. That made us vulnerable to foreign steel imports, and it spurred some steel companies to diversify into industries where global competition was less intense.

At best, import restriction will produce the same pattern: steel companies will add a billet caster to one mill, a rolling mill to another, but they will run out of investment capital well before they've upgraded all their outmoded facilities.

Thus, the current policies will only serve to intensify the steel industry's crisis. "Marginal" mills will be shut down—among them Southeast Chicago's South Works, Bethlehem's Lackawanna and Johnstown facilities, and almost the entire United States Steel complex in the Pittsburgh region. A huge chunk of western Pennsylvania and eastern Ohio will be devastated. Other steel producers will follow LTV into bankruptcy. Meanwhile overseas, rival steelmakers, aided by their governments, will continue to outspend U.S. firms. The gap between foreign and domestic steel producers will continue to widen.

And there could be even worse results. Inland Steel Chairman Frank Luerssen has predicted that the industry will have to shut down more than 20 percent of its existing capacity by 1990. Many steel analysts have even begun to speculate that the entire hot-metal-making segment of the industry will soon be lost to low-wage countries like Korea and Brazil.

All the recent federal steel programs are doomed to failure because they are piecemeal responses to crises of the moment. Since political leaders hold fast to the idea that the steel industry is supposed to compete in a free marketplace, they propose only limited intervention. Their programs attack one aspect of the steel industry's problems—whether it's imports, or taxes, or interest rates, or declining demand—without addressing the others. As a result, they end up costing the government a lot of money, but they don't enable U.S. steelmakers to become world class.

If the steel industry is to survive as more than a shell of its former self, there's only one solution: there must be a comprehensive strategy that coordinates a series of remedial programs. Ad hoc policies aimed at stemming pressure for more drastic action will be inadequate.

A comprehensive program must deal with imports—but it also needs to take steps to increase the *demand* for steel in other ways. It must make sure that steel companies have the money they need to modernize—but it can't limit itself to quick fixes, like short-term loan programs or partial changes in tax policy. Rather it will have to reform the tax codes and restructure the credit markets so that private investors will want to finance steel's renewal—and the federal government will have to provide direct subsidies if there is a shortfall in private capital. Finally, any program to preserve steel will be fruitless unless the government follows macroeconomic policies that assure the prosperity of the rest of American industry, which is to say, the steel companies' customers.

The comprehensive program outlined below may seem radical, particularly in an era dominated by the ideology of free-market conservatism, but two things should be remembered: First, ad hoc solutions haven't worked and they won't work. And second, America's steel industry is the only one in the world that is expected to compete in a free marketplace. If the United States develops a comprehensive steel program, it will only be doing what every other steel-producing nation in the world has done. As a study prepared for the Bethlehem Steel Corporation points out, from Canada to Brazil, from Korea to West Germany, steel industries get massive, sustained help of the sort that is denied to domestic producers.

THE DEMAND SIDE

A comprehensive program for the steel industry should begin with the demand side. Demand for American steel had fallen from 100 million tons shipped in 1979 to only 74 million tons in 1984, a 26 percent decline. If it doesn't rebound from this low level, domestic steelmakers will have no incentive to modernize their mills.

The decline in steel sales was caused partly by a rise in steel imports to more than 25 percent of the U.S. market in 1984. But that was only one chapter of the story. Equally important was the sharp rise in imports of cars, tractors, subway cars and buses, machine tools, and other steel-containing products. Each time an American buys a Japanese automobile rather than one made in Detroit, he or she has reduced the demand for domestic steel. In total, steel-containing imports reduced the demand for American steel by 13.7 million tons per year in 1985, according to a recent study by Locker/Abrecht Associates.

A third chapter in the story was declining exports. The

United States lost almost 6 million tons of steel exports in the years 1979–1983 because of the overvalued dollar and slumping third world economic growth. Furthermore, when overseas sales of Caterpillar tractors or Harvester trucks decline, so does demand for American steel. If exports such as these had not declined in the years 1981–1985, American steelmakers would have been able to sell an additional 3.4 million tons annually, according to the same Locker/Abrecht study.

To boost the demand for American steel, federal policy would have to reduce American imports of industrial goods and boost our exports. In addition, it would have to promote research on improving steel products, and to stimulate other economic activities that consume steel.

To achieve these ends, a comprehensive program should bring down the value of the dollar, restrict imports, rebuild America's aging physical facilities, support research in product innovation, and transfer capital spending from military to domestic uses. Accomplishing those tasks would make steel look much more attractive to private investors.

The sharp decline in demand for American steel during the years 1979–1984 was partly the result of an economic phenomenon completely outside the control of American steel companies—the strong dollar. In just three years, from 1980 to 1983, the dollar's value increased 82 percent against the French franc, 78 percent against the Italian lira, and 41 percent against the West German mark. The dollar's new strength had a clear effect on U.S. competitiveness, according to a Data Resource Inc. study: "German labor compensation costs have moved from about 25 percent above U.S. costs in 1980 to about 20 percent below U.S. costs in 1982." That means that an American mill producing steel 25 percent cheaper than a German mill in 1980 might very well have lost orders to that rival in 1984, even if the domestic facility was more modern and efficient.

The strong dollar sapped the strength of many formerly strong manufacturing firms, a fact that has begun ringing alarm bells in the business community. Thus, when the recovery beginning in 1983 failed to improve the profits of widely respected corporations like Caterpillar Tractor, business sentiment began to shift. A faint suspicion slowly grew into firm conviction that America's industrial decline was not the inevitable result of free-market forces but was instead the result of faulty federal policies—the overvalued dollar chief among them. Republican strategist Kevin Phillips and economist Otto Eckstein both wrote books in 1984 that helped legitimate this view within the business community.

Overvalued dollars were the products of many different factors, but their chief cause was the strict monetarist policies of the Volcker Federal Reserve Board, which drove interest rates up to record levels that attracted funds from investors all over the world. Then, the huge budget deficits of the Reagan years kept the rates up. If American manufacturing industries, including steel, are to have any hope of survival in the long run, the federal government will have to give priority to keeping the dollar stable and realistically aligned in relation to our chief trading partners.

Even if the dollar stabilizes at realistic levels, the government will probably have to impose strong and permanent trade restraints to ensure that the demand for American steel is sufficient to induce domestic producers to modernize.

"Protectionism" is a dirty word in American political discourse. Yet the reality is that "free trade" hardly exists anywhere in the world today. Even the United States, the bastion of free-trade ideology, manages trade in many sectors of our economy. For example, the prosperity of the American auto industry in 1983–1984 was based on Japan's voluntary agreement to limit exports to this country.

Another example concerns the American textile industry. The United States erected trade barriers to protect domestic textile manufacturers in the 1950s. There is now a Multi-Fiber Agreement which limits annual import growth to 6 percent. Under this umbrella, American textile manufacturers have modernized and achieved productivity growth twice the average for American industry. Protection has not meant inflated consumer prices; textiles have risen at only half the average rate of the producer price index.

But America's sins against free trade are minor compared to those of our trade partners. Wolfgang Hager, an economic consultant to the Common Market, estimates 75 percent of the free world's trade is subject to quotas, export subsidies, barter arrangements, and other direct government restrictions.

The growth of third world industry has made the need for protection more urgent. During the past decade, multi-national corporations have begun to build modern manufacturing plants in the poor regions of the world. At the same time, governments all around the globe have been promoting basic manufacturing industries like steel, auto, and electronics. The result, Robert Kuttner observes, "is enormous over capacity, and competitive pressure to maintain profits, cut taxes and lower wages."

If America does not protect its manufacturing industries, can we expect Chicago steelworkers or Detroit auto workers to compete with Koreans whose wages are kept low by government decree, backed up by American arms?

Since American manufacturing began its recent decline, federal officials have begun protecting one industry after another. But because they are hampered by their adherence to free-trade principles, their efforts have been ineffective. A prime example is the trigger-price mechanism (TPM).

The Carter administration headed off steel industry suits for protection against foreign dumping of steel in the United States at below-market prices by proposing a trigger-price mechanism. But the government never established an effective enforcement apparatus, as the Mitsui case revealed.

Disgruntled employees of Mitsui and Co. (USA, Inc.), a Japanese trade firm, brought telexes of company transactions to U.S. Customs Service officials. The documents established that Japanese steelmakers had been mislabeling their exports to the United States so that they could sell them here for lower prices than the TPM would allow. One of the firm's customers was U.S. Steel, which was buying wire products from Japan at illegally low prices to fill demand that had been supplied by the corporation's Torrance, California, plant before it shut down.

On July 21, 1982, Mitsui pleaded guilty and agreed to pay $11 million in civil penalties to the treasury department. A supervisory special agent for the U.S. Customs Service later testified that "the best agents, the best auditors, or even the best import specialists would not have detected this scheme without the information we were being supplied" by inside informants.

The Reagan administration's Voluntary Restraint Agreement program, announced in 1984, is similarly flawed. It originally set 18.3 percent as its target for steel import penetration, but in the winter of 1985–1986, imports were coming in at a rate of 24.5 percent, and there was widespread evasion of quota restrictions. Even if the Reagan plan were enforced more effectively, it would still be seriously flawed by its temporary nature. Domestic producers will think twice about spending a billion dollars to build a new facility whose markets are assured for only five years.

Many Americans who accept the necessity of protecting our industries from unfair competition by subsidized Japanese or European producers believe that nothing can or should be done about competition from third world countries like Korea, Mexico, or Brazil. Now that these rivals have combined modern technology with low labor costs, the argument goes, there's no way U.S. manufacturers can compete with them.

Such thinking appears perfectly reasonable, but it contains assumptions that are questionable if not downright fallacious. South Korean and Brazilian mills do have modern technology, but nonetheless, their productivity still lags far behind that of U.S. mills. The difference can be read in statistics on man hours per ton: according to Locker/Abrecht

Associates, American mills use 3.6 man hours to make a ton of hot rolled band steel, for example, while Korean mills need 5.5 hours and Brazilian mills need 5.9. The reason rests primarily in the fact that American steelworkers are more experienced and knowledgeable in the art of steelmaking.

Third world steelmakers do have an important advantage over U.S. manufacturers, and that is low wage rates. In most of the third world, severe political repression enables export-oriented producers to keep workers' wages so low that they can never hope to buy the things they produce. Machine guns and police spies provide the foundation of the "labor cost advantage" that is eliminating the jobs of steelworkers in Southeast Chicago.

But isn't protectionism unfair to the poor workers of the third world? This question is more complicated than it seems. There's a lot of evidence that export platforms like Korea's steel mills and Mexico's auto parts plants, financed by the International Monetary Fund and the World Bank, are not unmixed blessings for their local economies. They draw people off the farms, create slums in the cities, yet don't ever seem to generate the kind of self-sustaining economic growth that creates steadily improving living standards. Encouraging the export of third world manufactured goods to the United States may be a good way of helping solve the international debt crisis, but it is disastrous for U.S. steelworkers, and of dubious benefit to the poor of the third world.

To protect U.S. steelworkers without making the workers of the third world carry the burden, the United States should enact an import tax based on the differential between what American workers need to live decently and what third world workers are paid. The taxes collected could be used for two purposes—to modernize American steel mills and to fund third world development projects. This would provide an incentive for countries like South Korea to develop their home market. They would have a choice of paying the tax or raising their workers' wages, thereby generating domestic demand.

This would help U.S. steelworkers one way or the other and might give workers in the developing world a shot at jobs that are not completely dependent on the vicissitudes of America's economic needs.

The prospect of permanent import restraints is not something most Americans are likely to welcome because we instinctively believe it will foster inefficient production methods, which will cost consumers billions. The example of Great Britain's nationalized and protected steel industry—whose losses were subsidized for thirty years, as the mills became more and more backward—is what we think of first. It doesn't have to be that way. Japan's protected steel and auto industries have outstripped ours; there's no reason why a protected American steel industry couldn't be modern and efficient too.

Equally important, protection will have to extend beyond the steel industry. It would not make much sense to exclude foreign steel if at the same time we allowed foreign manufacturers to flood U.S. markets with products containing a great proportion of steel, such as autos, refrigerators, machine tools, and tractors. To do so would leave American steel mills without markets. Clearly, a program to protect steel only makes sense as part of a larger policy to protect a significant sector of American manufacturing.

At the same time that our government seeks to limit competition from abroad, it must also take steps to increase domestic demand. One of the most dramatic opportunities to expand demand for steel would be a program to rebuild America's infrastructure—our basic physical facilities.

Since 1965, America's investment in public infrastructure has dropped 50 percent, from 4.1 percent of GNP to 2.0 percent. Decaying roads, bridges, and railroad tracks increase transportation costs and energy consumption and decrease the productivity of our entire society. In October of 1983, Clifford Garvin of Exxon and Lane Kirkland of the AFL-CIO released a report estimating that in the years 1983–1995, the cost of rebuilding America's highways and bridges, urban water supplies, and wastewater treatment facilities would exceed planned spending by $8.5 billion to $10.8 billion *annually*. If we add to this analysis America's deteriorated local roads, our ancient railroad beds, and our inadequate urban mass transit systems, we would end up with even larger shortfalls. A thoroughgoing rebuilding program would generate demand for more than 10 million tons of steel per year, according to the Midwest Center for Labor Research, a figure that would greatly boost the attractiveness of investment in the steel industry.

A program to increase substantially social investment in America's infrastructure probably sounds utopian today, when budget deficits overwhelm public debate. Yet the size of the current deficit should not obscure the fact that the federal budget embodies social choices: while current spending on infrastructure is inadequate to maintain public facilities, our investment in the military is up—way up. And this has profound consequences for the steel industry, for just as infrastructure spending consumes lots of steel per dollar, military spending consumes little. A recent study by Ann Markusen indicates, for example, that only 5 percent of American steel production is consumed by the military, while 55 percent of the output of U.S. TV, radio, and communication equipment producers goes for national defense.

The defense buildup of the Carter-Reagan years has shifted American investment away from steel and into computers and communication technology. If America were to begin transferring investment from defense to civilian uses, the domestic steel industry would benefit greatly.

All these proposals to assure adequate demand for American steel are interrelated. If America initiated an infrastructure rebuilding program without enforcing trade restraints, the orders generated by the program would be filled by foreign steelmakers. And if we instituted trade restraints when the dollar was overvalued, the price disparities between domestic and foreign steel would eventually force the import barriers to topple. If we increase demand for steel with piece-meal policies, the cost will be high and the benefits dubious. But coordinated action to ensure high levels of steel consumption would minimize the program's costs and maximize its effectiveness.

INVESTMENT IN MODERNIZING STEEL

Increased demand for American steel is a precondition for saving the industry, but it must be linked to a deliberate program to make sure that the steel companies have the capital they need to modernize. Stimulating investment in steel will require governmental action because the structure of the American economy currently discourages long-term investment in manufacturing industry.

In recent years, America's financiers and corporate executives have developed means of making profits that are largely unrelated to our social purposes. In the new system of what Seymour Melman has termed "profits without production," financial expertise was more important than production competence. Accountants and financiers began to rise to the top of the corporate hierarchy, while managers who concentrated on producing goods fell still further behind.

Government tax policies and a revolution in banking practices have encouraged the corporate flight from productive investment. To reverse that flight, the government must reform the tax code and reform the credit markets. It must also use public capital to leverage private investment. And it may even have to grant direct subsidies to the steel companies.

Government tax policies encourage corporations to transfer their capital around the globe. Kuttner notes that "at the same time that our government pressures Japanese automakers to restrict exports to the U.S. 'voluntarily,' the U.S. tax code gives Ford tax incentives to shift production from Detroit to the Mexican border."

Tax code preferences have other bizarre and antisocial consequences: they provided U.S. Steel with incentives to shut its mills so that it could take over Marathon Oil. And the tax credits the company received when it shut South Works and other mills in 1983 helped it pay off the debt which financed the acquisition of Marathon.

The tax overhaul of 1986 leaves in place many of the incentives to corporate flight from productive investments. A genuine tax reform program would eliminate tax incentives for unfriendly mergers, conglomerate takeovers of unrelated business, and plant shutdowns, thereby making steel and other manufacturing industries more viable.

But tax reform without reform of our nation's credit markets is only half a solution. In the 1960s, banks became aggressive buyers and sellers of money; their search for depositors drove up interest rates—and the steel companies had to pay more to borrow the money needed for modernization.

The transfer of billions of dollars from Western consumers to OPEC accelerated the banking revolution by creating a huge pool of highly mobile capital available for investment in high-yield, short-term instruments. The frenzied buying and selling of new forms of paper drove up interest rates, further increasing the cost of industrial modernization.

The banking revolution and the rise of paper entrepreneurialism should have alerted federal officials to the need for increased supervision of the banking system, but the opposite occurred. "Deregulation" was the name of the game in banking just as it was in trucking, communications, and air travel. In the meantime, new forms of financial paper and speculation appeared every month, and the gains to society were hard to fathom.

The Congress and the Federal Reserve have the power to discourage bank financing of hostile takeovers, excessive foreign investment, and commodity speculation, but they are failing to exercise it. (The Federal Reserve Board's move against "junk bond" financing of hostile takeovers is a lonely exception.) It is urgent that they act, not only to help ensure the solvency of the banks but also to curb the wasteful use of capital needed for the more important task of modernizing industry.

But even if we enact real tax reform and control of the credit markets, there might still be insufficient incentive for private capital to invest in the modernization of industry. The federal government must use public investment as a lever for private investment. Such a strategy could shift billions of dollars of private funds into modernization projects and make America's industries world class once again.

Pension funds are one available source of public investment. Currently, $700 billion of America's capital lie in pension funds. The way our financial system now works, the private capital markets use this huge pool of public capital to finance corporate takeovers and other forms of "profits without production." But pension fund assets could be invested with an eye to creating jobs and modernizing industry; indeed, the Building Trades Department of the AFL-CIO already has developed a program to funnel pension funds into the mortgage market in order to stimulate construction activity.

The military budget is a second potential source of funds for leverage on private capital. Currently, federal defense spending harms American industry rather than helping it. Cost-plus Pentagon contracts have diverted manufacturers from cost-minimization practices, thereby rendering them unable to compete with foreign producers. Tens of thousands of engineers are taken out of civilian employment to work on military production. National spending on research and development is skewed to defense applications.

If America cut back its military budget by just 10 percent, the savings would reach nearly $30 billion per year. That sum could be diverted to rebuilding basic industry and infrastructure in a way that would leverage greater sums of private capital.

Such a proposal may sound unrealistic in the 1980s, when

public support for national defense is at an all time high, but a look at recent history suggests that the current situation is not immutable. The rapid military buildup that has produced huge Pentagon budgets and massive federal budget deficits began in 1979, and it followed five years of much lower spending. As Americans come to grips with the social consequences of oversize military appropriations—with their consequences for farmers threatened with the loss of their land, for communities threatened with the loss of their mills, and for elderly people threatened with cutbacks in their retirement incomes—it is possible that these diverse constituencies will join with those opposed to the arms race. The resulting coalition could push back the pendulum and moderate the pace of defense expenditures.

If all these parts of a comprehensive steel program were implemented—if demand for steel were increased, tax policy reformed, interest rates reduced, and private capital leveraged for industrial modernization—the steel industry might be able to make it on its own. Increased demand for steel and import curbs would drive up steel prices; reform of the capital markets would make funds for long-term industrial investment both cheaper and more plentiful.

But if this program were not implemented in toto, the steel companies would need direct federal subsidies. According to a study by the AISI, $3 to $4 billion annually would be required in the absence of a comprehensive program. The total amount needed depends on what kind of industrial policy for steel our nation adopts.

Most Americans, be they left, right, or center, don't want to subsidize firms like U.S.X. and Armco. When they got tax breaks in 1981, they used their windfalls to diversify, not modernize: why give them more money now?

These objections contain more than a grain of truth. If the federal government and the steel corporations continue to do business as usual, subsidies will promote price gouging and further diversification.

Subsidizing steel can work only if the public participates in corporate decision-making. To do so, government, labor, and community representatives would determine how much subsidy the steel industry needed. Then they would bargain with the steel companies. The contract that emerged from this planning process might specify three things: corporate commitments to modernize particular mills, government investment schedules, and the unions' agreement to moderate wages and modify work rules.

INDUSTRIAL POLICY

The comprehensive steel program presented above can work only if the government coordinates decision making about trade, monetary policy, regulatory policy, and public investment. It would also require coordinated government action on behalf of the auto and machine manufacturing industries, for steel can't be saved if its customers all die. In other words, we need an "industrial policy."

Politicians and labor leaders began to look at Japanese and European planning models when America's international trade position faltered in the early 1980s. By 1982, "industrial policy" had ceased to be an academic slogan and moved into the mainstream of Democratic party discussion. Even more surprising was the shift on the right: *Business Week*'s challenge to the corporate community's traditional commitment to free-market doctrine was joined by the conservative political strategist Kevin Phillips.

Talk of industrial policy was shelved only two years later, with the presidential election heating up, and economic recovery under way. It was the victim of Americans' traditional distrust of "big government" and planning bureaucracies, which we equate with inefficient Communist regimes. We prefer to rely on the free market to serve as arbiter of the myriad projects initiated by individual entrepreneurs; that's the American way.

Yet even while we adhere to laissez-faire rhetoric, millions of Americans appeal to the government for programs to serve their special needs. Farmers call for price supports; steelworkers call for import protection; businessmen call for tax incentives; shipbuilders call for subsidies. All of them believe in federal action, but only on their own behalf. As a result, Congress enacts thousands of programs to aid special interest groups. This isn't really the free market in action. As long as the government intervenes in the economy, there should be one agency of government making sure that different programs don't cancel each other out.

But how do we coordinate the needs of competing interest groups without developing a bureaucratic agency that is removed from the pushes and pulls of the democratic process? Here, the much-heralded Japanese model of industrial promotion offers little guidance. Japan's Ministry of International Trade and Industry is just the sort of elite planning mechanism Americans rightfully distrust. When it formulates programs to initiate new industries and abandon old ones, affected workers and neighborhood residents are excluded from the decision-making process. According to Robert Reich, "Japan's powerful economic ministries . . . are run by permanent administrative vice-ministers. These senior bureaucrats and the business leaders who were their old Tokyo University classmates form an impenetrable 'old boy' network that in effect governs Japan."

Sweden, Austria, and West Germany provide better models of industrial policy. In West Germany, for example, ever since World War II, the federal government has followed a "social market" policy which establishes the laws and social priorities within which the "free market" is allowed to operate.

Within the framework of the "social market" policy, the German national development bank (KW) invested in rebuilding war-torn basic industries like coal and steel. When this was accomplished, the Federal Republic began modernizing German industry. To that end, the Parliament created the Ministry of Technology in 1972, to fund research and development projects that could advance the nation's business position. By 1979, the ministry's direct cash grants totaled $3.2 billion, with the largest share going to the mechanical engineering industry.

While the Ministry of Technology makes the final decisions, committees of government officials, independent consultants, and representatives of industry and labor screen all proposals. They give priority to businesses that can support a high wage rate. Financing usually is reserved for projects too risky or too large for an individual company to undertake on its own. The ministry limits its funding to 50 percent of project cost, so that the private firm is subjected to risk—unlike Envirodyne Holding Company.

All this planning is done without a huge bureaucracy. For example, the Ministry of Technology uses a network of independent experts drawn from business and education to make decisions about funding new research; only five government officials staff the entire urban transportation section.

Planning in Sweden is carried out through a labor-market policy aimed at maintaining full employment regardless of fluctuations in the business cycle. The policy is conducted by a system of labor-market boards which create jobs, relocate workers, and coordinate job training and placement. To accomplish these tasks, the boards can offer employers wage subsidies, create temporary public jobs, finance the stockpiling of goods, and offer early retirement. The result has been low rates of inflation and unemployment and a high rate of economic growth; indeed, Robert Kuttner reports, for two entire decades, the 1950s and 1960s, "Sweden's annual rate of productivity growth was exactly double the American rate."

Austria offers a third model of industrial policy-making, one that relies on government planning and allocation of capital more than the West German and Swedish models do.

Austria's planning is accomplished through "social bargaining" involving employers' federations, centralized labor organizations, and government bodies. Over the years, these forces have learned to find the ground of common advantage: unions accept slow wage growth, businesses pay high taxes, and government maintains high levels of social spending. This arrangement kept inflation below 7 percent and joblessness below 4 percent through the worst years of the West's stagflation.

None of these three models of industrial planning are perfect, nor are they easily adaptable to American society. But they do point to directions we might explore, and above all, they affirm that coordinated decision-making can be effective.

For Americans attracted to the idea of "industrial policy," the problem is to devise a planning process that encourages popular participation, escapes bureaucratic ossification, and resists becoming just another political pork barrel. Gar Alperovitz and Jeff Faux warn us that industrial policy could become merely an extension of "the broker state": the planning mechanism will help business use state intervention to advance their own narrow interests at the public's expense.

If industrial policy is to be more than a feeding trough for narrow interests, we need planning boards which allow all those with a vital interest at stake to participate. It won't be enough to seat businessmen, labor leaders, and government officials on that board, for none of these can adequately represent the myriad of local organizations that spring up when communities are threatened. Community organizations must be allowed to participate in planning their future.

THE POLITICS OF SAVING STEEL

Any perceptive observer of the contemporary American political scene will find it difficult to imagine that an industrial policy of this scope could win acceptance—no matter how

great the need. Although even some conservatives have begun
to call for the preservation of our industrial strength and to
recognize the necessity for planning mechanisms to facilitate
that process, we are still very far from the kind of political
consensus necessary for embarking in the direction outlined
above.

Up to now, it has been all too easy for our national leadership to evade responsibility for the economic destruction
that is being wrought in Youngstown, Johnstown, and Southeast Chicago. Once, 4 percent was considered a high unemployment rate; today, 7 percent is considered "acceptable."
Politicians have transformed an ancient biblical maxim into
a contemporary political axiom—the "unemployed you will
always have with you." A moderately high unemployment rate
is now but a minor political irritation. Statistics showing that
the jobless are among those least likely to vote only increase
acceptance of the new unemployment as a fact of life.

In this era of the yuppie, of the venture capitalist, of the
MBA, unemployed steelworkers are no more than luckless
relics of an earlier age. So goes the conventional wisdom.

The weight of this "wisdom" has inhibited the growth of
political forces that could challenge the loss of industrial jobs,
the decimation of industrial communities, and the decline of
our industrial strength. Even in the churches, union halls, and
taverns of Southeast Chicago, there are few who dare dream
of a national program to save their community. Men like Mike
Ally and Don Stazak, whose entire working lives have been
given to the steel companies, believe that the mills are irrevocably doomed. And many of the people fighting to reverse
their community's decline don't always feel they can challenge
the corporate decisions that erode their best efforts. Nor do
they make the connections between their immediate concerns
and such seemingly remote issues as "industrial policy."

But if change is to come, it must begin in places like
Southeast Chicago. The American public will never accept a
planning program solely on the say-so of economist theorists

and government bureaucrats. To win such a new public consensus will require that displaced industrial workers themselves begin to insist that their voices be heard in the national
political debate.

Furthermore, even if an industrial policy for steel were
instituted tomorrow by administrative fiat, it would not
work—because labor union and community forces would not
be strong enough to participate on an equal footing with
corporate executives in shaping that policy. The organizing
campaigns in which these groups are now engaged are a critical training ground: learning that they can challenge national
policy, developing sophisticated economic analyses, building
coalitions among diverse forces. This process of growth is
essential if a system of democratic planning for economic
growth is ever to emerge in the United States.

There are signs that such a process is under way—that
some local groups are beginning to seek ways to take control
of the fate of their communities, and in so doing to impact
on national policy. The first such effort was in Youngstown,
Ohio. Mill closings there began in 1977, and by 1979, the
workers and community were organizing. Steelworkers went
to Washington to enlist government support for their efforts
to buy the closed mills. With the help of community and
religious leaders, and technical assistance from the Center for
Economic Alternatives, they developed a sophisticated proposal for community ownership of the mills. Local banks and
grocery stores joined with the churches to stimulate support
for a community-owned venture. However, the plan was turned
down by the Carter administration, and with no alternate
sources for the needed loans, the mills were shut down. Despite its failure, the Youngstown campaign provided a brief,
riveting glimpse of what is possible when local forces join
together and start to think big.

By 1984, the locus of resistance had shifted to the Monongahela Valley. Here, for the first time, the pieces all began
to fall into place. Local church leaders, unemployed steel-

workers, and policy experts organized the Tri-State Conference on Steel and devised a comprehensive plan to keep the
region's steel mills alive through community-worker buy-outs
combined with a program for rebuilding the bridges, canals,
and roadways of western Pennsylvania, Ohio, and West Vir-
ginia. Popular local union leaders mobilized their members
to stage colorful demonstrations that won widespread media
coverage. And the Steelworkers International union joined
the battle, providing funds for a feasibility study of the United
States Steel Duquesne Works, to test the viability of the Tri-
State plan. Their combined efforts brought enough pressure
to halt the corporation's plans to demolish the Duquesne blast
furnace and force its consideration of the union's proposals
for an employee buy-out to convert the mill. As of May 1986,
the efforts to save the Duquesne mill had failed, but the movement to halt corporate America's abandonment of manufacturing had spread throughout the Pittsburgh region.

The Monongahela Valley experience offers a clear indication of the forces of resistance to steel's decline—unions,
community-based groups, churches, and politicians. These
are the forces that will have to grow at the local level all across
the country, until they can merge into a force with national
political clout.

The USWA and other unions can provide funds, technical
resources, skills, and access to the national media. Perhaps
most importantly, they can bring to these battles the heritage
of solidarity, of decades of shared struggle.

Furthermore, the nature of the new battles to save the
steel industry is forcing the USWA to reevalute its previous
strategy of cooperation with the companies, its reliance on
high-level lobbying, and its removal from local union struggles. This current crisis is bringing the union back in touch
with its grass roots.

Community-based groups, many made up of unemployed
steelworkers, bring to this battle a willingness to take risks
and to test new directions. They are often the first to lead a

demonstration, to consider a buy-out proposal, to raise the issue of unbridled corporate power over their neighborhoods. Don't these corporations owe us anything, they ask, for all the years we helped them to prosper? It is a simple question, but also one with radical implications. Most of these groups are made up of people who have never before been politically active, who do not have any political philosophy, who are certainly not looking for a fight. Yet they have decided that they will fight before their communities are destroyed—and that determination may be one of the greatest weapons in this struggle.

Religious leaders make up another crucial element in this emerging resistance. Local clergy have seen their congregations devastated by the impact of plant closings and many have responded. In some cases, they have sought to meet basic human needs, through food banks or counseling programs. But in others, they have moved to take on larger issues, to draw on basic church teachings about stewardship—the importance of conserving our resources and using them wisely; about justice—the right of people to a job and a decent standard of living; and about community—people sharing their work and their lives as a means to spiritual growth. These teachings have moved some clergy to take an activist role in seeking new responses to deindustrialization, and to question the entire sweep of our nation's economic policies. Clergy of all denominations have joined with community groups and local unions in seeking to save jobs and neighborhoods.

Local politicians of both parties know that plant closings can devastate the economic base of their communities. And so, while few have taken the lead, many have responded to pressure, and have followed the lead of unions and community forces. The support of these local politicians can be critical. Although they have only limited resources to bring to bear against a large corporation, their involvement signals that plant closings do not have to be accepted passively, and that government does have a role to play in challenging them.

When local communities assert the need for action through their elected representatives, they can help to influence public debate at state and national levels. Equally important, frustrated local political leaders can play a role in reshaping the ways in which their national leaders and parties respond to the problem of industrial decline. At a conference of religious leaders in December of 1984, the Republican mayor of Cleveland described the damaging impact of unemployment on his city and called for a public jobs program aimed at repairing our ailing infrastructure. Voices like his need to be heard—not least, in the upper levels of his party.

These are not insignificant human and material resources with which to begin a movement to halt the decline of basic industries. But on their own, they are probably insufficient. Steelworkers and steel communities are simply too small a part of our country to spark a movement for fundamental change. The possibility does exist, however, that as steel communities mobilize, they will find allies in other Americans similarly threatened by the recent drift of the U.S. economy. Farmers faced with bankruptcy are obvious candidates for such an alliance; so are Detroit auto workers, Southern textile workers, Northwestern lumbermen, and Southwestern copper miners.

To be sure, challenging the way America does business will not be an easy process, or one with any guarantee of success. But if these local efforts grow and spread, if the jobless continue to insist on their rights, if communities continue their fight to survive, it may yet be possible to forge a new public consensus: the preservation of stable families, secure employment, and healthy communities are essential to a strong democracy.

It is Christmas Eve, 1984, a cold blustery day, but the sun is shining and the sky is a sharp, bright blue. The streets of South Deering are quiet, almost deserted. There are no signs of the normal holiday bustle. Only the giant eighteen wheelers rolling down Torrence Avenue shatter the stillness.

The remains of the Wisconsin Steel mill stretch out along the community's edge. Most of the structures are still standing, but mammoth holes now punctuate the siding. The fence that once kept out all unauthorized intruders has been torn down and it is easy to wander onto the intricate network of rail lines still dotted with abandoned coal cars.

There is an air of utter desolation about the place; it is hard to remember the days when it was abuzz with activity, hard to imagine that it could come alive once again.

But just half a block down from the main gate, there's a corner where the mill meets the rest of South Deering. On that corner is an old shack, and on top of the shack, a community group has erected a Christmas tree, just as it had done for so many years past when the mill was in operation.

The tree sways limply in the crisp winter air, its tinsel clinging desperately to its branches. Beneath it, a worn sign proclaims Seasons Greetings.

The truck drivers roll by with hardly a glance, but the display isn't really meant for them. Its message is not for those who are passing through, but for those who have remained.

Notes

Prologue

PAGE 3: On job loss in 1982–1984, see Bureau of National Affairs, Inc., *Layoffs, Plant Closings and Concession Bargaining: Summary Report for 1982*, Washington, D.C., March 1983, and "BLS Reports on Displaced Workers," U.S. Department of Labor, Bureau of Labor Statistics, Press Release, November 30, 1984, pp. 1–2.

PAGE 3: On job loss in the steel industry, see U.S. Department of Commerce, *U.S. Industrial Outlook*, 1985, p. 19-2.

PAGES 4–5: On displacement from the textile industry, see Barry Bluestone and Bennett Harrison, *The Deindustrialization of America*, Basic Books, New York, 1982, p. 97.

PAGE 5: For quote by Emma Rothschild, see Emma Rothschild, "Reagan and the Real America," *New York Review of Books*, February 5, 1981, pp. 12–18.

PAGE 5: For the growth in service sector jobs, see *The DRI Report on U.S. Manufacturing Industries*, McGraw-Hill Book Co., New York, 1984, p. 45.

1. The World as It Was

PAGE 16:   On deaths at South Works, see William Hurd, "Making Steel and Killing Men," *Everybody's Magazine*, November 1907.

PAGE 22:   For data on eight Chicago neighborhoods see Richard Taub, *Paths of Neighborhood Change*, University of Chicago Press, Chicago, 1984.

PAGE 23:   For quote about immigrants, see David Brody, *Steelworkers in America: The Non-Union Era*, Harper & Row, Publishers, New York, 1960, p. 119.

PAGE 23:   On churches of the Southeast Side, see John Conroy, "Milltown," a series of continuing articles, *Chicago* magazine, November 1976, p. 168.

PAGE 24:   On the role of the parochial school, see Dominic Pacyga, "Villages of Packinghouses and Steel Mills," Ph.D. thesis, University of Illinois at Chicago Circle, 1981, pp. 176–177, 186–189.

PAGE 24:   Quotation on South Chicago schoolchildren is from John Morris Gillette, *Cultural Agencies of a Typical Manufacturing Group: South Chicago*, University of Chicago Press, Chicago, 1901, p. 47.

PAGE 27:   Quotation by Edward Sadlowski is from Studs Terkel, *American Dreams: Lost and Found*, Pantheon, New York, 1980, p. 237.

PAGE 28:   On the importance of the family's good name, see William Kornblum, *Blue-Collar Community*, University of Chicago Press, Chicago, 1974, p. 210.

PAGES 28–29:   On the use of blacks as strikebreakers, see Brody, op. cit., pp. 254–255.

PAGES 30–31:   Quotation on community attitudes toward the Trumbull Homes is from Robert Bulanda, *The Historical Development of Three Chicago Millgates: South Deering*, Illinois Labor History Society, 1972, p. 48.

2. Shutdown at Wisconsin Steel

PAGES 39–41: On the early history of Wisconsin Steel, see James McIntyre, "A History of the Wisconsin Steel Works of the International Harvester Company," Wisconsin Steel Company, Chicago, Illinois, 1951, pp. 21–30; also see Robert Bulanda, op. cit., pp. 17–20, 56–63.

PAGES 43–45: On Wisconsin Steel's final years under International Harvester, see *Crain's Chicago Business*, November 8–14, 1982, pp. 211–243; also see *Crain's Chicago Business*, November 15–22, 1982, pp. 19–42, and *Business Week*, March 17, 1975, pp. 50–53.

PAGES 46–47: On Dr. Ronald Linde, see *Business Week*, September 12, 1977, pp. 96, 101.

3. South Works and the Decline of the American Steel Industry

PAGES 74–75: On forecasts of steel demand, Donald Barnett and Louis Schorsch, *Steel: Upheaval in a Basic Industry*, Ballinger Publishing Company, Cambridge, Massachusetts, 1983, pp. 23-29, 38.

PAGE 75: On the cost of greenfield modernization, Robert Crandall, *The U.S. Steel Industry in Recurrent Crises*, The Brookings Institution, Washington, D.C., 1981, pp. 86–91.

PAGE 76: On the incompetence of steel industry executives, see Robert Reich and Ira Magaziner, *Minding America's Business*, Harcourt Brace Jovanovich, New York, 1982, pp. 160–166.

PAGES 78–79: On U.S. Steel's decision to build a rod mill, Interview with Donald Barnett, August 10, 1983.

PAGES 81–82: *Fortune* quote in *Fortune*, June 1936, p. 64.

PAGE 82: *Fortune* quote in *Fortune*, June 1936, p. 157.

PAGE 82: On preserving U.S. Steel's eastern mills, see

Ann Markusen, *Profit Cycles, Oligopoly and Regional Development,* unpublished manuscript, Chapter 8; also see *Fortune,* April 1936, pp. 127–129.

PAGE 82: On the high prices paid by steel users, see *Fortune,* April 1936, pp. 130–131.

PAGE 83: On U.S. steel's complacency, see Crandall, op. cit., p. 23.

PAGE 83: On Fairless Works, see Barnett and Schorsch, op. cit., p. 63.

PAGE 84: On the surge in imports, see Crandall, op. cit., pp. 22–23.

PAGES 84–86: On Japanese steelmakers, see Verner, Liiphfert, Bernhard and McPherson, "Government Promotion in the Japanese Steel Industry," a report prepared for the Bethlehem Steel Corporation August 1983, pp. 54–57.

PAGE 86: On the growth of minimills, see Barnett and Schorsch, op. cit., pp. 199–201.

PAGE 87: On competition in steel prices, see Crandall, op. cit., pp. 46-71.

PAGE 87: On import levels, see U.S. Congress, Office of Technology Assessment, "Technology and Steel Industry Competitiveness," U.S. Congress, Washington, D.C., 1980, p. 30.

PAGES 87–88: On import restriction, see Barnett and Schorsch, op. cit., pp. 238–242.

PAGE 88: David Roderick quoted in *Business Week,* September 17, 1979, p. 81.

PAGE 88: On the closing of integrated steel facilities, see *Business Week,* June 13, 1983, p. 94.

4. **Dark Days**
PAGE 97: On the health impact of unemployment, see Bluestone and Harrison, op. cit., p. 65.

PAGE 98: The survey of local health providers was conducted in the summer of 1983 by the South Suburban Task Force on the Health Impact of Unemployment and Low Income under the auspices of the Suburban Cook County–Du Page County Health Systems Agency.

PAGE 99: Data on median family income was compiled by the Steelworkers Research Project under the auspices of the Research and Advocacy Department, Hull House Association, Chicago, "Chicago Steelworkers: The Cost of Unemployment," January 1985, pp. 10–11.

PAGES 102–103: On the impact on black steelworkers, see the report of the Steelworkers Research Project, cited above, pp. 13–14.

PAGES 105–106: On hazardous waste dumps, see Ben Joravsky, "Dumpers Swamp City's Southeast Side With Noxious Toxic Waste," *Chicago Reporter*, August 1983, p. 1.

PAGE 116: Quotation by John Ortiz is in Linnea Myers, "Closing of South Works Mourned," *Chicago Tribune*, January 1, 1984, p. 13.

5. **Local 65's Painful Dilemma**
PAGE 124: On working conditions in turn-of-the-century mills, see Brody, op. cit., pp. 154–158.

PAGE 125: On the 1919 strike, see Brody, op. cit., pp. 215–262; also see Pacyga, op. cit., p. 13.

PAGES 125–126: On U.S. Steel's labor policy during the depression, see *Fortune*, May 1936, p. 141.

PAGE 126: On George Patterson, see Alice Lynd and Staughton Lynd (eds.), *Rank and File*, Princeton University Press, 1981, pp. 91–93; also see Conroy, op. cit., December 1976, p. 218.

PAGES 126–127: On the organization of U.S. Steel, see Irving Bernstein, *Turbulent Years*, Houghton Mifflin, Boston, 1969, pp. 457–467; also see Robert R.R. Brooks, *As Steel Goes*, Yale University Press, New Haven, 1940, *passim*.

PAGES 127–128: On Tom Girdler, see William J. Bork, "The Memorial Day Massacre of 1937," M.A. thesis, University of Illinois at Urbana-Champaign, 1975, pp. 45–47.

PAGE 128: On working conditions at Republic Steel, ibid., p. 52.

PAGE 128: On munitions for Republic Steel, ibid., p. 72; also see Bernstein, op. cit., p. 483.

PAGE 128: On the Memorial Day Massacre, see Bork, op. cit., pp. 95–110; also see Bernstein, op. cit., pp. 485–490.

PAGE 129: On the triumph of SWOC, see Bernstein, op. cit., pp. 727–731.

PAGES 131–132: On George Patterson's story, see Conroy, op. cit., January 1977, p. 116.

PAGE 132: On the pursuit of labor-management harmony, see Clinton Golden and Harold J. Ruttenberg, *The Dynamics of Industrial Democracy*, Harper & Bros., New York, 1942, pp. 29–30.

PAGES 132–134: On Edward Sadlowski, see Conroy, op. cit., February 1977, pp. 106–185; also see Philip W. Nyden, *Steelworkers Rank-and-File*, Praeger, New York, 1984, *passim*.

6. **The Limits of Clout**

PAGE 154: Quotation by John Buchanan is from Conroy, op. cit., February 1977, p. 111.

PAGE 160: Quotation by Mayor Jane Byrne is from the *Chicago Sun-Times*, October 7, 1980.

PAGE 164 Quotations by Edward Vrdolyak are from *The Daily Calumet*, April 18, 1980, and April 28, 1980.

7. Down but Not Out

PAGE 193: Quotation by Edward Vrdolyak is from *The Hegewisch News*, August 19, 1982.

8. Saving Steel

PAGE 204: On job loss in 1979–1984, see "BLS Reports on Displaced Workers," pp. 1–2.

PAGES 204–205: On the bifurcation of the labor force, see Bluestone and Harrison, op. cit., p. 97; also see AFL-CIO, Committee on the Evolution of Work, "The Future of Work," August 1983, p. 11.

PAGES 205–206: On union impact on wage standards, see Richard Freeman and James Medoff, *What Do Unions Do?*, Basic Books, New York, 1984, pp. 48–63.

PAGE 206: On the health impact of unemployment, see Bluestone and Harrison, op. cit., pp. 63–65.

PAGES 206–207: On the cost of steel's decline, see "Social Costs of the Decline of the Calumet Steel Industry," a report prepared by the Midwest Center for Labor Research, Chicago, September 1983.

PAGE 209: On New Deal reforms, see Robert Kuttner, "A Working Economy," Citizen Action, Chicago, 1983, p. 6.

PAGE 210: On communities and democracy, see Gar Alperovitz and Jeff Faux, *Rebuilding America*, Pantheon Books, New York, 1984, pp. 262–267.

PAGES 212–213: Marcus and Luerssen quoted in *Business Week*, January 14, 1985, p. 84.

PAGE 214: Verner, Liiphfert, Bernhard and McPherson, op. cit.

PAGE 214: On steel-containing imports and exports, see Locker/Abrecht Associates, Inc., *Confronting the Crisis: The*

Challenge for Labor, United Steelworkers of America, Pittsburgh, 1985, pp. 50–51.

PAGE 215: DRI quoted in *The DRI Report on U.S. Manufacturing Industries*, p. 45.

PAGE 216: On the Multi-Fiber Agreement, see Robert Kuttner, "The Free Trade Fallacy," *The New Republic*, March 15, 1983, pp. 19–20.

PAGES 215–216: On faulty federal policies, ibid.; also see Kevin Phillips, *Staying on Top*, Random House, New York, 1984, pp. 3–6.

PAGE 217: Wolfgang Hager's estimate of the extent of protectionism is cited in Kuttner, "The Free Trade Fallacy," p. 21.

PAGE 217: On the ineffectiveness of the trigger-price mechanism, see testimony of James W. Smith to the Subcommittee on Oversight and Investigations of the Committee on Energy and Commerce, Hearings on "Impact of Illegal and Unfair Foreign Trade Practices on U.S. Commerce: Steel Dumping," House of Representatives, Washington D.C., September 21, 1983, pp. 14–15.

PAGES 217–218: On the Mitsui case, ibid., pp. 1–164.

PAGE 218: On the flaws in the Reagan VRA program, see Locker/Abrecht Associates, Inc., op. cit., p. 62.

PAGES 218–219: On the productivity of third world steelmakers, ibid., p. 37.

PAGE 221: On investment in public infrastructure, see Kuttner, "A Working Economy," pp. 44–45; also see The Labor Management Group, *A Consensus on Rebuilding America's Vital Public Facilities*, October 1983, p. 6.

PAGE 221: On a thoroughgoing rebuilding program, see "Infrastructure and the Steel Industry," Midwest Center for Labor Research, Chicago, January 1984.

PAGE 221: On the military use of steel, see Ann Markusen, *Steel and Southeast Chicago*, Northwestern University Center for Urban Affairs and Policy Research, Evanston, Illinois, 1985, pp. 96–98.

PAGE 222: On profits without production, see Seymour Melman, *Profits Without Production*, Knopf, New York, 1983 *passim*.

PAGE 223: On changing the banking system, see L. J. Davis, *Bad Money*, St. Martin's Press, New York, 1982, pp. 77–117.

PAGE 224: On pension funds, see Kuttner, "A Working Economy," pp. 8–9.

PAGES 224–225: On the military budget, see Seymour Melman, op. cit.

PAGES 225–226: On modernizing the steel industry, see American Iron and Steel Institute, "Steel at the Crossroads," Washington, D.C., 1980, pp. 47-54.

PAGE 227: On industrial policy's appeal to the right, see "The Reindustrialization of America," *Business Week,* June 30, 1980, ff.; also see Phillips, op. cit., pp. 131–142.

PAGES 227–228: Robert Reich quoted in Reich, *The Next American Frontier*, Times Books, New York, 1983, p. 277.

PAGES 228–229: On West German industrial policy, see Andrew Levison, *The Full Employment Alternative*, Coward, McCann and Geoghegan, Inc., New York, 1980, pp. 108–118; also see Reich, *The Next American Frontier*, p. 220.

PAGE 229: On Swedish industrial policy, see Robert Kuttner, *The Economic Illusion,* Basic Books, New York, 1984, pp. 150–153.

PAGE 229: On the broker state, see Alperovitz and Faux, op. cit., pp. 9–28.

Index

245

246   Index

Community:
    impact of deindustrialization, 208–
        210
    ownership, 231–232
    role in industrial planning, 232–235
    (*See also* Southeast Chicago)
Costello, Therese, 182–183
Crandall, Robert, 75
Cronin, John, 28, 100, 117, 179, 180
Crowel, Robert, 52–53
Cruz, Jessie, 97

Daily Calumet, The, 14–15, 159, 165,
    166, 173, 184, 193
Daley, Richard M., 34, 152, 156, 168
Defense spending, 224–225
Deindustrialization of America, The
    (Bluestone and Harrison), 4–5
Democratic party (*see* Machine politics)
Devine, David, 106
Doyle, James, 45, 46, 47, 52, 61, 67, 68
Drakulich, Mike, 41, 51
Drexel Burnham Lambert, 158, 159

East Side, 14, 31, 104
East Side Clergy Unemployment
    Committee, 182
Eckstein, Otto, 5, 216
Economic Development Administration
    (EDA), 56–62, 63–65, 66–67, 158,
    159, 160, 162, 165–166, 167, 211
EDC Holding Company, 50–51, 57–58,
    60, 61, 63, 64, 68, 69, 194
Employment:
    of displaced workers, 4–5, 204
    in manufacturing sector, 204, 205
    in service sector, 5, 204–205
Envirodyne Industries, 2, 42
    acquisition of Wisconsin Steel, 46–51,
        162–163
    and federal loan guarantee program,
        57–62, 63–65
    management of, 55, 60, 64
    plant shutdown by, 67–70, 194
    and Progressive Steelworkers Union
        (PSWU), 54–55
ERISA Act of 1974, 52, 53, 54, 163

Faux, Jeff, 210, 229
Federal Reserve Board, 73–74, 211,
    216, 224
Fish, Jim, 139–140
Fitch, Jim, 158, 161, 185, 186
Fitzgibbons, Kevin, 36, 150, 153, 154

Fleming, Thomas, 157–158
Foley, Jim and Gail, 189–190
Francisco, Joe, 198
Freeman, Richard, 205–206
Friess, Jack, 78

Galuzzo, Greg, 183
Garcia, Mary, 96, 99, 118
Gary, Judge Elbert, 81, 82
Geaney, Father Dennis, 178
Geoghegan, Tom, 195, 196
Germano, Joe, 34, 131, 133, 168
Girdler, Tom Mercer, 127–128, 129
Gomez, Dorothy, 97, 99
Gomez, Jaime, 109
Gonzalez, Mary, 99, 105, 111–112
Gonzalez, Mary (Galuzzo), 183
Gonzalez, Victor, 95–96
Gooch, Alice, 102
Graham, Thomas, 141
Grande, Chuck, 39, 40, 42–43

Hager, Wolfgang, 217
Hall, Robert, 59–60, 64–65
Hammer, Ruth, 101, 175
Harrington, Bob, 108, 112, 113, 114
Harrison, Bennett, 4–5
Hartigan, Neil, 139, 142, 144, 169, 170
Hayes, Charles, 196, 199
Hegewisch, 14, 31, 104, 189
Hegewisch News, The, 189
HUD, grant to Wisconsin Steel, 63, 64,
    65, 161

Import restriction, 87–88, 90, 211–212
Industry:
    impact of deindustrialization, 3, 5–6,
        8, 202–210
    information/service sector, 3–4, 204–
        205
    policy, 6, 226–230
    community participation in, 230–235
International Harvester Corp., 1–2
    blamed by unemployed, 116
    decline of, 44
    management of Wisconsin Steel, 39–
        42, 43–45
    participation in federal loan
        guarantee, 61, 62, 66
    sale of Wisconsin Steel, 42–43, 45–51
    pension liability in, 42, 45, 48, 51,
        52–54, 162–163, 194, 195
    UAW strike at, 65–67
    and Wisconsin Steel shutdown, 68, 69

248   *Index*

Politics (*see* Machine politics)
Progressive Steelworkers Union
(PSWU), 1
agreement with Harvester, 52–54,
194, 195
blamed by unemployed, 115
contract with Envirodyne, 54–55
and Harvester management, 41–42
leadership of, 51

Reagan, Ronald, 74, 114, 169, 211–
212, 218
Regular Democratic Organization (*see*
Machine politics)
Reich, Robert, 227
Republic Steel, 14, 92
unionization of, 127–129
Rice, Rudolf, 32
Richards, Eric, 61
Roderick, David, 88–89, 136, 138–139
Rodgers, Richard, 64
Rodriquez, Bob and Lolly, 179–180
Rodriquez, Petra, 22, 32, 187, 190
Roque, Leonard ("Tony"), 149, 166
agreement with Harvester, 52–54,
194, 195
and plant closure, 157, 158, 163,
192–193, 194
and Vrdolyak, 51
Rostenkowski, Dan, 144, 169
Rothschild, Emma, 5
Royko, Mike, 153

Sadlowski, Ed, 27, 115, 132–134, 155
St. Vincent dePaul Society, 179–181
Samano, Bob, 77
Savage, Gus, 156, 163–164, 196
Save Our Jobs Committee, 193, 194–
196
Scanlon, Andy, 148, 149
Schlesinger, Henry, 103–104, 105, 108,
115
Schopp, Father George, 17, 18, 107,
182, 183, 191. 200
Schorsch, Louis, 79
Schwartz, Wayne, 21
Sealey, George, 47–48, 52, 57, 60
Slag Valley, 13, 31
Smetlack, Joe, 1, 6, 98, 114, 164, 195,
196
South Deering, 13–14, 39–40, 45, 46,
103
commercial decay in, 104

South Deering (*cont.*):
racial tensions in, 30–32
waste dumps in, 107, 187–189, 191–
192
South Deering Improvement
Association, 148
South Works, 2, 13, 15, 16
decline of, 71–72, 73
efforts to save, 169–171, 198–200
mismanagement of, 76–78
modernization of, 72–73, 75, 79
partial shutdown at, 72, 89, 143
rail mill plan for, 121, 123–124, 136–
145
Southeast Chicago:
barriers to mobility in, 27–28
Catholic Church in, 23–25, 176–179,
182–183
commercial deterioration in, 104
commercial revitalization in, 185–187
community organizations in, 35–36,
175–192
community stability of, 22–23, 105
crime and delinquency in, 104–105
The Daily Calumet, of, 14–15
family life in, 25–26
future of, 9–10, 116–118, 200–201
history of, 12–13, 15
impact of deindustrialization, 6–7,
36–38, 92–93, 209–210
(*See also* Unemployed workers)
insularity of, 28
landscape of, 11–12
neighborhoods of, 13–14
political life in, 32–36, 147, 150–151
(*See also* Machine politics)
racial discrimination in, 30–32
waste dumps in, 34, 105–107, 187–
192
Southeast Chicago Development
Commission (SCDCom), 185–187
Sowell, Margaret, 65
Stazak, Donald, 135, 136, 137, 138,
139, 140–141, 142, 143, 144, 197,
199
Steel industry:
abandonment of competition in, 80–
82, 90
community/worker ownership in,
231–232
comprehensive program for, 213–
214
infrastructure spending in, 220–
222